Table of contents

A note on the nature of the text:

In 1898 the book *The Play of Animals* by Karl Groos came out, and in 1901 the same author produced *The Play of Man*. His theme was that all mammals, man included, learn through play. In the first of those books, he said, "Animals can not be said to play because they are young and frolicsome, but rather they have a period of youth in order to play; for only by doing so can they supplement the insufficient hereditary endowment with individual experience, in view of the coming tasks of life."

I adhere to the theory that mammals learn through play, and dear reader, I dare hope that you are a mammal. I believe that the occasional bit of playfulness will make this book a better instrument for learning new things, because to delight in learning is our nature. Please do not take this as a sign that the information presented is not accurate or the theories propounded are not rigorous. No doubt there will be errors, as there are in the most serious tome, but I have attempted to present accurate information and interesting ideas in a playful manner, rather than writing either a farce or a text so dry the words crumble in your memory.

Preface: A republic, if you can keep it

America is the most successful large Utopian experiment of all time.

The events of Jan. 6, 2021, showed how easily we could lose the benefits of that experiment. President Donald Trump had rescheduled a rally nearby to occur shortly before Vice President Mike Pence was to go before congress and certify the election of Trump's replacement, Joe Biden.

Trump directed his followers to march to the Capitol Building, where Pence was to engage in the ceremony. They marched to the building, set up a (not very well built) gallows, overwhelmed the police guarding the Capitol Building, and invaded the building. Some seemed to be there on a lark, others came in full G.I. Joe cosplay, equipped with Flexcuffs and communications gear, apparently ready to take congressional representatives and senators captive. The Capitol Police succeeded in evacuating the elected officials, and only five people died in the attempted putsch, none of them elected representatives or senators.

They were attempting a sort of counterrevolution. The United States of America was an effort to find a better, more rational way for people to govern themselves than the ethno-religious states that had preceded it. When Trump's followers said they would 'make America great again,' what they aspired to was a nation dominated by Christian Whites. Yet the Constitution, in the Bill of Rights, said there would be no establishment of religion. Those claiming America is a Christian nation have probably forgotten the evils of an established church, which at one point led Christians to burn booksellers for selling English-language Bibles (see Chapter 13.)

It is no coincidence that the Jan. 6, 2021 riot, or attempted putsch, or whatever it was (I favor the term 'beer belly putsch,' but I doubt that will make it into the Associated Press stylebook), happened at a time when Whites and Christians were both declining as the defining groups in American identity. As long as those groups dominated, it was easy enough to paper over one of the most radical aspects of the American experiment, the fact that the country was not based on ethnicity or religion. It now begins to appear that the next effort to paper over that radicalism will be an attempt to entrench minority rule by disenfranchising people who are not part of the concurrent White Christian majority as it fades into minority status.

The entire premise of the attempted putsch was silly. Had the participants managed to "hang Mike Pence," the intention they chanted, and prevented him from formally recognizing that Joe Biden won the presidential election, Biden would still be the president-elect, and Trump would still be the loser. It's as if an aspirant to power had heard of "seizing the throne" and decided that possession of the right piece of furniture would give them power over all the land. But however delusional the putsch may have been, the intentions behind it are tearing America apart.

Nick Fuentes, leader of the Proud Boys, one of the groups that was accused of organizing the putsch, followed the keynote speech at the Conservative Political Action Conference about six weeks later with a speech in which voiced support for the putsch. He explained the goal of the participants this way:

> *"If [America] loses its white demographic core ... then this is not America anymore," the AFPAC founder told the crowd. Fuentes went on to praise the Capitol attack, boasting about it leading to a delay in the certification of the election results. "While I was there in D.C., outside of the building, and I saw hundreds of thousands of patriots surrounding the U.S. Capitol building and I saw the police retreating ... I said to myself: 'This is awesome,'" Fuentes said to the applause of the crowd... "To see that Capitol under siege, to see the people of this country rise up and mobilize to D.C. with the pitchforks and the torches — we need a little bit more of that energy in the future," he said.*[*]

For Fuentes and his comrades, America would not be America if it were not ruled by White Christians. But this was not the essence of the American revolution.

When the Constitutional Convention of 1787 was wrapping up, Elizabeth Willing Powell, who maintained a salon that attracted some of the brightest minds of the age, asked Benjamin Franklin what sort of government the delegates had come up with, a monarchy or a republic. Franklin famously replied:

"A republic, madam, if you can keep it."

It is now fashionable on the right to tell people that America is a republic, not a democracy, as a justification for making the country less democratic. They usually quote James Madison as authority, even though

Americas is generally considered a pioneer among what are now called liberal democracies. Madison, in fact, made it very clear that what he opposed was direct democracy, in which people vote directly on every political issue. He was a believer in elites, and advocated elected representatives. When he helped found a political party, it was called the Democrat-Republican Party, embodying two ideals he held dear. For short, I will be referring to the system of liberal democracy as liberalism. It is a system based on social contract theory. The idea is that the government gains its legitimacy from serving the people it governs, in a social contract periodically renewed by elections in which the people may choose to keep their current representatives or elect new ones.

Up until America's founding, most nations were made up of territories where a majority of people belonged to one ethnicity, whose language, religion, customs, and appearance were similar enough that people could recognized their fellow citizens as "one of us." This was one of the major differences between nation states and multinational empires such as the Austrian, Persian, or Roman empires. Ethnic homogeneity had become the new requirement for a coherent political unit.

In contrast, consider this charge against King George III listed in the Declaration of Independence:

> He has endeavoured to prevent the population of these States; for that purpose obstructing the Laws for Naturalization of Foreigners; refusing to pass others to encourage their migrations hither, and raising the conditions of new Appropriations of Lands.

Not only were they building a new country not based on ethnicity, America's founding fathers were upset that the king was not allowing them to encourage people who were not English to come to this land and become citizens.

America was founded not as an ethno-religious state like those of Europe, but as an experiment in building a society based on reason. Americans would have no king, no nobility, no state religion. People could worship as they saw fit, they could speak their minds, and they could select their leaders -- or, should they find their leaders needed to be removed, they could remove them without violence. The American constitution provides two ways of removing a bad president, elections and impeachment. In adopting impeachment, they were following the example set in the English Civil War, when Charles I became the first head of state to be impeached.

The theory was that there might be a need to remove a head of state between elections, either before they could do more damage, or because they had corrupted the means of replacing them by election. Locke argued that people have a right to revolution when a bad leader could not be removed by other means, and the American constitution was written to make revolutions unnecessary.

There was nothing else like it in the world. There had been democratic and republican states in the ancient world, but not states without a state religion. Even the Netherlands, governed as a republic after 1649 and considered a bastion of free speech, was an ethnically homogeneous state founded in a war between Catholics and Protestants.

There are countries where more than one language is spoken, such as Switzerland and Belgium, but America never has had an official language. The Pennsylvania Dutch (ethnically Deutsch, that is, German) developed their own version of German. Our 8th president, Martin Van Buren, spoke Dutch as his first language, as did most of the residents of Kinderhook, N.Y., where he grew up (he was the first president born after the American revolution, therefore the first president born an American citizen.) Thorstein Veblen, one of America's most famous academics and the inventor of the concept of conspicuous consumption, spoke Norwegian as his first language and only started to learn English when he went to school (he was born in Wisconsin to Norwegian immigrant parents and had plenty of Norwegian-speaking playmates.)

And as a bookseller, I frequently get old books in German that were published in Chicago, because many German-speaking communities in America wanted books in their language.

The term "melting pot" was not at all common until about Word War I, when war propaganda made preserving German culture less popular.

The truth is, 18th and 19th century America was more multicultural[*] than melting pot, which was fine, because America was not founded to be an ethnic or religious state. It was intended to be a bold experiment to find a better way for humanity to live together, to reduce conflict and increase happiness. Consider the second paragraph of the Declaration of Independence:

> We hold these truths to be self-evident, that all men are created equal, that they are
> endowed by their Creator with certain unalienable Rights, that among these are Life,
> Liberty and the pursuit of Happiness. — That to secure these rights, Governments are

instituted among Men, deriving their just powers from the consent of the governed, — That whenever any Form of Government becomes destructive of these ends, it is the Right of the People to alter or to abolish it, and to institute new Government, laying its foundation on such principles and organizing its powers in such form, as to them shall seem most likely to effect their Safety and Happiness.

No medieval monarch would have recognized this as a proper way of governing. The sovereign served God, not the people, and God's earthly representatives gave their approval (or not) to the sovereign's reign.

We have lived so long by the founders' principles that we no longer appreciate how unique the experiment is. Faced with enemies who wish to frame conflicts in ethnic and religious terms, some wish to respond in kind instead of playing to America's strengths, such as a tolerance of differences that allows us to absorb instead of conquer, and a freewheeling, vibrant culture that attracts others, instead of subjugating people outside of it.

Keep in mind during our journey, those who held these ideals were human, inconsistent, and as prone to failures as we who live today. But ideas have their own life; they spread and grow more like a forest than a subdivision, not because of coordinated effort but because they found fertile minds.

Chapter 1: The radicalism of liberalism

Politics is the means by which our moral sense is translated into law. How we select our rulers, the laws they pass, and how they conduct the business of the people, is the way the personal ethics of many people becomes the official version of what is right, enforced by the state. A slow-motion revolution in how this is done, in progress since the 17th century, has made a clean break with the past. People are still fighting and dying in that revolution

In this book, we will take 'liberalism' to mean the system and logic of liberal democracies. In liberal society, rather than be united in an ethno-religious grouping, individuals have joined to secure their ability to live a good life by forming a social contract in which government exists to serve the governed, and that contract is renewed by periodically holding elections on who is to take on the tasks of government.

Members of society should be able to live as a person without being arbitrarily deprived of life, a dictum that has caused great difficulty because of differing views of when one becomes a person, and who shall be regarded as a person.

To be a member of society, one needs to be part of the web of rights, obligations, and prohibitions about the use of things that we call property. When we speak of inalienable rights, those are the rights we cannot alienate, that is, that is, transfer ownership rights to another person. You cannot function as a person in society if you do not have possession of your own life, which is why your right to life and property are inalienable, although you may alienate any property other than yourself.

Liberty is a word not used as much as it was a couple hundred years ago. Jean-Jacques Rousseau defined it in terms of being subject to a law of one's own making. John Locke defined it much the same way, though less epigramatically, saying "People are free from the dominion of any will or legal restraint apart from that enacted by their own constituted lawmaking power according to the trust put in it." He also had some very specific views on what constituted legitimate government for the making of laws.

Two of the most important works of liberalism were written by men (Thomas Hobbes and John Locke) who at some point lived in exile from their native country, and both men had reason to fear for their lives based on their politics. If they were writing today, they would find that there are still parts of the world where expressing their ideas of the rational, free, and secular state can get you killed – which is why so many of the surviving Bengali bloggers live in exile. Those still in Bangladesh risk being hacked to death for expressing secularist views. Even in countries where the revolution has already taken place, the battle is still being fought.

Thomas Hobbes concluded that governments gain their legitimacy from the service they provide the governed. John Locke realized that religious strife comes not from people believing different things, but from trying to get them all to believe the same thing.

Those concepts are the basis for the successful democracies that now exist. They lead to a way of life that has secular government and religious freedom. Those things are so revolutionary and disruptive that in many societies, you can die for advocating them.

You can die for expressing liberal ideals of freedom of conscience, freedom of speech, and rule by consent of the governed in a variety of places, not just places like Bangladesh or the late Islamic State "Caliphate," but in countries that are important U.S. allies, such as Saudi Arabia. This is because liberalism is radical, a clean break from most of human history, and a threat to many people who want an older tradition of rule.

The great conflict in the world now, and within American society, is between people who want society to be based on religious and ethnic identity, and those who want a more inclusive society with room for people with different beliefs and ethnicities. This book will trace the history of the idea of a free and inclusive society from the Protestant Reformation, through the founding ideas of liberal democracies such as the United States, the evolution of liberal democracies in parallel with the evolution of capitalism, and the way economic elites have exploited the politics of religious and ethnic identity to take a greater share of the nation's wealth. It will also explore the conflict between tolerance and the politics of religious and ethnic identity.

People with views similar to those who hacked Bengali bloggers to death flew jetliners into the World Trade Center in Sept. 11, 2001 and blew themselves up after murdering random people in Paris in November 2015. In these cases, it is not what individuals have said, it is an attempt by fanatics to get a response from the enemy they wish to provoke: Liberal democracies. They want to change the dynamic from the live-and-let-live ethic of the liberal democracy to one in which the battle lines are drawn by religion, ethnicity, and culture, and the outcome depends not on elections, but on force.

The reason they want liberal democracies to act as their enemies, and resort to such extreme measures to get them to act like enemies, is that in the natural course of things, such societies tolerate Muslims' faith without much difficulty. That creates what Islamic State called a sort of "gray zone," where Islam exists without dictating how people live unless they want it to.

In a statement after the *Charlie Hebdo* massacre of 2014, Islamic State argued that terrorism in European countries would "compel the Crusaders to actively destroy the gray zone themselves. . . . Muslims in the West will quickly find themselves between one of two choices, they either apostatize . . . or they [emigrate] to the Islamic State and thereby escape persecution from the Crusader governments and citizens."[*]

In either the case of an attack on an individual or an attack on a society, those who want religion to rule society regard liberal democracy as the enemy. And this has been the case as long as the idea of a government whose legitimacy did not rely on religion has been involved in politics. The enemies of free and open societies are not those who attack the religion of some of the people in them, but those who attack the very idea of a society not defined by religion.

It used to be that pretty much all governments claimed to serve God or the Gods. The idea that the government should serve, instead, the people it governs, is a threat to those who arrogate to themselves the power to decide how God wants people ruled. And threats of death against those who proposed secular sources of legitimacy for governments have been a feature of public life since at least the 1640s, when Thomas Hobbes fled his former allies among monarchists in fear that they would kill him.

For centuries, it has served the purpose of those in power in Western countries to make it seem that liberal democracies are a normal, ordinary, logical way of governance, and to obscure how radical its ideas were and are. But liberal democracy represents a clean break from most of human history, a new way of thinking about the legitimacy of governments. For most of human history, we have been ruled by force, faith, and custom.

Force is easy enough to understand. The man on horseback in the expensive armor, helped by his knights, could physically compel commoners into doing his will (and for most of history, it was men who held this role, especially in young dynasties where someone had to establish dominance.)

Faith is more complicated. Religion concerns itself with the greater questions about why we exist and how we should live our lives. It is also concerned with our concept of virtue more intimately than most institutions.

The question of virtue is the question of who is acting rightly. The role of deciding who is acting rightly is a position of great power, determining who shall be stoned to death in the public square and who shall be heaped with praise and rewards. Virtue addresses the question of who may act legitimately and how, and who, if they act, will be acting illegitimately.

It takes a lot less force to rule a willing people, so if the holder of force can get the arbiters of virtue to approve their rule as legitimate, the ruler will have greater stability and require less expenditure on force.

When someone comes along and questions the legitimacy of the Gods themselves, that person is a threat to both church and state. Athens executed Socrates on charges of impiety and corrupting the minds of the youth, because he questioned the accepted notions of justice. Those notions came from the Gods, according to the state and the state religion.

I find it revealing that this happened during a period of Athenian decline, when they were being defeated in the Peloponnesian wars. It is when a society most needs a major rethink that those who have led it into decline are most eager to suppress those who would question their wisdom. Perhaps that is why we so often see this behavior in places where people fear they are weak, such as Germany during the Depression or Islamic State, which viewed Islam as under siege by Western culture. If you think this is a trick elites use to keep power, please review how one gets power in a society such as Athens, famously a democracy. One of the more effective means is to see which way the mob is headed, get in front of them and shout "This way!" while pointing in the direction the mob was going. The problem is that in a time of decline, it isn't just the leaders who feel threatened. A sizable chunk of the body politic is likely to feel the values on which they've based their lives are threatened.

Part of the problem was that Socrates did not live in a secular society, and with no separation of church and state, there was every incentive for those who could use the force of the state to kill him to do so on behalf of those who were the arbiters of virtue. Socrates was a threat to religious authority not just because he questioned their judgment, but also because of the way he did it. He started from a position of doubt, and tried to determine the truth through reason.

Reason is not always a friend to power, and it has not been the dominant means of organizing society for most of human existence.

For most of the time there have been humans on this earth, living with their strange, symbolic world of language and culture, the world has been explained in terms of myth and metaphor. These things deal with truth in a very different way than reason does.

Consider the evolution of culture. Does culture need to be rational or even explicable in order to work? In theory, you could have the people of a culture believing things that are neither rational nor, in any rational or empirical sense, true, and those beliefs could get people to act in ways that produced an orderly, productive society that is able to perpetuate itself and produce generation after generation that hold those same beliefs.

Such a society might not be terribly adaptable or able to deal with a rapidly changing world, but as long as things are stable, this might be the best way for a society to function. For example, little changed in the 1,500 years of the Old, Middle, and New Kingdoms of Egypt. In such a society, kings were gods and priests were servants of God, and things went smoothly, all great and good fun until someone invents iron.[*]

The Golden Age of Greece followed the Late Bronze Age Collapse, a dark age in which populations fell and knowledge was lost. The old ways stopped working, the new technology of iron was creating new winners in the world and the old Gods were falling. Doubt set in, and new thoughts flourished. When the old ways didn't work, people had to find new ways of thinking. Until, or course, the vibrant new civilization started to get old, and to fear the questioning of its arbiters of virtue. From the beginning of the late bronze age collapse in about 1200 BCE to the trial of Socrates in 399 BCE took about 800 years.

But it turned out the Greeks were real pikers when it came to fearing those who questioned the arbiters of virtue. Later Europeans made a regular practice of killing people who questioned the arbiters of virtue, and gained great power by this tactic. And great power led to corruption, and rebellion against corruption, and reformation. One of the things that happened was a 30-year long war that killed off so many people in parts of Europe – Germany in particular – that they had a third fewer people at the end of it than at the beginning.

Does questioning the wisdom of an established religion cause violence? John Locke, in *A Letter Concerning Toleration*, argued that differing religious views are not the cause of violence, it is the attempt to prevent people from holding non-sanctioned views that brings on violence. That points to a society where religion does not dominate the state, and the state itself is not the ultimate enforcer of religious orthodoxy (such as when a judge in Scotland ordered Thomas Aikenhead to be hanged for making atheist statements in 1697, and an executioner employed by the government did so.)

Locke's insight still holds. Islamic State hoped that a few terrorists could change the way the liberal democracies treat Muslims, and they hoped this would make the very regime some Muslims are fleeing seem more attractive to them. Only if they could spread intolerance would they have a chance of being proved right.

In fact, the tactics of religious terrorists are designed to force their enemies to frame the conflict the same way they do, as if those who hold differing religious views were a direct threat of disorder. Framed in John Locke's logic, it is the effort to impose religious uniformity that causes conflict. Framed in Islamic State or Al Qaeda's terms, only one faith can win, and only people living with one belief system can live in peace. Refusing to accept the religious extremist's frame is how the West became wealthy, peaceful, and free.

Locke's insight came from the painful experiences of the Reformation, and the wars that went with it. So, to understand liberalism, we must first review the religious conflicts that made it necessary.

Now, it may seem I'm going far afield, but the Reformation played a vital role in the invention of liberalism, in part as a way to put an end to centuries of bloodshed.

The spiritual upheaval that made liberalism necessary

To understand how tumultuous the Reformation was, you must first understand that the Catholic Church was a very different sort of institution back then, and rebellion against it could be fatal. It had grown from the oppressed faith of a few poor people into the richest and most powerful institution in Europe. It had changed from a faith preached by a few poor men who told variations on the teachings of Christ to an orderly and regimented instrument for the control of human minds that was quite willing to kill to save souls. The story of how that happened, and the crisis of faith that broke the pattern, is the background to what made liberalism essential for the peace and prosperity of Europe.

When Christianity first became a state religion under Emperor Constantine, he convened a council of bishops in Asia Minor in 325 A.D. at Nicaea (now the Turkish city of Iznik) which produced a universal doctrine, the Nicene Creed. That doctrine transformed Christianity from a term referring to churches with a variety of points of view to single a church with a set dogma. The Nicaean Council attempted to "anathematize the heresiarchs" (that is, make the heretics anathema – exclude people who didn't agree to the dogma from the community of faith) but found that secular powers would often not cooperate.

By the 13th century, things had changed. Excommunication had become a powerful way of undermining the legitimacy of secular power. Pope Innocent III at first sent missionaries to deal with the heterodox views of a group now known as the Cathars ("the pure ones," although they seem to have referred to themselves as "good men" or "good Christians.") But when his emissary to Count Raymond VI of Toulouse excommunicated the Count for being too lenient to the Cathars, he was murdered while coming home. The Pope decided it was time to kill these folks.

The Albigensian Crusade lasted from 1209 to 1229. Perhaps the most famous incident of that conflict was the massacre of Béziers in 1209. Prior to the battle, Papal legate and Cistercian abbot Arnaud Amalric feared that as they tried to kill all the heretics, some Cathars would pretend to be Catholic to avoid the sword. So he gave the order, "Caedite eos. Novit enim Dominus qui sunt eius." usually translated as "kill them all, God will know his own." Catholic forces put about 20,000 people to the sword, regardless of age, gender, or religion.

No doubt the Abbot felt he was doing the faithful a favor, sending them on early to heaven. The soul, after all, was more important than the "vile body."[*]

The Church had made heresy a capital crime in 382. The burning of heretics was first declared in the 11th century and the synod of Verona in 1182 made it a duty of bishops to ferret out heretics and hand them over to the local secular power. The secular power could be excommunicated for being too lenient, which is what gave the Church doctrine of burning such force.

After the Albigensian Crusade, the Church found a more humane way of dealing with heresy. Instead of killing whole towns, they would put the question to individuals. Individuals who declined to confess and recant usually became more cooperative under torture, but it was for the their own good (immortal soul versus vile body again.) This, of course, was the Inquisition.

At that point, the power of the Church was immense. No one had freedom of conscience or of speech, and those who did not profess the dogma of the Church could lose their lives. Secular authorities who refused to cooperate could be excommunicated, delegitimized, even obliterated, as the Albigensian Crusade had demonstrated. You will notice that I am now referring to the Church, capitalized, as if there were no other, because this was indeed the case.

All power corrupts, and this certainly happened to the Church. Rodrigo Borgia is said to have become Pope Alexander VI (1492-1503) by buying more votes than his opponents, in one case the bribe amounting to six mule-loads of silver. There is some doubt about the bribes being the definitive factor, because his opponents were as willing and capable of bribery as he was. But bribery was not his only skill; as we shall see, he had a talent for alliances. Upon ascending to the papacy, the theoretically celibate Borgia had his son Cesare succeed him as archbishop of Valencia, a post which brought with it one of the highest incomes in Europe.

Cesare was a 17 year old student at the time.

Now, the name Borgia may be familiar to you because of the much-maligned Lucretia Borgia. She was accused of incestous relations with her father and brother and of poisoning people in the interest of the family fortunes. It is probably more accurate to say that her father and brother made use of her to form political alliances through marriage, and when her husbands had stopped being useful they saw nothing wrong with killing them so they could marry her off again.

The politics surrounding popes were lethal, not just for their daughter's suitors, but to all involved in the wars they participated in. Which is why Pope Alexander VI (AKA Rodrigo Borgia) kept needing new allies. And you must understand, Popes back then did not live like kings. They lived like Roman emperors. They were the richest men in Europe. Every Christian in Europe was subject to Church taxes, secular authorities helped collect them, and some Church dignitaries could make good money by selling Church offices.

But as the lifestyles of the rich and holy became more lavish, more money was needed. The openhanded Leo X, in particular, was a bit hard up after a war that established his nephew, Lorenzo de Medici, as Duke of Urbino.

So, he had the church give a special sale of indulgences in 1517. For a small fee, the Church would give complete absolution and remission of all sins but, wait, there's more! Also preferred treatment for their future sins. The putative purpose of the sale of indulgences was rebuilding St. Peter's Basilica. Profits would be shared with the Archbiship of Mainz, Albrecht of Brandenburg, who was deeply in debt to the Fuggers.[*]

The chief agent of this sale was a Dominican friar named Johann Tetzel. He traveled from town to town with a brass-bound chest and some printed receipts. William Manchester, in *A World Lit Only by Fire*, describes him as a sort of proto-P.T. Barnum, who would set up in the nave of the local church and say, "I have here passports...to lead the human soul to the celestial joys of paradise." Anything could be forgiven, and one example he is said to have given was that if a youth slipped into his mother's bed and spent his seed inside her, "the holy father has the power in heaven and earth to forgive that sin, and if he forgives it, God must do so also." This also worked for departed family members who had died unremorseful of their sins, and abided in purgatory because of this.

The printing press had enabled the mass production of passports to paradise, and the Church was literally offering heaven to motherfuckers for half a florin. Tetzel always exceeded his sales quota.

This did not always seem reasonable to the customers. Some brought their passports to the celestial joys of paradise to a monk (and professor of theology) named Martin Luther to make sure they were getting value for money. He pronounced them frauds.

Tetzel, assuming some skinny, bookish academic would scare easily, denounced him. Luther responded with the strongest move an academic could make. He wrote a thesis. In fact, he wrote 95 of them. It was customary, in a time before academic journals, to pin a paper describing any new theological thesis to the door of the church. It was not generally the custom to post them on a day when there would be a crowd, and distribute pamphlets with the theses translated into German so any literate person could read them, rather than just other churchmen, or to send a copy to the Archbishop of Mainz.

Luther wasn't claiming the passports to paradise were forgeries, he was claiming that the power of the Pope did not reach beyond the grave, and he could not force God to forgive sinners. He also questioned why, if the pope had such power, he did not empty purgatory for the sake of the suffering souls there rather than for money.

The sale of indulgences collapsed. Worse, Luther had brought into question the entire economy of sin and the theology that supported it. Indulgences were based on the theory that good works, such as giving the Church money, could get you into heaven. Luther argued that only faith would get you there.

So, if faith is what gets you into heaven, why do you need that priest who's always asking for money? Luther said that the final authority was holy scripture, and eventually did a translation of the Bible into German that helped shape German as a national language.

This was a philosophy that appealed to the most religious people, disgusted by the increasingly material Church, but it also had a sound financial basis. After all, a German church would not pay taxes to the Roman church, and the German princes would all be better off (there was no country called Germany until 1871, although there was a loose confederation of German kingdoms and duchies formed in 1815.) Not that the peasants would find this pleasant, the aristocracy in central Europe at the time was busy pushing them off their land and making them into serfs.

It took four years for the followers of Luther and the followers of the Church to formally split. The Diet of Worms[*] produced an edict that condemned Martin Luther and anyone who propagated his ideas. Anyone who fingered someone advocating his views got to keep half of the accused's stuff, the other half going to the Holy Roman Emperor. Luther, who had given testimony at the Diet, faced arrest. An ally spirited him away to the dermitologically named Wartburg Castle, where he started his translation of the Bible.

Now, it is beyond the scope of this study to provide a blow-by-blow of the wars that followed. Luther used his influence to keep peace as much as possible until he died in 1546, and war broke out between two Lutheran princes in 1547, leading to their defeat and the oppression of Lutherans by the Holy Roman Emperor (Charles V, one of those Habsburg boys, son of Philip the Handsome and Joanna the Mad. We really need to get back to giving our politicians colorful names.) But Charles V was not the most enthusiastic prosecutors of the Lutheran persecution, because he could see where the Pope might throw his weight around a little less if he had some competition. He gave the Lutheran princes some territory in a peace signed before he died, about a decade after Luther. I should perhaps mention that the Holy Roman Emperor did not rule an empire, but held some kingships himself and held together an alliance of Catholic states.

But tensions grew, religious riots killed people, and Bohemian protestants threw representatives of their new Catholic king (and future Holy Roman Emperor Ferdinand II) out of a window of Prague Castle in what is charmingly called the second defenestration of Prague in 1618, beginning a series of conflicts that would last until 1648.

Prague was at this time the capital of the kingdom of Bohemia, and faced with the majesty of the Holy Roman Empire's wrath, they sought allies among the Protestant Union and even the Ottoman Empire (through the good offices of the Prince of Transylvania. This has the makings of a really colorful video game.)

By 1625, armies from Spain to Denmark were involved. As more and more of Europe became involved, the contestants began running out of money. Armies began to rely on theft and sack to provide provisions and even pay. Famine and disease may have killed more people than arms did, as armies stripped the land bare to feed the troops and left civilians to starve.

Remember the story of stone soup? Three soldiers come into town and when the people say they have no food, the soldiers say they will make a soup from a stone. They taste the boiling water and say, "not bad, but it would be better with some leeks," and a curious onlooker comes forth with a leek. Soon, the soldiers have tricked enough villagers to have a hearty soup.

No doubt the soldiers in the 30-Years' War had a good laugh about that, but it represented a softening of the reality of armies marching without provisions and stripping the land, leaving starvation and death in their wake.

Religious wars were making the case for the secular state by undermining the system of combined rule by religion and state.

Chapter 2: Thomas Hobbes, the Beast of Malmesbury

Few people have anything nice to say about Thomas Hobbes these days, which might seem strange, because he laid out the subjective system of value that underpins our society.

One wonders whether Hobbes was really a nice man. Late in his career, he was known as 'the beast of Malmesbury,' because he was willing to think the unthinkable.

He was a scientist and scholar who seems to have thought the world of himself, a materialist in a world being torn apart by religion, one of the great minds of his time, but unwilling to follow the logic of his own thought to one particular uncomfortable conclusion.

Hobbes was math tutor to Charles II, pretender to the throne of England following the unfortunate death of his father, Charles I, who was beheaded in 1649 by order of parliament during the English Civil War. He was beheaded because he refused to accept a constitutional monarchy rather than the absolute monarchy he had abused to the point of causing a civil war.

Europe at the time Hobbes wrote *Leviathan* (Published in 1648) was convulsed by the 30-Years' War. Everyone's grievance eventually got a look in, but the war was mainly about religion, as Catholic and Protestant settled the matter of who should rule over peoples' souls.

So, when Hobbes, in *Leviathan*, talked about the war of each against all, he wasn't describing some hypothetical state of nature with cave men thinking, "You know, the way we're living just ain't right. We ought to start a society." He was describing the breakdown of society that had engulfed most of Europe during his lifetime. In the breakdown of society, he saw a kind of chaotic individualism which prevented people from acting fully human, that is, exercising their natural rights. For Hobbes and Locke, individualism was a problem to be faced and solved. The war of each against all that Hobbes observed was caused by a breakdown in one of the important ways people cooperated, a shared religion.

Curiously, many people now blame Hobbes and John Locke for the radical individualism sometimes displayed in American politics. Hobbes and Locke were both dealing with the problem of *too much* individualism. Hobbes argued that without the restraints of society, the individualist nature of man led to the war of each against all, where only one's personal strength could defend one's right to live. A contract to form a society, Hobbes argued, was the only way to minimize the risk of being killed by some random stranger. The Leviathan, in the form of a sovereign who could enforce laws against murder and banditry, was therefore the only solution to the problem of excess individualism.

Let's apply this to a modern example, the need in the year 2020 to reduce the toll of the sometimes lethal Covid-19 virus. Public health officials eventually realized that wearing a mask covering the nose and mouth reduced the chance of the disease spreading through aerosols.

As soon as companies and governments started requiring people to wear such masks, there were instances, sometimes violent, of people claiming they had a right not to wear a mask. But the American government is based on social contract theory. The whole point of a social contract is to be able to set limits to individual rights so that they will not interfere with the rights of others. The sovereign power has a duty to limit the tendency of some people to endanger others, so that all may have a right not to be killed, according to Hobbes, and Locke went further with the rights the sovereign should protect.

One peculiar thing about the masking debate is that the anti-maskers tended to have a near-religious belief that Covid-19 was a hoax or a plot, or something designed to allow the government to enslave them by making them wear masks. I cannot help but think that this is connected in some way to the old governing formula of force, faith, and custom. After all, a great many people have been killed for believing the "wrong" things.

The Rights of Lollards

Protestants wanted to be closer to God, not to rely upon priests to intervene on their behalf with God, but to know His word more directly. To that end, they wanted Bibles translated into their own languages. The Church preferred to use the Vulgate Bible, which had been translated into Latin about 500 A.D. so that the Romans could read the text in their own language. By 1500 A.D. Latin was a dead language understood mainly by priests. Before Henry VIII broke with the Catholic Church, British people were put to death after they were found reading scripture in English. The church sentenced them to death for heresy, because those reading the scripture in their own language tended to admit they disagreed with the Church's interpretations of scripture. Under the means of interrogation in use at the time, people would admit to pretty much anything.

There is a very good account of many instances of this in *Actes and Monuments of these Latter and Perillous Days, Touching Matters of the Church*, more commonly known these days as *Foxe's Book of Christian Martyrs*, published in 1563. Foxe wrote about how, despite the Church's prohibition of reading the Bible in their own language, some people gathered in private, reading scripture to each other in such low tones that they became known as Lollards, after a Dutch term for "mutterer." Reading loudly might attract the attention of neighbors who could collect a reward for turning them in.

Protestants rebelled against such abuses. In England, Henry VIII had dealt with the interference of the Catholic Church by starting a sort of "Catholic light" Anglican Church, which transferred much of the wealth of the Catholic Church in England to his followers and ended the practice of burning heretics until Queen Mary I a few years later brought back Catholicism.

But even the new Anglican Church demanded adherence to its tenets and attendance at its services. Worse, it was riven with conflicts between the high church, which wanted to remain pretty much Catholic but with the king of England at the head of the church instead of the Pope, and the low church, composed of people who wanted to purify the church from Catholic practices. Neither were big fans of freedom of religion. The Puritans even started colonies in the New World where they could discriminate against anyone with different religious views (one of my ancestors, I'm told, was kicked out of the Puritan church for giving Quakers shelter from a storm. He became a Quaker.)

And putting the king at the head of the church did not resolve the issue of legitimacy, either. Kings tended to think they should rule by divine right, that is, that their actions could be judged only by God, in whose service they ruled. Parliament tended to think this was pretty high handed and that they should have something to say about matters such as who the country warred with and how money was raised and spent.

This brought on civil war between the supporters of the king, Charles I, and the Puritan-infected parliament. The parliamentary forces included a variety of religious dissenters, including Diggers, Ranters, Levelers, Quakers, Muggltonians, and other colorfully named sects.

In such an environment, the claim to absolute rule by a monarch that was based on divine right bestowed by God was unworkable, even though both Charles I and Charles II claimed to rule on that basis.

Hobbes sought to justify restoring the monarchy and putting his pupil on the throne, but he was more philosopher than politician, so he approached the problem as a philosophical one.

Hobbes was, among other things, a physicist and a chemist. Most of all, he was a materialist. He therefore approached the problem of the legitimacy of the ruler in a materialistic manner. He imported the logic and values of the marketplace into the political sphere, viewing society more as a company than as some sort of spiritual union. Based on what he had seen of Europe in the age of the 30-Years' War and the English Civil War, he wrote of the war of each against all:

> Whatsoever therefore is consequent to a time of Warre, where every man is Enemy to every man; the same is consequent to the time, wherein men live without other security, than what their own strength, and their own invention shall furnish them withall. In such condition, there is no place for Industry; because the fruit thereof is uncertain; and consequently no Culture of the Earth; no Navigation, nor use of the commodities that may be imported by Sea; no commodious Building; no Instruments of moving, and removing such things as require much force; no Knowledge of the face of the Earth; no account of Time; no Arts; no Letters; no Society; and which is worst of all, continuall feare, and danger of violent death; And the life of man, solitary, poore, nasty, brutish, and short.

In short, without some way to keep order, the benefits of civilization are lost. Hobbes perceived that the old system of order had broken down. When the central myth of a society becomes fractured, there are a couple ways to fix this. The usual method is to fight until one side wins. Thus, the Albigensian Crusade of 1209-1229 was not against Muslims, as was usual in those days, but against a Christian splinter group – the Cathars.

When the Church was killing Lollards for reading scripture in English, this was a continuation of a traditional policy of annihilation of sects that competed with the Catholic Church to determine what was right, and therefore, who could legitimately rule. Protestants were executed as heretics as recently as the 16th Century in Britain. Queen Mary I, AKA "Bloody Mary," had 283 protestants executed as heretics, mostly by burning. Mary had promised parliament when she acceded to the throne that she would not require her subjects to follow her religion (Catholic), but she must have had her fingers crossed. In 1554, she got parliament to make Catholicism the state religion again and re-enact the penalties against heresy, and by 1555 she had begun having people burned. The first was a biblical scholar named John Rogers who, on Mary's accession, preached against "pestilent Popery, idolatry and superstition." His heresy was denying the divine character of the Roman Catholic Church. Eventually she was burning a butcher here, a bricklayer there, a fisherman, a draper, and other people who might have brought little attention to themselves if they'd been left alone. Some died on purely doctrinal grounds, such as denying the trinity, a position certain dissenting churches took. Mary had returned Roman Catholicism as the established church of England, so the distinction between the church and the state executing these people was moot.

After Mary died, Queen Elizabeth I had the heresy laws revoked.

It must have been evident to Hobbes, writing nearly a century after Mary's death, that as long as the legitimacy of rulers depended on religion, wars based on religion would continue to convulse Europe. He took a different tack, and decided to describe a purely materialistic justification for civil order.

Karl Marx looked at the misery ministry brought to man, and thought the solution was to eliminate religion, but did not propose a working system of values to replace it. Hobbes, instead of proposing the elimination of religion, simply showed what source of government legitimacy might replace it, perhaps understanding that if the sovereign was legitimate regardless of religion, that would mean religious conflict could be confined to the civil sphere, and not involve armies marching against each other. He saw that somehow, we had to find a way for a government to legitimately govern a society as divided by religion as England or Germany, a lesson nations split between Shiite and Sunni might benefit from.

But how could government be legitimate if the sovereign wasn't God's chosen?

Well, the 30-Years' War had certainly shown that some sort of government capable of keeping order was needed to keep us from being murdered in our sleep, or worse, when we were awake and could see it coming. If you could hire guards to protect you, why not hire an entire government to protect you? All you had to do was get most people to agree to making a social contract with someone to keep order.

Once you had s sovereign who could legitimately act to keep order, the next problem was that this person could not do this alone. Therefore, though the sovereign was the author of acts to keep order, the sovereign could lend his authority to underlings to act in the interest of keeping order. Hobbes is accused (by Leo Strauss) of being an authoritarian thinker, but we should remember that he had a personal agenda, which was to see his friend and pupil, Charles II, installed to be the author of all acts to keep order in Britain. Although his student was a believer in rule by divine right, Hobbes felt that this could not continue as a system for legitimate government. He invented nothing short of a new form of governmental legitimacy.

This would require a completely different value system than the one humanity had relied upon for thousands of years. He began by reinterpreting certain cherished values in purely materialistic ways. In the marvelously cynical Chapter X of *Leviathan*, Hobbes brought some of the most cherished shibboleths of chivalry into the realm of the market.

> The Value, or WORTH of a man, is as of all other things, his Price; that is to say, so much as would be given for the use of his Power: and therefore is not absolute; but a thing dependant on the need and judgement of another. An able conductor of Souldiers, is of great Price in time of War present, or imminent; but in Peace not so. A learned and uncorrupt Judge, is much Worth in time of Peace; but not so much in War. And as in other things, so in men, not the seller, but the buyer determines the Price. For let a man (as most men do,) rate themselves as the highest Value they can; yet their true Value is no more than it is esteemed by others.

This sounds terribly philistine, but the remarkable thing here is that Hobbes was describing a subjective system of value, "dependent on the need and judgment of another," not on God as interpreted by His priests, not to be determined after your death, but here and now and judged by your fellow man.

If the ruler's fitness is to be judged by this standard, no church is needed to determine the divine right.

Further, Hobbes said of honor:

"The manifestation of the value we set on one another, is that which is commonly called honoring, or dishonoring."

And that means that a great many cherished illusions about nobility are nothing but manifestations of power.

"Honorable is whatsoever possession, action, or quality, is an argument or sign of power," Hobbes wrote.

There is a whole list of interpretations that undermine the notion that nobility and honor are somehow spiritual. One of the more striking is what he says about being well born:

"To be descended from conspicuous parents, is honourable, because they the more easily attain the aids, and friends of their ancestors. On the contrary, to be descended from obscure parentage, is dishonourable."

So much for your noble blood, the breeding that has made you a superior person. All those of noble birth are, then, are people born with advantageous connections.

There is something mischievous in the way Hobbes reinterprets the notions of nobility and chivalry into the tawdry values of the marketplace.

And his theory was not well received at first, because it undermined all religious basis for government. The royalist faction he belonged to, for the most part, insisted on the divine right of kings, which claimed that kings ruled by the will of God and only God could judge a king. This was a doctrine adopted by kings both Catholic (Louis XIV) and protestant (James I, Charles I, Charles II.) While he was in exile, his fellow royalists reacted so strongly to *Leviathan* that Hobbes feared for his life and was forced to appeal to the parliamentary government for safety and flee to England.

This new exile was uncertain enough. Oliver Cromwell, one of the signers of the death warrant for Charles I, later Lord Protector of the Commonwealth of England, Scotland and Ireland, was a sample of the sort of people running England during the interregnum, and he firmly believed God guided his victories. He styled himself the "Puritan Moses." And as absolute ruler of England, Scotland, and Ireland, he brought the sort of order to the area he ruled that Hobbes had touted as the advantage of having a sovereign. Some royalists insisted that this meant Hobbes was justifying the rebellion, but when Hobbes was writing *Leviathan* Cromwell was not yet in power, and his campaigns in Ireland and Scotland were still under way. *Leviathan* was published in 1651, and Cromwell did not use force to expel the Rump Parliament and take power himself until 1653. For Hobbes, making his peace with the English Commonwealth must have depended to some extent on members of the Rump Parliament not reading his work too closely. They were ruling Britain as a republic, and he was an advocate of monarchy.

Hobbes, although he had come up with a secular justification for the legitimacy of the king, argued that a nation needed a state religion and had a right to enforce the adoption of said religion. This would come back to haunt him. You see, if there is a state religion, the state is placed in the position of deciding who is practicing that religion. And while Hobbes felt quite sure he was Church of England all the way, there were those in parliament who disagreed.

Once Charles II was safely on the throne, parliamentarians who had read *Leviathan* took issue with the seldom-read second half of the book, which deals with theology. You see, Hobbes was such a dedicated materialist that he even insisted that, since only the material world exists, God must be a material being. And England at that time was ready to pass blasphemy laws as strict as any ayatollah could desire. (And about as strict as had been used under its Catholic kings and queens. The Marian persecutions had burned 283 protestants as heretics from 1553 to 1558. Thus the sobriquet "Bloody Mary.")

By denying the existence of the entire spiritual world, some said, Hobbes had committed blasphemy and should be killed. In 1666 the House of Commons considered a law against blasphemy and atheism, and the committee to which the bill was referred was ordered to consider in particular "the book of Mr. Hobbes called the *Leviathan.*"

Now, you might think they would have to pass a law, arrest Hobbes, and try him under that law. But between 1321and 1798, parliament could simply pass a bill of attainder (which in effect declared a person tainted, and deprived them of their civil rights) and execute them without a trial. This is specifically prohibited in the American constitution, because it was too often used as a convenient way for rulers to dispose of inconvenient people without a trial. So the fact that parliament was considering a bill that would declare Hobbes a blasphemer was a direct threat to his health and, should he be beheaded, his height.

But Hobbes had one particularly powerful connection, King Charles II, and by his own peculiar definition of honor, it was perhaps honorable that the king interceded and prevented him from being prosecuted. However, he never again published any work relating to human conduct in England, preferring to publish in Amsterdam, and he did burn some of his papers as a precaution.

Hobbes, who had essentially ridiculed the world of honor, chivalry, and nobility, had by his definition dishonored God by demoting him to the status of a sort of superman, but there was one line he never crossed. He never followed his argument to its logical conclusion.

After all, if society is formed by a sort of contract in which you hire a ruler to keep order, what happens if he's bad at his job? Shouldn't you be able to fire him, or if he refuses to leave power, depose him? Well, that's where we come to the criminal, one might even say terrorist, John Locke, a radical who also argued that the state should not enforce religious belief by force and that its citizens had the right to kill the king under certain circumstances.

In particular, Charles II. He was alleged to have conspired to kill *that* king.

Chapter 3: The Outlaw John Locke

The social studies version of John Locke is that he was a rather boring person who lived a long time ago and taught that society is based on property. This is one of those partial truths intended to make the teaching of liberalism safe for students who will not disrupt the classroom or the society that nurtures them.

Locke wrote at least part of his most famous work, *Two Treatises of Government*, while in exile after escaping charges of treason, and he did not allow it to be published under his own name during his lifetime. This prudence was well justified. He was wanted in connection with an attempted regicide, and it wouldn't have done to make conspicuous his connection to texts that first, argued that there was no divine right of kings, and second, that if the king ruled badly and could not be replaced by other means, citizens were justified in killing him. Even after the Glorious Revolution put a king more to his liking on the throne, a text which included a right to revolution against bad kings was unlikely to make him any friends among those with death warrants in their desks.

Locke was not an epigrammatic writer, but Thomas Jefferson was, on occasion, and one of those occasions was when he put Locke's ideas into the American Declaration of Independence:

> "We hold these truths to be self-evident, that all men are created equal, that they are endowed by their Creator with certain unalienable Rights, that among these are life, liberty, and the pursuit of Happiness, – that to secure these rights, Governments are instituted among Men, deriving their just powers from the consent of the governed – That whenever any Form of Government becomes destructive of these ends, it is the Right of the People to alter or abolish it..."

That's a pretty good summation of Locke's views on the matter, which is why he had to flee his native country. The reason it is not a counsel for complete anarchy is that it applies only when government cannot be replaced by other means. The right to revolution is a last resort, not a first one when you don't like the outcome of an election.

When Locke lived in exile, he was wanted in connection with the Rye House Plot of 1683. Rye House was a sturdy stone structure with a moat. The plan was to trap the carriage of King Charles II in the courtyard in front of it and rain down musket fire until all within the carriage were dead. (And yes, that's the same Charles II that Hobbes had taught math to and for whom Hobbes had invented a new form of legitimacy.) The king's route changed (because Newmarket, where he planned to watch some horse races, burned down,) the plot was uncovered, and the participants were hunted and some were killed. Quite a few were hanged, drawn, and quartered,[*] some had the more gentlemanly death of beheading, and many were pardoned for giving evidence that got their co-conspirators hanged, drawn, and quartered.

Locke fled to the Netherlands. Charles II died in 1685, and was briefly succeeded by his brother James, (a Catholic) who was simultaneously James II of England and Ireland and James IV of Scotland. In 1688, he was overthrown in the Glorious Revolution, which was a reaction to James attempting to give equal rights to Catholics and dissenting Protestants. Since the time of Elizabeth I, people had to be Church of England to hold public office or an officer's commission in the military. Locke accompanied across the English Channel one William of Orange, who was invited to invade the country by some Protestant noblemen. (The invasion ended in a bloodless coup. Some of the forces James commanded switched sides, and although James still commanded the larger force, he was unsure of their loyalties and chose not to fight.)

Charles II, as I've mentioned, wasn't buying any of this social contract nonsense. He was an avowed believer in the divine right of kings, which was sort of the point of Locke's writing the *First Treatise of Government*. Locke pretty well demolished the theory of divine right in that one. James II was also an advocate of his own divine right.

But it's the *Second Treatise of Government* that is mainly read today. That's the one in which he tackled the social contract.

Hobbes had argued that we need a social contract to form a government in order to free us from the constant threat of violent death. That's all well and good, but it's not specific to human society. Wolves manage to have enough of a society to avoid killing each other, and they are really *good* at killing. Apparently, no philosophy is needed to form such a society, only as much sense as the Good Lord gave a wolf.

Locke's concept of the social contract is more specific to human society, in that he founded it on the human institution of property.

Locke's theory was that we are all born owning property in our own bodies, which we cannot sell (or, as Locke was wont to put it, "alienate.") We could make more property by applying our labor to nature.

Locke thought we all have a right to life, liberty, and property. Perhaps this is best understood as what is required to be part of human society. To be a person, you must have individual agency. Once born, you must be allowed to live, you cannot help but think, and you must at least be sufficiently engaged in the web of rights, obligations, and prohibitions about the use of objects to at least own yourself. In a way, it all comes down to property.

Strangely, Locke never exactly defined property. The current understanding of property is that it is not objects, which exist whether they are owned or not, but rather it is the rules, rights, and obligations that regulate the use of objects by persons. An "object" might not even be a physical thing, it might be a computer algorithm or any image that resembles to a sufficient degree a certain corporate-owned cartoon character.

Given this definition, Locke's concept of all of us owning ourselves makes the notion of inalienable rights more understandable. After all, if you sell a chair, it will never rebel. It will allow its new owners to do what they wish with it. But we will always be in our bodies as long as we live, and we will never be able to lose interest in how our bodies are used while we live, and perhaps even after we shuffle off this mortal coil.

This concept of people being born owning themselves also had a kind of ticking bomb inside it. In Locke's time, to have full rights of citizenship and be able to vote, you had to own property. If we all owned property in ourselves, this became an argument for universal suffrage.

No doubt, dear reader, you are asking yourself, "why was the bomb ticking, rather than exploding as soon as it was created?"

I suppose the answer is that you first had to be considered enough of a human being to own yourself. Locke, like many philosophers, did not necessarily live by his own precepts. He wrote the constitution of South Carolina in which chattel slavery was enshrined in law, and owned stock in the Royal African Company, which was in the business of buying slaves in Africa and transporting them to the New World.

He did write a justification for slavery in the *Second Treatise of Government*, but it did not justify the sort of slavery in which he was complicit. In the chapter on slavery, he says that if someone commits a crime so great that their life could be forfeit, their life may belong to the authority that would have taken that life.

This in no way justifies the sort of system he wrote into law and participated in, which provided for people to be born into slavery. Perhaps he did not regard Africans as people. Or perhaps he was one of those rare people who become more radical as they get older.

People are complicated, and it could be that both racism and radicalism are involved. In any case, we can say that well after he had written the South Carolina constitution and sold off his holdings in the Royal African Company, he was writing about slavery in a way that did not justify the sort of slavery he had seen. In writing about what conditions might justify slavery, he made it clear that those conditions did not apply to slavery as it was practiced in his day, which was a finger in the eye of slave owners.

The *Second Treatise of Government* gave us a way of thinking about people that meant, as soon as you recognized their humanity, you no longer had any justification for treating them like things, like objects that can be bought and sold.

That's a way of looking at humanity that caused another revolution. For pretty much all of recorded history, human beings have either kept slaves, known about slavery without objecting to it, or been slaves. The Athenian Golden Age was supported by the wealth generated by silver mines worked by slaves. Granted, the chattel slavery of the New World was many times worse than the slavery of Europeans by other Europeans, but it has never been a good deal to be a slave. The very notion of slavery is that you are held against your will, forced to do work not of your choosing, and the fruits of your labor belong to your master.

But if you own yourself, and cannot alienate, that is, sell, your property right to own yourself, you are your own master. It is a responsibility you cannot evade, and a right that cannot be taken from you. That is, as long as people recognize your humanity, which was the problem for slaves.

Just as Hobbes did not follow the logic of his social contract to the natural conclusion that the people should be able to change their rulers, because it would be inconvenient for his personal goals, Locke did not follow the logic of his theory of inalienable rights to the conclusion that the slaves should be set free.

Others did, leading to the abolition movement.

Slaves were not the only people affected by the property paradigm. Abraham Lincoln's father hired him out to work for other farmers, keeping any wages earned for himself. His property rights over his son allowed him to treat him in a manner Lincoln later characterized as being like slavery.

Until the Married Women's Property Act of 1882, under English law all property a woman may have owned prior to marriage became the property of her husband.

Marriage, the household, and the rights of fathers over children and husbands over wives were defined to a great extent by the conventions of property. The words, "You belong to me" are still uttered by men to women, but back then, the meaning was more literal.

So, the concept that people owned themselves was a lever that could pry apart old conventions and remake our institutions in a more egalitarian spirit. Centuries after Locke, we are still remaking our world based on the idea that we each are our own master.

In a household where the father was the master, relationships tended to be defined in property terms. The wife and children belonged to the household, the father was the master of it. This goes back a long way in history. The polygamous households of biblical times were very much defined in this way, which in fact is how polygamy has generally worked in the societies that have practiced it. Modern marriage defines the relationship in terms of partnership.

So, strangely enough, Locke's system of thought was based on the notion of property, but it has freed us from a tradition of treating people as property.

One might say, "property" is what objects mean to us. Just as marriage is the institution that regulates our urge to mate, property is the institution that regulates our desire to possess.

Our concepts of what is property and who owns it can change dramatically, as it did with the abolition of slavery. Property, after all, is only one province in the realm of meaning. Our society is constantly redefining the meaning of things and therefore the shape of our institutions. But how does that happen?

Well, we have institutions that interpret things. Courts interpret law, adapting it to new circumstances. When an established church was entwined with the state, it defined virtue, and said who was acting as God willed, and who was acting against God's will.

Sometimes power has a great deal to do with such changes. When the textile mills began to demand large quantities of wool, the lord of a local manor sometimes got an "inclosure act" passed, which meant that land that had been the village commons, that is land anyone could graze a cow on, became property of the local lord. This had the effect of impoverishing commoners to enrich their masters (there's that word again) and producing expanses of grass closely cropped by sheep. Even now, a lawn of closely cropped green grass is a status symbol, even in countries such as the United States and Canada that saw an increase in immigration because of the inclosure acts.

But liberalism is a child of the Enlightenment. It is an attempt to apply reason to matters that previously might have been settled by the power titled landowners exercised on the courts, or decisions by the Church about who was acting virtuously.

A Letter Concerning Toleration

There was more to Locke's philosophy than property. One of his more insightful works was about religion, and was published without his consent.

The "caliphate" of Islamic State appears, at this writing, to have collapsed. At the same time, there are people in the United States insisting that America is a Christian nation.

There are reasons that the founding fathers chose to write a constitution that bans any religious test for holding office, and in 1797 unanimously passed the Treaty of Tripoli, which states in article 11 that "the Government of the United States of America is not, in any sense, founded on the Christian religion."

First, they had been ruled by Britain, which had a state religion, and decreed that only members of the Church of England could be officers in the military or hold public office. Many of those who settled this nation did so to practice religion as they saw fit, not as the government saw fit.

Second, the Constitution and the Bill of Rights were written by men who admired John Locke, the most influential of the liberal theorists.

Locke is most famous for the Second Treatise of Government, which laid out his theory of the social contract. But another work laid out his thoughts on the relationship between church and state.

This was *A Letter Concerning Toleration* written originally in Latin to a Dutch intellectual named Philipp van Limborch, who thought so highly of it that he had it published. He did so without Locke's knowledge or permission, embroiling Locke in a dispute with High Church members of the Anglican clergy.

They argued that the state has a right to force dissenters to reflect on the Anglican Church as the one true religion.

But wars were fought over which was the One True Faith. The 30-Years War depopulated parts of Europe as effectively as the Black Death had three centuries earlier.

Which is why, in his letter to Philipp van Limborch, Locke argued that:

> It is not the diversity of opinions (which cannot be avoided), but the refusal of toleration to those that are of different opinions (which might have been granted), that has produced all the bustles and wars that have been in the Christian world upon account of religion.

Further, he argued for separation of church and state. The argument rests, in part, on his definition of the role of civil authorities:

The commonwealth seems to me to be a society of men constituted only for the procuring, preserving, and advancing their own civil interests.

Civil interests I call life, liberty, health, and indolency of body; and the possession of outward things, such as money, lands, houses, furniture, and the like.

Locke was not inclined to write briefly, and the argument has many parts, but the most important aspects were:

A) Religious wars are caused not by people believing different things, but by trying to make them all believe the same thing, and

B) The state has no particular expertise at knowing the true religion, and

C) You can compel people to act as if they believe in your religion, but you cannot compel them to actually believe, therefore they do not have faith that will save them, even if the state picks the right religion, and

D) When there is a state religion, the state intervenes in religion, and religion intervenes in the state.

On the matter of religion intervening in the state, he wrote:

What can be the meaning of their asserting that kings excommunicated forfeit their crowns and kingdoms? It is evident that they thereby arrogate unto themselves the power of deposing kings, because they challenge the power of excommunication, as the peculiar right of their hierarchy.

On the state intervening in the church, Locke wrote:

> But, to speak the truth, we must acknowledge that the Church (if a convention of clergymen, making canons, must be called by that name) is for the most part more apt to be influenced by the Court than the Court by the Church. How the Church was under the vicissitude of orthodox and Arian emperors is very well known. Or if those things be too remote, our modern English history affords us fresh examples in the reigns of Henry VIII, Edward VI, Mary, and Elizabeth, how easily and smoothly the clergy changed their decrees, their articles of faith, their form of worship, everything according to the inclination of those kings and queens. Yet were those kings and queens of such different minds in point of religion, and enjoined thereupon such different things, that no man in his wits (I had almost said none but an atheist) will presume to say that any sincere and upright worshipper of God could, with a safe conscience, obey their several decrees.

The framers of the Constitution were, for the most part, admirers of Locke. They understood that to practice your own religion freely, you must be free of other peoples' religions. This is why the first amendment to the constitution reads:

> **Congress shall make no law respecting an establishment of religion**, or prohibiting the free exercise thereof; or abridging the freedom of speech, or of the press; or the right of the people peaceably to assemble, and to petition the Government for a redress of grievances.

The boldfaced part is called the establishment clause. It means that the government cannot establish a religion, that is, make one religion the state religion. That is why a senate comprised of people who had been alive during the Revolutionary War and in many cases fought for America's freedom were happy to unanimously pass the Treaty of Tripoli, which as mentioned above, stated that "the Government of the United States of America is not, in any sense, founded on the Christian religion."

What they knew, and many people apparently do not know now, is that one of the things that made America revolutionary was that the state did not dictate what religion would be approved and in some ways dictated by the state to the people. This meant that you could practice any religion you liked.

Events like the Marian Persecutions were still well known at that time, whereas most people no longer know about them.

Queen Mary I was Catholic, and came into power after the deaths of

Henry VIII, who had founded the Church of England and seized the property of the Catholic Church, and his son, Edward VI, who had established the Protestant church. Mary made Catholicism the established church of England again, and started burning Protestants at the stake for heresy.

Mary had 283 people burned at the stake, ranging from Church of England Bishops, even the Archbishop of Canterbury, to working-class men and women who confessed to beliefs in conflict with Catholic doctrine.

For example Guillemine Gilbert and Perotine Massey, sisters living on the island of Guernsey, were arrested on suspicion of stealing a golden goblet. While they were found innocent of the theft, under interrogation, they admitted to beliefs that, while common among Protestants, were contrary to Catholic doctrine.

The women were sentenced to death for heresy. John Foxe (author of a book now usually called *The Book of Christian Martyrs*) recorded that Perotine Massey was "great with child," and that when she was burned at the stake, "the belly of the woman burst asunder by the vehemence of the flame, the infant, being a fair man-child, fell into the fire"

Foxe was not there, and I do wonder if perhaps the baby was born in a more usual manner by a mother who must have been writhing in pain, but that's what the eyewitnesses said. They also said the child was rescued from the flame, but the bailiff had it thrown back into the fire. The Guernsey Martyrs had a great deal to do with the rise of Calvinism in the Channel Islands, and the diminishment of Catholicism in the same place.

Given that this could be the face of establishment of religion, the founders of the American nation wanted none of it. The problem is, once you say that yours is a "Christian nation," or for that matter, an "Islamic state," the apparatus of state force can be used to enforce someone's notion of what that religion consists of. This is why Islamic State was killing people for being Shia Muslim rather than Sunni Muslim, and killing Yazidi men and enslaving Yazidi women for not being Muslim at all.

The logic is the same as applied to Bloody Mary's actions. The state does not serve the people, it and they serve God, and only God can judge their ruler. Therefore, once you have a state-accepted religion, it is the duty of the state to punish unbelievers. No elections are needed, because the state serves God, and his earthly representatives can tell the people who God has appointed to rule them.

This also means that it is imperative for rulers to either be on good terms with God's representatives, or choose those representatives themselves. In killing the upper ranks of the Church of England, Mary I was choosing which of God's representatives should rule on her own legitimacy, and sending an unmistakable message to those who replaced them.

The people who founded America had no use for a system that could produce anything like the Guernsey Martyrs, or the many indignities short of that. They took Locke's advice and separated the state from religion, allowing the peaceful coexistence of different sorts of believers. There had, in colonial times, been individual colonies with established religions, sometimes leading followers of an entire faith to be disenfranchised. In 1718 Maryland, which had been founded by a Roman Catholic, passed a law depriving Catholics of the right to vote, reflecting in-migration of protestants, who had become a majority. Catholics did not regain the right to vote until 1776.

A Letter Concerning Toleration is not much studied today, but it should be. It contains the solution to religious strife, and the logic of the secular state, which are inseparable.

Another figure who, like Hobbes, wrote during the English Civil War, proposed a way to settle matters of what is true that differed quite substantially from Bloody Mary's method of relying on the Catholic Church for doctrine and torture for evidence. John Milton, a poet, champion of the Puritan cause, and advocate of the freedom to divorce, advocated a new and revolutionary way of arriving at judgments of truth or falsehood. He suggested we should have free and open discussion. But before we get to him, let's talk about how Locke's conception of who we are continues to reshape our lives.

Chapter 4: Polygamy, gay marriage, and the liberal mindset

For a lesson in traditional marriage, we should no doubt look to the Bible.

King Solomon is said to have had 300 wives. I have pledged to settle down and get married as soon as I find the right 300 women to allow me to marry in the traditional style (that is, always outnumbered, always outgunned.)

But although the Bible is replete with references to polygamous marriage, modern Americans are more comfortable with the notion of gay marriage, which is mentioned nowhere I know of in the Bible.

There are practical reasons for this. Conservatives fighting against gay marriage found it difficult to find proof that children raised in gay households are harmed by them. Opponents of polygamy seem to suffer from no such difficulty. Communities that practice polygamy have been accused of forcing under-aged girls into marriage with older men, exploiting children and having them do unsafe work, being abusive to children, and kicking teenage boys out of the community when they start showing an interest in girls so that the girls will be available to older men. The boys are shunned by their families and forced to live in a world they know almost nothing about outside the community.

The reason boys were expelled was simple math. If some men have many wives, others must have none, unless they are eliminated. Male elephants not connected to females are called "rogue males." It is certainly in the interest of human society not to have too many rogues in it, because they are disruptive.

But I don't think such practical matters are really the key to why polygamy is less acceptable than gay marriage to the modern Western mind.

The key is a revolution in how we think of people, codified by the philosophers of the Enlightenment, and especially the thinkers of liberalism.

Thomas Hobbes laid out a new system of value, that it "is not absolute, but a thing dependent on the need and judgment of another."

We were now to be valued by each other, not by the priest or by the position of our birth.

John Locke, writing at the end of the 17th century, noticed that not only did we value each other, our relationships were often subject to the rules of property. The master of a household had something like a property right to those within it under the law of his time.

A married woman, for example, was regarded as a "feme covert," that is, she became, for property purposes, one with her husband, and subordinate to him. (A widow would be a "feme sole," in charge of herself.) If a woman at that time (and in fact until the late 19th century) in England held, for example, a copyright, it passed to her husband when she married and would not be returned to her if she divorced. In fact, all of the household's property remained with the husband, and a divorced woman would usually be impoverished unless a very good prenuptial agreement were negotiated.

Property was also connected intimately with the notion of citizenship. To vote in England at the time, you had to own property.

I have mentioned that Locke's *Second Treatise of Government* contained a ticking time bomb, because he proposed that we all own property in our own person, and cannot alienate – that is sell – that particular property. Every person, therefore, had inalienable property rights to themselves, that is, we are each of us our own master.

All that remained was to decide who was a person. A dawning realization that slaves are people meant that they must logically be their own masters, and slavery must be immoral. The Womens' Rights movement brought about property rights for married women before it brought them the vote. The Married Womens' Property Acts were not completed in England until1882, though earlier acts had set the pattern.

But polygamous marriages worked, to the extent they did, because women and children were regarded as property of the master of the household. If wives are recognized as their own "master," this relationship no longer exists.

The term "feme covert" seems at first glance to have promise. One pictures a Thurber cartoon, with the wife in ninja clothing and the ineffectual husband looking on, the caption reading, "When you married me I was a blushing maid, but now I am a feme covert, Mr. Johnson!"

One of Thurber's main themes was "the war between men and women," which he seems to have lost to his domineering first wife. But by then, the feme covert was a thing of the past; community property was the future.

We still see conflict over the nature of marriage. Traditionalists still advocate "traditional marriage," sometimes even polygamous marriage. What they mean by this is a return to the concept of the feme covert, subordinate to her master. It is no coincidence that the same people often worry about keeping control of their children, worried that exposing them to public schools would cause them to learn things they shouldn't know, like evolution, and expose them to a system of values that would be distressingly modern. This could give them dangerous ideas of autonomy.

Birth control has meant that marriage doesn't have to be about child rearing, and many of the tasks of the household that used to consume a great deal of women's time, like spinning and weaving and sewing clothing, have been moved outside the home. Marriage is less about property and child rearing than it has ever been before, and more about love, and a partnership between equals.

As people are recognized as equals, old barriers have fallen. Miscegenation laws fell because, if African Americans are not a lesser race, why should they not marry whites, if that is who they love? As the humanity of homosexuals has been recognized by society at large, the question comes up, why should they not marry who they love?

What was once common knowledge, that the master of the household is the master of all within it, has fallen before the revolutionary idea that we are all our own masters. Few people have read Hobbes or Locke, but their ideas permeate our society and are still reshaping it. Ideas travel though a society less by formal indoctrination than by a sort of mimetic contagion. It is "common knowledge" now that we are our own men and women, when in an earlier age, it was common knowledge that this was not the case. The older "common knowledge is associated with patriarchy.

The most remarkable thing about patriarchy is that after millennia of organizing societies around it, we have now become uncomfortable with it.

A remarkably large number of human societies treat people as things. It is a foundation of patriarchy, a system in which dominant males treat women and children as property. There is even a debate about whether such behavior is innate or socially conditioned (full disclosure, I come down on the socially conditioned side of the debate.)

Abraham Lincoln was rented out as a laborer by his father for 10 cents to 31 cents an hour, and wages earned by him were paid to his father. "I used to be a slave," is the way he described the situation in an early political speech.

The legal situation that allowed this was part of what we now call patriarchy. While American society never allowed men to buy and sell children or wives, fathers and husbands long held a dominant property position in the family. Under the doctrine of coveture, when a woman married a man, they became, for purposes of property, one person, and that person was the man. Any property the woman had passed to the man, and in event of a divorce, would remain property of the man unless there were an ironclad prenuptial agreement. This meant that for a very long time, divorce meant ruin for a woman.

Being, essentially, property, meant that you were not treated as fully human. Neither slaves nor women got to vote until they got property rights, and the first property right is to own yourself. And who would not want to own themselves? I'm not aware of any slaves that wished to remain a thing used by others. I am aware that a few women prefer traditional gender roles. Perhaps it is comforting to know your place and not have to invent your own place in the world, but it seems to be a comfort few wish to avail themselves of.

Patriarchy played a role in the justification of monarchy, and is perhaps part of what attracts people to all autocratic forms of government. No one needed to justify the right of kings to rule until it came into question, but when it did, some of the justifications founded the king's authority in parental authority. In fact, a book some considered the definitive defense of the divine right of kings was titled *Patriarcha, or the Natural Power of Kings.* In it, Sir Robert Filmer argued that Adam had complete power over his descendants, including the power of life and death, and it was from this basis that kings could trace their power. Filmer had a son, who seems to have survived his parenting.

John Locke, who never married or had children, seemed to have a better understanding about how families work. He pointed out that the father shares his authority over the children with their mother, and his power is not absolute. Locke argued that we are all born owning ourselves, and that fathers do not have the power of life and death over their children, because such authority is not needed for the purpose of the relationship, which is to care for and nurture children until they reach the age of reason, and can be responsible for themselves and embrace their freedom.

It is fashionable to study the ethics John Stuart Mill and Immanuel Kant, who addressed the question of how we may know right from wrong directly, attempting to codify behavior that was already accepted. But Locke's ideas changed the way we conceive of people, and changed the way we treat them. He changed what we regard as ethical in a way no ethicist could.

Once we encounter Locke's idea that we are all born owning ourselves, and cannot sell the rights to ourselves as property, it seems intuitively obvious. A pot has no mind to care who cooks with it, or whether the food is good or bad, a chair cannot resent the weight it bears, but we cannot help but care how we are used. Once we understand this about ourselves, we cannot escape a natural human empathy to others who are used as objects are used, and we sympathize with their plight. Slavery, an institution probably as old as war, becomes an abomination. Coveture, and parallel institutions in other patriarchal cultures, becomes absurd.

The process of the logic of liberalism spreading through human institutions has not been terribly rapid, but it has been inexorable, and the effects of its logic continue to change traditional elements of our society.

Consider Locke's theory of property. We apply our labor to nature, and this makes property. Now consider the patriarchal way of life. A man plants his seed in the land, and makes it fruitful, he plants his seed in a woman and makes her fruitful. In each case, the land and the woman, both the thing he plants his seed in and the fruit of his planting becomes his.

Clearly, this is more a founding myth than how the world has ever worked, but myths are the way we understand the way the world is *supposed* to work. The patriarch is supposed to build a little world in which he owns the land, governs his family, and provides for all. This is a model for the larger society, as well.

Not all men could do this, particularly in a world where most of the land was already owned. One solution to this was to have disenfranchised men who had little or nothing, and wealthy men with many acres, cattle, chattel, and wives. The entire system was based on perpetuating little empires of property, and the relationship to most of the things in a household was one of the patriarch's ownership. Traditional institutions of law and government existed, to a great extent, to adjudicate and enforce this system of property, and thereby bring order to society. Men of property wielded great power in such societies. Women of property, and therefore women of power, in many societies did not exist. Instead of owning property, they were property.

Not owning yourself, of course, has a spiritual side, but more obviously, it has a physical side. If you do not own yourself, you do not own your body, and you do not control what is done with your body. When Ohio Republicans blocked an amendment that <u>would have made it illegal to rape one's spouse</u> while they are drunk, drugged, or incapacitated,[*] this was part of the same philosophy that caused them to pass a law banning all abortions, even in cases of rape or incest, if a heartbeat can be detected (usually around six weeks after conception, often before the mother is aware of the pregnancy.) In either case, the object is to keep women from having control of their bodies.

I'm not sure to what extent there is a conscious realization among the people doing these things about the connection between women controlling their bodies and and women owning themselves and having agency and power in the world. One would think that people who find abortion abhorrent would favor availability of birth control, which makes abortion less necessary, but this is not the case. Nor is it the case that they consistently advocate for society to provide better prenatal care for the unborn or for children after they are born. The logic of their actions does not support the notion that what they care about is mainly children. However, in matters of birth control, abortion, and marital rape, the same group of people act on a unified theory that women should not control their bodies.

Granting them control of their bodies grants them ownership of themselves, which in turn means granting them agency and power in the world. Changing who owns the woman's womb challenges the entire traditional edifice of a society based on a system in which women and children were property.

And if men of property really *should* wield great power in a society, power over women, over those who have less property, and over those who previously were property, that at last explains the mystery of why poor whites have been voting for a political party that gives benefits mainly to those who have a lot of property. They are voting for a traditional society in which patriarchs run things, because something deeply embedded in our society tells them this is how it should be.

Locke's idea that we are all born owning ourselves is deeply subversive, even more subversive than he realized in his lifetime (and Locke knew it was explosive enough that it could cost his life or liberty, which is why he never allowed his Treatises on Government to be published under his own name during his lifetime.) Property, after all, is not things, it is the set of rules about how we use things, about our rights and responsibilities in relation to them.

When you decide that a person is not property, you change a great deal about how that person is to be treated. And when you do that, you change the very structure of society.

We are in the midst of a slow-motion revolution that is changing first our minds, then changing everything else. We must not underestimate the disruption this is causing, or the resistance it will engender. The imperatives of a society in which we each own ourselves are very different from those of traditional societies, and we will find ourselves reinventing ourselves and our societies.

Liberalism, therefore, is not for the faint of heart. There is no certainty that what the logic of liberalism leads to is even possible. This reinvention of society is a product of the enlightenment, and it will require courage and persistence to avoid sinking back into the dark age in which we were governed by force, faith, and custom.

How do these ideas spread and change our minds? Through another change in the way we think, championed by another 17th century malcontent; John Milton, the poet, champion of the Puritan cause, advocate for the right to divorce one's spouse, and sometime Secretary for Foreign Tongues for the Commonwealth that ruled England during the Interregnum between the beheading of Charles I and the restoration of Charles II.

Milton's revolutionary idea was that we could arrive at truth through free and open discussion, rather than the old method that had involved dismembering people who disagreed with the sovereign or burning at the stake those who disagreed with the Church.

Chapter 5: John Milton and the many shapes of truth

John Milton is today mainly remembered as a poet, but he was also a political actor in the English Civil War, writing many tracts in support of the Puritan and parliamentary cause, eventually serving as the Secretary of Foreign Tongues for the Council of State. Under this remarkable title, he handled most of the council's correspondence in, you guessed it, foreign tongues, but also wrote pamphlets in defense of popular government and the regicide of Charles I. His clear and powerful Latin prose made him a reputation in Europe.

He also wrote one of the founding documents of liberalism, *Areopagitica*, to my way of thinking the definitive defense of free speech.

In 1644, when he wrote the *Areopagitica*, the war was going badly for the parliamentary forces, and their ultimate victory would only be achieved after their army was completely reorganized in 1645. In such times, rulers typically worry about what gets said and written, not just in terms of military secrets, but in terms of propaganda and morale. Parliament had the power to censor, and Milton urged them not to use it.

He had personal reasons for this. In 1643 Milton married, at the age of 35, 16-year-old Mary Powell. After only a month of living with a difficult older man, she left him and returned home. Milton wrote a series of pamphlets saying that divorce should be legal, which got him in a bit of trouble, which seems to have prompted him to write in defense of free speech. Not, mind you, that he only wanted to be allowed to continue agitating for a policy that he at the time he thought he wanted (Mary returned to him in 1645 and they had three children together, she dying in childbirth with the third.) Milton seems to have firmly believed that there should be no prior censorship for people, no matter what their views, with one exception.

We all have our limits, right? The "no censorship" rule sounds fine until some child pornographer comes along and tries to use this freedom to publish something really gross. For Milton, there were limits as well. Anyone should be able to voice their opinions, he believed, except Catholics.

Remember, there was a war on, and it was very much about religion. The Catholic Church was so opposed to the Bible being translated into English that at one point the Bishop of London bought up as many copies as he could of William Tyndale's English translation of the Bible and burned them (Tyndale used the money to print a new edition with some corrections he had wanted to make. Ecclesiastical rank does not automatically confer on one a deep understanding of economics.) The Church hunted William Tyndale until he could be strangled, and had his remains burned so that he could not be resurrected on Judgment Day.

A more forgiving man than Milton could take a dim view of that. Tyndale's translation of the Bible was the basis for the Great Bible, published under King Henry VIII, and what is now called the King James Bible, because the scholars who followed recognized his genius. Milton saw the argument that censorship was a Papist import as one that would resonate with parliament.

As it happens, in my misspent youth I studied the fashionable theorists of that time, among them Jürgen Habermas, one of the leading theorists on the subject of discourse. It struck me at the time that Harbermas (whose work has been criticized by Marxists for being bourgeois) had a theory that was in many ways like Milton's, but not as well written and far less radical. Habermas, by the way, is at this writing still alive, and one of the most influential philosophers around, bridging the gap between Anglo-American and Continental philosophy. I will say that his philosophy is far more complete than Milton's. It should be, he packs a lot into every sentence and *The Theory of Communicative Action* runs to two volumes that seem to weigh more with every word one reads. And that's just one of his books.

Habermas claims that if you could achieve undominated discourse, the result of such a dialogue would always produce the same answer, which would be the truth. This always struck me as a dubious proposition. What if no one present thinks of the right answer? What, we may ask, if everyone present is stupid, or at least not clever in the right way? I have a Manx named Bunny who is brilliant at being a cat, but faced with a logical argument her only response is to bring my attention the feather-on-a-string toy. In short, she is helpless before my logic. I tell her that the feather-on-a-string toy argument is so far beside the point that she's not even wrong, but we end up playing her game in the end. I will admit that Habermas is worth any ten other theorists of the Critical School, but his logic and Bunny's steely resolve about the toy would not produce the same result as a conversation between him and Jacques Derrida. No doubt, the result would be better.

Milton had greater faith than Habermas in the truth:

> And though all the winds of doctrine were let loose to play upon the earth, so Truth

Unlike Habermas, Milton was willing to accept the notion that truth
"may have more shapes than one." England and Europe as a whole were rent
by religious strife. If each sect insisted that only its truth was acceptable, the
strife would continue. The notion that ones countrymen could profess a
different faith and not be persecuted as apostates was a path to peace, just as
Hobbes' effort to find a secular path to the legitimacy of government was.

The method Milton proposed, allowing publication without prior
censorship, is the basic method adopted by liberal democracies everywhere.
Sure, you can be sued, fined, even jailed for saying some things, but there is a
very high bar the state must achieve to justify censorship prior to publication.

To understand the landscape of English discourse, it helps to know
that truth was not a defense in cases of libel against the sovereign. Consider,
for example, the case of John Stubbs.

In 1579, he published a racy little number called *The Discovery of a
Gaping Gulf whereunto England is like to be swallowed by another French
Marriage, if the Lord forbid not the banns, by letting her Majesty see the sin
and punishment thereof.* In it, he argued that Queen Elizabeth should not
marry the brother of the King of France. Stubbs argued that at 46, the Queen
was too old to bear children, and had no need to marry. He argued that such a
marriage to the Catholic Duc de Anjou would entail a return to Catholic
orthodoxy and undermine English liberty. (See Bloody Mary, reign of.)

Elizabeth thought he should die for that. She was persuaded to show
mercy, so on Nov. 3, 1579, she had his right hand cut off (they used a cleaver
and a mallet.) Stubbs is said to have responded by raising his hat with his
remaining (left) hand and saying "God save the Queen!" before fainting. He
was then imprisoned for 18 months before resuming his publishing career.

In Elizabethan times, there was a system of prior censorship, as publishers were required to be registered stationers. Stubbs' offending pamphlet was burned in the stove at Stationer's House, apparently to show that they hadn't vetted it prior to publication and did not approve.

Milton proposed that instead of returning to a system of prior censorship and post-publication dismemberment, parliament should allow what we now call a free market of ideas.

The value system involved was about truth, not property. Parliament was planning to reinstate licensing laws for publishers, and you were not "the press" unless you owned one, so property rights were involved, but for Milton the search for truth was not about property at all. He even urged parliament to recognize that bad ideas must be published. In the section on the value of wrong ideas, he uses the Biblical story of Adam and Eve's fall in a way I find reminiscent of Prometheus:

> Good and evill we know in the field of this World grow up together almost inseparably; and the knowledge of good is so involv'd and interwoven with the knowledge of evill, and in so many cunning resemblances hardly to be discern'd, that those confused seeds which were impos'd on Psyche as an incessant labour to cull out, and sort asunder, were not more intermixt. It was from out the rinde of one apple tasted, that the knowledge of good and evill as two twins cleaving together leapt forth into the World. And perhaps this is that doom which Adam fell into of knowing good and evill, that is to say of knowing good by evill. As therefore the state of man now is; what wisdome can there be to choose, what continence to forbeare without the knowledge of evill?

Wisdom, then, is having the knowledge of good by knowing evil, knowledge that Adam and Eve gained from the apple. What had been, in the Catholic Church, evidence of man's sinful nature, became in the *Areopagitica* the source of essential knowledge. The Catholic Church had an entire economy of sin, of which indulgences were one small part. But in the mind of this liberal thinker, the lesson to be learned was that God wanted Adam, Eve, and all mankind to make choices, not to be denied them.

We have several entwined sources of authority and value in our culture. The law is a system of value about who is responsible for what, one might even say, it is about who is to blame. Property is about the rights and obligations between people and the things they have and use, one might say the meaning of things. Speech, discourse, scholarship, are all about truth, and truth is one of the most difficult and important concepts in any culture.

I like to think that truth is a word we use to describe that which we believe without question. We are not free to choose what we believe, because belief is an emotion akin to love (no wonder truth and beauty are so often seen together.) I may wish to believe my lover is faithful, but the truth whispers through each door I close on it, seeps under the window sash when I try to shelter from it, and I must in the end believe what I do not wish or choose to believe. Milton maintained that we should never close truth out.

The problem with truth is, you cannot necessarily know it without discussing various notions of what it is, and at the end of the discussion, people may still disagree. If you say, "Politicians should be required to tell the truth!" the matter remains unresolved. Consider those who still insist that Barak Obama was not born in the United States, despite all the evidence that has been provided (an example of a belief that is professed as a tribal shibboleth rather than a reasonable supposition of truth.) If we live in a world where they cannot say such things, we will also live in a world where political competition will focus on who gets to say what is true.

Milton, by the way, lost his vision as he got older, probably from glaucoma. He had to dictate his later works to assistants, as portrayed in an 1826 picture of him with his daughters. He did not attend any religious services near the end of his life, having become alienated from the Anglican Church and objecting to the intolerance of the Dissenters (churchmen who did not accept the Book of Common Prayer.) He was exactly the sort of person he said should be tolerated.

He advocated what is now referred to as a "marketplace of ideas," but we should remember that the marketplace was itself not well understood. We could, in Milton's day and even in Adam Smith's, not even explain why diamonds cost more than water.

Chapter 6: Adam Smith, moral philosopher of the marketplace

In 1776, two important documents in the evolution of western culture were published: The *Declaration of Independence* and *The Wealth of Nations*.

The *Declaration of Independence* is a political document, based on a legal system of values. It is almost entirely about who was to blame (hint: his first name was George, and he lived in a very large dwelling in England.) A great deal of it has to do with the king's efforts to keep the colonies from governing themselves. The quartering of soldiers, outlawed in our Constitution, was one of the things they objected to, because they were being required to give a place to live to the very troops that were burning their towns (for example, Falmouth, Maine, located on the site of modern-day Portland, burned on Oct. 18, 1775.)

The Declaration objects to the King preventing the colonies from naturalizing new citizens, or encouraging their migration, because apparently the colonists did not regard themselves as entirely English or want only English subjects to immigrate. In short, they were saying that they were not exactly part of the English tribe, and should be allowed to absorb people of other ethnicities. That's a fundamental difference in their view of who they were, and not one the king was likely to welcome.

Adam Smith, on the other hand, was not so concerned with law, which may at first glance seem strange, because he was by profession a moral philosopher. He was at one time the Head of Moral Philosophy at Glasgow University, and his major work there was *The Theory of Moral Sentiments*. In short, he was a man interested in values. Through the good offices of David Hume, a fellow philosopher of the Scottish Enlightenment, he got a very well-paid position as tutor to Henry Scott, the Duke of Buccleuch, which makes me very happy to be writing this rather than trying to pronounce Buccleuch. This enabled him to travel the continent and meet such great minds as Voltaire, Benjamin Franklin, and François Quesnay, a prominent physiocrat.

It always struck me as odd that the first widely recognized school of economics should be the physiocrats, who considered only the agricultural sector productive of wealth. This is a view they share with Confucius, strangely enough. The physiocrats divided the world into the proprietary class, the landowners, the productive class, those who worked the land, and the sterile class, the merchants and artisans. They were influenced by Vincent de Gournay, French Intendent of Commerce in the 1750s, whose motto was *Laissez faire et laissez passer, le monde va de lui même!* (let do and let pass, the world goes on by itself.) In Thomas Jefferson's mistrust of cities and idealization of the independent yeoman we see the influence of the physiocrats, in Alexander Hamilton's advocacy for the role of the government in developing the nation we see the influence of the mercantilists.

Mercantilism focused on the balance of trade, on the wealth of kings, and the accumulation of gold. The current economic policies of China might be said to have evolved from the physiocrat phase, in which intellectuals were sent to work with the peasants because this would teach them what was truly of value, to the mercantilist phase, in which the goal is to get more wealth from the world than you give up.

But in any case, it set Smith's mind to work on the issue of how values work to produce wealth. Unlike the physiocrats, he did think merchants and craftsmen could produce wealth. Like the physiocrats, he thought people acted in their own self-interest, producing the public good as a side effect:

> It is not from the benevolence of the butcher, the brewer, or the baker, that we expect our dinner, but from their regard to their own interest. We address ourselves, not to their humanity but to their self-love, and never talk to them of our own necessities but of their advantages.

But he also foresaw the concept of market manipulation:

> People of the same trade seldom meet together, even for merriment and diversion, but the conversation ends in a conspiracy against the public, or in some contrivance to raise prices.

And why is this bad? Because it is an attempt to pervert the system for expressing value judgments that we've been discussing, the value system Hobbes adapted from commerce to give secular legitimacy to sovereigns and stop the religious wars that were tearing England and the rest of Europe apart. Coercion and deception are morally objectionable because they are efforts to corrupt the system of values on which commerce is based, therefore parasitic and a threat to the system's proper functioning.

The worth of things is expressed in the marketplace with prices, and an effort to rig prices is an effort to pervert social values; a sort of lie. Smith laid out the moral justification, in other words, for anti-trust law, because one of the the intersections of the legal and market systems of value was at the points where markets were not allowed to function. Smith was not a fan of the laissez-faire advocated by Gournay, because he thought the participants in any trade would prefer to pervert the system of social values rather than have to deliver value for money. Thus, regulation of some sort was needed, but even that could be perverted.

Today, pundits like Matthew Yglesias argue that a great deal of our legal structure is designed to protect economic incumbents from competition, and Smith would have agreed, as he wrote:

> The proposal of any new law or regulation of commerce which comes from this order, ought always to be listened to with great precaution, and ought never be adopted till after having been long and carefully examined, not only with the most scrupulous, but with the most suspicious attention.

So if people, for example, who do cosmetic things to fingernails and toenails say that their profession should require licensing, and the license should require X years of working in the field, we should ask if bad cuticle treatments are a major medical problem, or if this is intended to raise the incomes of people who do nails. What's important about this is that it shows Smith understood that a market is a made thing, a social artifact that can be perverted by social means such as lies and coercion. Without the legal system of values to place blame for such behavior and punish wrongdoers, could markets survive?

And if the markets are subjected to arbitrary political intervention, what begins as a political problem, described again in the Declaration of Independence...

> He (George III) has obstructed the Administration of Justice, by refusing his Assent to Laws for establishing Judiciary powers.
> He has made Judges dependent on his Will alone, for the tenure of their offices, and the amount and payment of their salaries.

... becomes an economic problem, to the point where stout merchants dress up in disguise and throw tea into Boston Harbor. If the courts are not just, but corrupted by the power and purse of the sovereign, can property be secure? If the sovereign's navy bombards your town with incendiary shot, then sends in the marines to finish burning the town, what does the deed to a piece of property mean? The values of the marketplace can create wealth, but only when there is a functioning legal system to ensure stable property rights and a market not perverted by power. This is a problem for the notion that society is formed to protect property: Until such protection exists, even the concept of property is incoherent, and only the passion to possess exists.

In fact, to bring the discussion to the present day, I think one of the problems with modern Russia is that the advisers they brought in to help them form a market economy had lived so long in a society with functioning laws and courts, they did not realize how important these things are to the functioning of capitalism. As a result, *Laissez faire et laissez passer* was the motto of the new Russian state (until the oligopolists became entrenched and the state went back to being repressive.) Add to that the fact that they had spent generations convincing themselves that capitalists were gangsters, and their interpretation of capitalism soon became a society in which economic activity resembled a criminal enterprise, the courts were corrupted by those in power to reward their friends, and the wealth of the nation was lost as all the evils that old moral philosopher Adam Smith warned of were realized.

Capitalism at its very beginnings faced a dilemma, that it needed regulation to function properly, but the regulation itself could produce mischief that would either unfairly benefit or unfairly penalize commerce. And that's important, because the system of values Smith described was a system for rewarding or penalizing behavior to produce actions that would benefit society as a whole rather than just the individual. A lack of regulation, excessive regulation, or regulation designed to unfairly benefit certain people was a corruption of the way we negotiate the meanings of our actions.

We speak of commercial speech in terms of advertising, but commerce itself is a kind of speech designed to answer the question, "how much does that item mean to you?" And if the question cannot be answered honestly because of lies or manipulation, our actions cannot accurately reflect this meaning.

Chapter 7: Physiocrats and Mercantilists: The economic philosophies of the founding fathers

It is curious how confused people become about liberalism and the economic systems that can be associated with it.

Liberalism was born when the old sources of government legitimacy, faith and tradition backed by force, were failing. Thomas Hobbes brought a fresh source of legitimacy in from the marketplace – the sovereign deserves his job because he performs for you the valuable function of imposing order and thereby preserving you from violent death.

So, we might suppose capitalism is the natural economic system for liberal political systems. The trouble is, although markets have become entangled with capitalism in our minds, markets are much older. The terms capitalism, liberalism, and socialism are all 19th century inventions.

Prior to that, people had markets, fought over trade routes, paid taxes and made arrangements for the common defense, for the construction of roads and bridges and ports and canals, in complete innocence of the possibility of a science of economics and of ideological battles that would one day be fought over what the best economic system is.

The United States was founded near the end of this period of ideological innocence. Adam Smith's *The Wealth of Nations* was published in 1776, and his ideas were not immediately and universally adopted. It is a curious thing, but not one of the founding fathers of the United States would have called himself a capitalist. That's because capitalism hadn't been invented yet. The invention of capitalism started about the time of the Revolutionary War, and capitalism as a system got its name (from Karl Marx, of all people) in 1850.

In fact, the Virginia planter class that gave us presidents George Washington and Thomas Jefferson was influenced more by the French physiocrats. From Vernon L. Parrington's *Main Currents of American Thought*:

> The conception that agriculture is the single productive form of labor, that from it alone becomes the produit net or ultimate net labor increment, and that bankers, manufacturers and middlemen belong to the class of sterile workers, profoundly impressed the Virginia mind, bred up in a plantation economy and concerned for the

welfare and dignity of agriculture.

Franklin had first given currency to the Physiocratic theory in America a generation earlier, but it was Jefferson who spread it widely among the Virginia planters. He did more: he provided the new agrarianism with politics and a sociology. From the wealth of French writers he formulated a complete libertarian philosophy. His receptive mind was saturated with romantic idealism which assumed native, congenial form in precipitation. From Rousseau, Godwin and Paine, as well as from Quesnay and Condorcet, came the idea of political justice and the conception of a minimized political state, assuming slightly different forms from filtering through different minds. The early doctrine of laissez faire, laissez passer – a phrase given currency by Cournay, the godfather of the Physiocratic school – proved to be curiously fruitful in the field of political speculation, as in economics. From it issued a sanction for natural rights, the theory of progress, the law of justice, and the principle of freedom. The right of coercion was restricted by it to the narrowest limits, and the political state was shorn of all arbitrary power. "Authority," the Physiocratic thinkers concluded, "should only employ the force of the community to compel madmen and depraved men to make their conduct conform to the principles of justice."

But of course, while the physiocrats favored laissez faire, minimal regulation of the economy, they also considered agriculture the only producer of value. Alexander Hamilton was our first Secretary of the Treasury and is said to have been influenced by Smith. Hamilton was distinctly *not* a believer in laissez faire. He favored high tariffs to protect fledgling American industry, a national bank, and public credit. The Sinking Fund Act of 1790 bailed out states in debt from the revolutionary war, established federal taxes to pay off those debts and in the process created a market for securities that would become an engine for economic growth.

Hamilton's *Report on the Subject of Manufactures*, presented to congress in 1791, recommended means to stimulate the economy and ensure the nation's continued independence. It recommended policies similar to those of Jean-Baptiste Colbert, Louis XIV's finance minister, a pioneer mercantilist. Hamilton's report would become the basis for the American Way, sometimes called the American System, though it had little to do with the American System as the term applied to manufacturing with interchangeable parts. This interventionist approach to economic development was, however, associated with industrialization, and became associated with abolitionism. Both were in the Republican platform under Abraham Lincoln.

In short, the founding fathers were split between the physiocrats, who favored laissez faire policies but saw little value in banking, commerce, or industry, and the mercantilists, who saw value in manufacturing, banking, and commerce as well as in agriculture, but were interventionist in their policies.

Once you realize that the United States was founded by people who were not, in the modern ideological sense, capitalists, certain things start to make more sense. It's easy to see how Southern planters would take to the physiocrats' notion of all real value coming from the land, and a philosophy of *laissez faire, laissez passer* had a certain unsubtle appeal for owners of slaves at a time when much of the country was already questioning the validity of the institution of slavery.

Theirs was the losing side in the Civil War. It was the mercantilist side that won, the side that was more inclined to build railroads and the rolling stock that traveled them, to build ships and their steam engines, not the side where a few people lived like feudal lords and ladies, supported by the slave labor of people who were not even allowed to own themselves.

But even after the Civil War, the modern style of individualist capitalism as a theoretical construct was not fully developed. Economists tended to talk about how classes of people would act, much as Marxists still do, rather than about how individuals make economic decisions.

It all sounded very erudite, but it did not explain why water, which we all need, is worth less than diamonds, which really aren't that useful.

A decade after the Civil War, the marginal revolution changed that. The theory of diminishing marginal utility gave economists who studied markets an actual, working theory of value, one that explained why diamonds cost more than water and a great deal else. Karl Marx, then reading everything he could in the British Museum and using what he learned to write *Kapital*, never formulated a response to it, nor did his own theory of value ever show itself as useful.

The basic concept of the marginal revolution was marginal utility. Consider Adam Smith's paradox of water and diamonds. Water is essential to life. In fact, anyone who has insufficient water for very long is, by definition, dead. So most of us have more than enough water, and a gallon more or a gallon less matters to our lives very little. Many of us have no diamonds, and they are scarce. If more people want diamonds than have them, one more diamond could make all the difference to them.

Now, I personally couldn't care less about diamonds. If I had one, which I don't, I'd gladly part with it. This is the basis for trade; the marginal utility of diamonds to me is less than it is to, say, a young fellow getting engaged. The difference in the marginal utility of diamonds to him and to me is what makes trade desirable.

Now capitalism had an explanation for how its value system worked, and it didn't need to talk about classes of people. It could even take its explanation down to the level of the individual. The marginalist's model of human nature is what we now think of when we think of capitalism having a concept of how the world works. It was sometimes called the "psychological" school of economics, and it gave economists a powerful tool for understanding the workings of markets and society that was not matched by Marxist thought. It gave us such useful things as the demand curve, and revolutionized micro economics, the economics of the firm. In fact, micro economics now is so important to the field, many journals show a strong preference for macroeconomics that is micro founded. One wonders if physics could survive an environment in which journal articles on astrophysics had to be quantum founded. Large systems don't necessarily act like aggregations of small systems; one need only see how differently a mob acts from the way the same number of individuals act to know this.

Mercantilism could be evaluated with this new tool, and has not entirely died out. Modern Chinese economic policy resembles it more than just a little. The physiocrats, however, now look so far off track that they were, like my Manx, not even wrong. They are simply irrelevant.

Yet the cultural legacy of those French thinkers and the Southern planters they influenced lives on. When conservative politicians rally voters against big-city values and ways of doing things, when they treat rural voters as the only "real Americans," part of that, it seems to me, echoes those old claims that only the soil produces anything of value. Of course, it also ties in with the more chilling doctrine of blood and soil, which in Germany in the 1930s and '40s became a justification for racism and anti-Semitism, but we can't blame the physiocrats for everyone who admires rural values. We can't even blame rural values for that.

In 1776, the founding fathers would not have called themselves capitalists, but they based the philosophy of the Declaration of Independence on the writings of John Locke, who had a thing or two to say about economics.

Locke believed in natural law and natural rights. The most fundamental of these rights was owning yourself, and therefore, your labor and the property produced by your labor. For the quiet enjoyment of your property, you needed a sovereign power to enforce your rights to life, liberty, health and property. But there was another condition that is less well known. Here's how Locke said it in the *Second Treatise of Government*:

> Nor was this appropriation of any parcel of land, by improving it, any prejudice to any other man, since there was still enough and as good left, and more than the yet unprovided could use. So that, in effect, there was never the less left for others because of his enclosure for himself. For he that leaves as much as another can make use of, does as good as take nothing at all. Nobody could think himself injured by the drinking of another man, though he took a good draught, who had a whole river of the same water left him to quench his thirst. And the case of land and water, where there is enough of both, is perfectly the same.

Just as you have a right to live, but not to kill others, you have a a right to apply your labor to nature and acquire property, but not to prevent others from acquiring property. It's a natural outcome of Locke's theory about natural rights, but it also did not describe the property situation in England or anywhere else at the time. Locke didn't really explore the implications of this aspect of his philosophy, but it's a major difference between Locke and the other economic philosophies current in the American colonies at the beginning of the war for independence. The mercantilists and the physiocrats thought the source of wealth was resources. Mercantilists emphasized the state's role in developing those resources. Locke said that nature was just there, but its value as property was created by labor. This is similar to the emphasis Adam Smith placed on labor as a creator of value.

But at what point does your acquisition of property interfere with the rights of others? According to Locke, at the point where it interferes with others gaining property. Harvard professor Robert Nozick, a libertarian, dubbed this the "Lockean proviso."[*]

Nozick argued that the limit to one's acquisition should be at the point where it makes someone else worse off, but Locke argued that the limit should be at the point where it interferes with others' ability to create wealth. Both would have been offended by the behavior of 19th century railroads that acquired monopoly power over railroad lines, then raised the price of moving farm produce to market to the point where farmers were nearly destitute. But it was those following Locke's views that argued that inherited wealth was a problem, and instituted the inheritance tax to place individuals on a more even footing in building wealth.

Nozick argued that a minimal state was needed to preserve life and property and enforce contracts, and anything beyond that was illegitimate. He even argues that taking more than required for this minimal state is theft, and the notion of taxes as theft has become a persistent theme on the right. Nozick's work seems to have contributed to a change in capitalist ideology. While business interests opposed the New Deal policies when they were instituted, after World War II society generally seemed to accept that government had an important role in making a capitalist system work. That consensus is no longer with us. I don't blame Nozick for this, but I do hold him up as an example of changing social attitudes, in that there was a ready audience for his ideas.

But if capitalism had not been invented as an ideology when Americans founded their republic, what preceded it, and what distinguishes capitalism from other systems of economic thought?

Chapter 8: Capitalism, so much more than markets

Capitalism is an economic system based on the private ownership of the means of production, with the goal of making a profit.

-- Wikipedia

Several political movements have been named by their opponents. "Liberal" used to be a term of disapproval before it became a term worn with pride, and then became a term of disapproval again. "Totalitarian" was a term invented by Fascism's liberal opponents and enthusiastically adopted by its followers.

Capitalism is a term invented by Karl Marx in about 1850 to describe something new in the world, something he thought evil. As the Wikipedia definition demonstrates, the term is now retrospectively applied to all systems in which there is private ownership of the means of production, a situation that has probably existed as long as the institution of property has existed.

But Marx was not describing prehistoric societies where flint knappers owned their tools and hunters owned their spears. Through most of history, there had been peasants who owned their land, their draft animals, and their plows, and artisans who owned the tools of their trade. The situation Marx invented a new term to describe was one in which no longer did each weaver own his loom; ownership of the textile mill belonged to the capitalist, a person who did not weave or spin, but whose profession was to own, and to manage or hire managers.

The capitalist was the creator and the creation of the industrial revolution. Prior to this, there had been a number of theories of how economics worked.

Thomas Hobbes believed that government made it possible for labor to create value. The war of each against all, like the 30-Years War, made it impossible for agriculture, navigation, or commerce to take place, which is why, apart from the preservation of our lives, we should form a social contract and value the sovereign who keeps us from violent death and ensures that those who plant can reap.

The physiocrats thought that all value came from the soil, and government should interfere as little as possible. The mercantilists thought the goal should be to bring as much wealth to their country as possible, which meant getting control of resources, providing the means to exploit those resources, such as roads and bridges for commerce, and steer the most profitable operations of business to their own country.

Capitalism adopted parts of all these philosophies, but grew from changes in technology. Frederick Law Olmstead, who traveled in the South from 1852 through 1857 writing for the *New York Daily Times*, considered that slavery and the inefficiency it enabled had impoverished the South, its wealth restricted to the few owners of large plantations. From *Journeys and Explorations in the Cotton Kingdom*, an 1861 abridgment of that series of articles:

> The citizens of the cotton States, as a whole, are poor. They work little, and that little, badly; they earn little, they sell little; they buy little, and they have little – very little – of the common comforts and consolations of civilized life. Their destitution is not material only; it is intellectual and it is moral... They were neither generous nor hospitable and their talk was not that of evenly courageous men.

In short, he viewed them as insufficiently capitalist. The slaves of the South were at that time worth more than all the factories and railroads in the entire nation,[*] but even so, they were not efficiently employed, because their cost was less than the cost of hiring free men. Not that the cost was low; about half the wealth of the South was in the ownership of slaves.

Capitalism did well enough out of slavery, with 80% of the South's cotton going to British textile mills and some of it coming back as fabric. But the semi-feudal society of the South did not reward labor well, so did not have sufficient demand to support its own industry.

As for the mercantilists, they saw conquest and the domination of other peoples as the key to gaining wealth. The West was won by people following those imperatives, using the nation's troops to conquer land for private ownership. The conquest of Indian land was not an enterprise for libertarians, it was a nation dominating by force people who commanded less force.

Frederick Jackson Turner declared the frontier closed in 1890. Perhaps it is no accident that in 1898, America tried to expand into a true empire by seizing most of the remaining colonies of Spain in the Spanish-American War.

The failure of America to become the sort of empire the proponents of the Spanish-American War had envisioned was really the end of the mercantilist dream, and the intellectual basis for an economic theory replacing mercantilism had been laid not that long before.

The theory of comparative advantage -- that is, the theory that if each nation produces what it makes best, and trades it to other countries, all will be better off -- was first examined in detail in David Ricardo's 1817 book, *On the Principles of Political Economy and Taxation.*

Ricardo suggested that such trade left both countries better off, in contrast to the mercantilists who advocated high tariffs to encourage domestic production of as many goods as possible. This was a very different view of how value is produced, and because it suggested that the production of value is not a zero-sum game, it was a major break from previous notions of how the world works.

The theory of comparative advantage has always been a hard sell, especially in hard times. But the powerful paradigm of the marginalists helped explain why capitalism is not a zero-sum game. The thing I sell means more to the buyer than to me.

The marginal revolution laid the basis for the economic consensus that gave us steady growth with only modest downturns from the late 1930s until 2008. In the early 1930s, there was a sizable leftist movement, reflecting that many people didn't buy into capitalism as the best way of life. The steady success of a kind of capitalism where government moderated the excesses of the markets and made it possible for people living in them to thrive undermined the socialist alternative, as did the less than brilliant performance of Fabian socialism and the wretched failure of the Communist economies.

The economic philosophies that asked government to moderate the effects of capitalism were first Keynesian economics, then monetarism. Keynes claimed that when the economy got into a liquidity trap -- that is, when the natural rate of interest is below zero -- fiscal stimulus is needed to get the economy running again. Monetarists claimed that monetary policy could do the job, making central banks the essential institution of capitalism.

But what has happened is that with the collapse of the socialist alternative, the left is defined by Keynesian and even monetarist ideas, while the right is defined by what amounts to pre-Depression economics. Although those on the right wish to portray this as an argument between socialists and capitalists, it is really an argument between different brands of capitalists.

When the only real alternative to capitalism is another brand of capitalism, you can say with some certainty that capitalism has won. Rhetorical efforts to label Keynesians as socialists remind me of the efforts of the Catholic Church to label the Goliard poets as "Bohemians."

The Goliard poets were rebellious clerics who wrote scandalous songs and poems often featuring "Father Golias," a figure who possessed all the flaws of the rulers of the Catholic Church. At the time they were suppressed (in 1289, the Church decreed that, "no clerks shall be jongleurs, goliards or buffons"), the Gypsies, so called because of the untrue claim that they were from Egypt, were moving into France, where they were called Bohemians, because of the untrue claim that they were from the kingdom of Bohemia. They were foreign, poor, transient, and often were accused of stealing things.

The Church began to refer to the Goliards as "Bohemians," in an effort to make them seem less socially acceptable. But the term bohemian has come to mean a rebel poet, which is pretty much what Goliard meant. The Church had managed to change the sign, but not the signified.

So those who now wish to associate a rather successful branch of capitalist economic theory with the term "socialism" should be wary that they may revive the legitimacy of the term "socialist."

The paleoeconomic right wants to "end the fed." It's my belief that in so doing, they would be well on their way to ending modern capitalism, which since 1913 has relied on the central bank to moderate the excesses of the market and guarantee some stability in the economy. The problem is that a system that relies on large accumulations of capital needs a market in debt that can be relied upon. Alexander Hamilton understood this, which is why the Funding Act of 1790 funded the debt rather than paying it off. Hamilton wanted to create a market for securities that could finance commerce. He proposed a Bank of the United States, which would accept deposits and make commercial loans. It was to take on the functions of the Bank of England, which had rescued the pound by acting as a lender of last resort in 1763.

Andrew Jackson, the Ron Paul of his day, denounced the Bank of the United States in 1828 and refused to renew its charter in 1836.

State banks took up the slack until 1863, when the Union, freed of Jacksonian southerners, chartered national banks. Currency issued by banks that were not backed by the U.S. government tended to be worth less the farther you got from the issuing bank, and a bank collapse could make your currency useless. It was an unstable time in American finance, and held the county back.

The panic of 1907 revealed that capital had become so important, and markets so unstable, that a central bank – the Federal Reserve system – was needed.

Jackson demonstrated that capitalism without capital fails, and the Panic of 1907 revealed that to have stable capital markets, we need a lender of last resort. So let's add that to the components of capitalism. It needs central banking.

When Marx coined the term "capitalism," it was a flawed and sometimes brutal system. He correctly forecast that it would have to change. What he missed was that the beast could be tamed, with the advancing arts of economics and central banking, and policies of social insurance making it not only tolerable, but preferable to other systems. The danger now is that we will forget the lessons we learned in an earlier and more brutal time, and eliminate those elements of capitalism that make it function well enough not to call for its replacement.

When you take the tools from the weaver and concentrate them in the hands of the textile mill owner, you take control of working conditions away from those who make the fabric. Democracy has a pretty good history of fixing that problem, with the actions of capitalists restrained to a level that keeps revolutionary urges in check. It is inherent in the nature of capitalism that the ownership of the means of production is concentrated in few hands, often in the hands of a person who is a legal fiction, the corporation. This is at the core of capitalism, and it is the need for such large investments that makes the management of capital so important.

In 1811, William Blake published the following words:

And did the Countenance Divine,
Shine forth upon our clouded hills?
And was Jerusalem builded here,
Among these dark Satanic Mills?

Yet somehow, among paleoeconomic conservatives, those dark Satanic Mills have become a vision of paradise. I would say they were not even capitalism, only the precursor to our capitalist system.

It is important to remember, not all institutions can or should be capitalist. Some are simply not something private ownership can do well.

One of the more peculiar things about the current state of American politics is that an entire political party devalues all things public (except police and the military) and valorizes all things private.

Like many Netizens, I spend too much time arguing with idiots on the internet. One exchange involved me and an Australian librarian discussing the need for libraries with a business consultant, who argued that libraries are not needed.

"Where's the market failure?" he asked, as if no form of human organization was legitimate unless it could not be provided by the market. Markets Über Alles has long been the cry of business conservatives, but other than assuming that markets are superior, they don't seem to spend much time justifying this choice.

The truth is, we have centuries of experience and thought that help us understand the difference between public and private institutions, but few people seem to avail themselves of this knowledge.

Markets work very well when used for goods from which people can be excluded, both physically and morally. The example usually cited is lighthouses. Everyone can see a lighthouse and use it in navigation, but because no one can be excluded, it is difficult to collect a fee for the services provided by the lighthouse. In England, private companies built lighthouses, then found they could not collect money from those who used their service, so they got the ports to collect port fees to support lighthouses. Then, the profit incentive was to spend as little as possible on maintaining the lighthouse while still using the power of the state to collect the fees. Eventually it was discovered that only government had the means to collect the fees and the incentive to provide decent service. This is the essence of a public good.

At one time, excluding people from health care services was considered morally tenable. Physicians served the rich, barber-surgeons served the rest, and neither had an enviable record of curing people, so home remedies were often as effective as medical care in any case. John Locke argued that natural law shows we all have a right to life, liberty, health and property, and he first gained a powerful patron by acting as a

physician to Anthony Ashley Cooper, Lord Ashley, not long after getting a medical degree at Oxford (Locke got the medical degree in 1665 and treated Ashley in 1667.)

As medical care improved, it became increasingly evident that to exclude someone from medical care could result in them losing their health or even their life. If we are all born owning ourselves, depriving us of such things interferes with our fundamental right to exist and our property right to ourselves.

In 1986, Ronald Reagan signed the Emergency Medical Treatment and Active Labor Act, which said hospitals could not refuse treatment at their emergency rooms for people because of citizenship, legal status, or the ability to pay, in order to end the practice of "patient dumping," that is, discharging patients because they might cost the hospital too much money. It was possible to physically exclude people from treatment, but was in morally acceptable?

Theodore Roosevelt in 1912 campaigned on a promise of social welfare insurance, including a national health service (he founded the Progressive Party, better known as the Bull Moose Party, for the purpose of running.) Medicare, Medicaid, and the Reagan-era emergency room mandate were all patchwork attempts to deal with the failure of American politics to provide a path to universal access to healthcare when it had ceased to be morally acceptable to exclude people from healthcare. The Affordable Care Act (AKA Obamacare) attempted to solve the same problem more comprehensively while not eliminating the private-sector actors in the insurance and health care industries.

We have, at this point, spent more than 100 years trying to solve the problem of medicine becoming good enough to be worth having, while private enterprise could not provide the service in a morally acceptable way. Medical care has made a transition from private good to public good.

Oh, and returning to the business consultant's question, where's the market failure that justifies the existence of libraries?

First, no market failure is required to justify people's desire to have a public amenity. We are free to organize our society however we want, provided we don't infringe on the rights of our citizens. If we elect a government to build public institutions and keep electing those who found and fund libraries, we are free to spend our money though taxes just as we are free to spend our money in markets.

Second, libraries provide goods from which it is immoral to exclude people. They provide knowledge, both in the form of non-fiction and in the form of literature, that people ought to have access to in order to realize their potential and to have sufficient knowledge to exercise their freedom of conscience.

What is socialism?

It seems socialism was a big issue for some voters in the 2020 election, particularly in Florida.

For example, in a Nov. 17, 2020, article New York Magazine recounted the following:

> "It was a McCarthyism type of pounding," said Congresswoman Donna Shalala, looking back on the election she narrowly lost this month. Shalala had spent eight years serving in the Cabinet of Bill Clinton, the paragon of Democratic moderates, but by the end of her reelection campaign, she told Intelligencer, people were coming up to her and saying, "You're a communist."

The smears relied heavily on lies, and on linking to the few people who caucus with the Democrats who embrace the socialist label, such as independent Bernie Sanders, a senator for Vermont, and Alexandria Ocasio-Cortez, elected to congress on the Democratic ticket in New York.

Part of the problem here is that socialism means different things to different people. From that New York Magazine article

> As Rick Wilson, a longtime Florida-based Republican consultant, put it: "Socialism broadly speaking in the United States is a bad brand. In Florida, it is a horrific brand." Wilson, who is now a leading "never Trump" voice through his perch at the Lincoln Project, noted that to south Florida Hispanic voters "socialism isn't universal health care and day care, socialism was secret police knocking at their door and shooting a family member in the head."

Wikipedia, that voice of consensus knowledge, says that socialism is characterized by social ownership of the means of production. This was most famously carried out in the Soviet Union and other Communist regimes, but the Fabian socialists associated with the Labour Party in the United Kingdom also advocated social ownership of the means of production, producing a National Health Service, nationalized coal industry, steel industry, and other industries. Most of their program produced terrible results, but the NHS is well loved, and produces results comparable to the American medical system at a fraction of the cost.

Social Democrats have embraced democracy, and in general have been more inclined to advocate for a social safety net without wanting to nationalize the whole economy. There is a huge difference between a Labour government in Britain or a social democratic one in Denmark and the sort of socialist government found in Cuba and Venezuela.

Social Democrats and Fabian socialists have embraced democracy, believing that their ideas would sell themselves to people once they saw them in action. When they failed to produce results, they were voted out of office, but some of what they did remained. No Conservative government has been able to privatize the NHS, though Margaret Thatcher did manage to privatize the coal and steel industries, where the socialist experiment had failed badly.

We actually know a great deal about what goods are best handled by markets and what goods are naturally public goods. Even the most radical of our elected conservatives would probably not advocate privatizing the military and having everyone hire their own mercenaries to prevent their turf from being invaded. The military is insurance against invasion, and the peace it ensures within those borders is not something you can easily exclude people from if they don't want to buy it. People are therefore not required to buy that peace in order to enjoy it, so markets are not practical as a means to deliver it.

But the rhetorical use of the term 'socialist' goes well beyond social ownership. For example, the conservative Heritage Foundation came up with a market-based system for reforming the provision of health insurance, and the Republicans adopted it in opposition to the Clinton administration's proposal for a reform based on having employers provide the insurance. Years later, President Barack Obama used that plan as the basis for the Affordable Care Act, better known as Obamacare. Republicans denounced it as 'socialist,' although it did not involve nationalizing anything, it was just a way of changing the incentives in the market for health insurance. The ACA also gave states the option of expanding Medicaid, a program for government payment of medical bills for those who cannot afford medical care. In states that have not availed themselves of this provision, hospitals absorb the cost and pay for it by raising prices on everyone else.

Most nations, in the end, have public and private sectors, and there is not much controversy about it. People drive on public roads and stand on sidewalks paid for with taxes while protesting against socialism. Few of them would prefer police departments be disbanded so that we could all hire our own guards. At the moment, Medicare seems sacrosanct, although conservatives claimed it was socialist before it became the law of the land.

In a 1965 speech, Ronald Reagan said, "[I]f you don't [stop Medicare] and I don't do it, one of these days you and I are going to spend our sunset years telling our children and our children's children what it once was like in America when men were free."

When he was elected president 15 years later, he knew better than to try to 'free' Americans from Medicare.

Providing medical insurance to the elderly was not profitable. Retired people tend to have less money than working people, and old people tend to have more expensive medical needs than a younger population. Yet Americans found it unconscionable to have people dying prematurely because they couldn't buy health insurance or pay for care out of pocket or afford expensive medical insurance.

Does one become more free or less free with the provision of Medicare? If you are not wealthy, surely Medicare makes you more free, as you can get your ills treated sufficiently to go about life in a normal fashion, rather than be bound to your bed by debilitating disease. Certainly Medicare is sufficiently popular that it would be difficult to reverse the policy based on the ideological argument that it is socialism. The other problem with this argument is that Medicare isn't socialism. Medicare owns no hospitals. It is a subsidy to those in need, not an effort to take over the means of production.

Sen. Mitch McConnell, leader of the Republican faction in the U.S. Senate, called the part of President Joe Biden's covid-19 relief plan providing for $1,400 checks sent to all taxpayers socialism. He did not call the $600 checks Republicans had voted to send the same people socialism, and he didn't call former president Donald Trump's call for the checks to be $2,000 instead of $600 socialism, but then when President Biden decided to pursue the same policy Trump advocated by topping up the amount so it would total $2,000, McConnell decided it was socialism.

This definition of socialism, then, means that socialism occurs when Democrats try to use government to help those not already wealthy and powerful. The same policies, when proposed by Republicans, are not socialism. By using the term this way, Republicans have a rhetorical cudgel they can use to claim that those who, for example, support higher funding for Medicare, are equivalent to violent, oppressive regimes along the lines of the one now ruling Venezuela.

Chapter 9: What is money?

I have stated that I believe property is not objects, but the system of rights, obligations, and meanings we apply to objects and ideas. But what is money?

This is a troubling matter for many people, and for the current crop of conservatives, it is a question they wish to forget. After all, if money were gold, it would be an object, and not so complicated. It would be harder for people to fool with it and somehow more concrete and easier to understand. This is a peculiar view, because gold is not valuable in and of itself, it is only valuable in that people value it. Value is not a property that objects have whether we measure it or not, like hardness or volume. Value is something with which only people can imbue an object, because it is people who value things.

Gold is a symbol of wealth, but then, so is a stack of greenbacks.

And we left the gold standard for good reason. It resulted in a system that undermined economic performance during the Great Depression. Getting rid of the central bank and going back on the gold standard has been tried with disastrous results. (See England, post WW I.)

Conservatives have long hated central banks. Virginia Senator John Taylor argued against a central bank when the Second Bank of the United States was legislated in 1816, saying, "...if Congress could incorporate a bank, it might emancipate a slave."

Why were these things linked? It was the merchants and industrialists who wanted a central bank. They were building industries that relied on free labor, and were more on the mercantilist than the physiocrat side of the economic divide. Mercantilists wanted tariffs, to protect nascent industries, and physiocrats wanted to ship cotton to England and have them ship back manufactured goods. They did not want a balance of trade that might encourage England to look elsewhere for its cotton, as it eventually did when the Civil War broke out. They understood that for England to buy from us, we had to buy from them, and were therefore not fans of industrialization.

Andrew Jackson hated the idea of a central bank, and though he was unable to muster the votes to kill the Second Bank of the United States, he managed to allow its charter to expire in 1836. This created chaos, because other banks, some with state charters and some without, started issuing promissory notes to use as money. There was a spurt of inflation, and Jackson responded by requiring land payments made to the United States government to be made in gold.

This created deflation and a recession. The nation struggled on with money issued by seigniorage, that is the minting of coins, and a variety of promissary notes. The notes might not be worth much if you were far from the issuing bank, or nothing at all if the bank failed.

We got a national currency again in 1863-64 with the National Banking Acts, which established a network of nationally chartered banks.

Money is really not a simple matter. Economists have several measures of how much money is out there, based on several definitions of what money is. The process by which money is created is not intuitive, if you are a believer in hard and unchanging values.

Consider the normal way money comes into being. A central bank loans money to a commercial bank. This money did not exist before the loan was extended, the bank created it by loaning it, and the commercial bank can destroy it by paying it back.

The notion that money can be created by issuing loans and destroyed by paying them back seems wrong to people who don't understand what money is.

Money represents a favor owed. We might call this the The Marquis de Carabas standard, after a character in the Neil Gaiman novel, *Neverwhere.* When the Lady Door needs his help, the Marquis asks what his payment will be. Lady Door answers, I will owe you a very big favor, and the Marquis is satisfied with that.

Because in fact, all trade is a trade in favors. If I buy you dinner, you will owe me dinner, or else some other exchange of favors is at work (perhaps you are my favorite nephew or niece, and I enjoy the favor of your company.) But perhaps I can say, no, buy my friend a meal, I owe him one.

Money makes favors fungible, and a fungible favor is one that any person can trade with any other person, rather than having to know each other and remember the favors we've done for each other. I am a bookseller, and I can do someone the favor of giving them the book they want, and instead of doing me a favor in return, they can give me a talisman that represents a favor, a symbol such as a $20 bill or even a favor represented, as someone writing on the Ron Paul blog once put it, nothing but "blimps on a computer screen." (That typo has since been corrected, but I find the imagery so appealing I wish it hadn't been.)

I can use these talismans representing favors to repay my landlord for allowing me to operate a bookstore in his space. The talisman is a symbol of the underlying meaning, and the meaning is that someone is owed a favor. That is the value money represents, a web of obligations between people.

It is important to remember that the talisman is not the favor. Most of the money in the world is not represented by coins or bills, but by entries in the electronic ledgers of banks. You can wire money from one country to another without sending suitcases of $100 bills precisely because the bills are not the money itself, but only a symbol representing money. They are used to communicate exchanges, just as gold and silver once served that role. Those who pine for a return to the use of gold forget this. Gold is a fine thing for making jewelry that doesn't tarnish, it makes excellent filings for teeth, and it is quite a good conductor of electricity, but in the end, it is simply a durable commodity. The value it has to people is based on how people feel and think about it.

This market in favors can be tricky. It represents the values of all those who participate in it, the value of a back rub from a skilled masseuse, the company of a courtesan, or a meal prepared by a cook or chef, which may vary in the quality of materials, the skill of preparation, and the surroundings in which it is consumed.

A system that allows us to trade favors with strangers has many pitfalls. Some are obvious, such as efforts to obtain favors, not by doing favors, but by force or subterfuge, such as robbery or fraud. Some are less obvious, such as the paradox of thrift: If everyone in a society tries to pay back their debts at once, it will impoverish society and leave everyone poorer, because just as money is created when debt is issued, it is destroyed when it is repaid without being loaned again.

Another problem is the debasement of currency, which can happen when a nation's central bank doesn't function properly. In *1493*, a book by Charles Mann about the Colombian exchange, Mann describes such a situation in China.

Paper money was invented in China, first with merchants issuing what amounted to letters of credit (an instrument still widely used in the shipping industry.) Then, the Chinese government discovered that it could issue paper money, and it needed to, because China's silver mines, which had supplied the material for its more valuable coins, were getting played out.

But China did not invent central banking. Repeatedly, Chinese governments issued too much paper money, causing inflation, effectively meaning its citizens were owed fewer favors for the currency they had saved than before the excess bills were issued.

So, they went back to using silver. But as you carry silver around and exchange it, there is wastage, silver wearing off the little bars you carry in your purse. China was faced with a shrinking money supply – not enough talismans to represent all the favors owed – which was a drag on the economy. Essentially, there were not enough talismans around to represent a growing number of favors, so each talisman had to represent more favors.

One way of thinking about the resulting deflation is that when we do a favor, we expect its value to decline over time with human forgetfulness. If I fed you yesterday, I'm more likely to get a reciprocal meal today than if I fed you 20 years ago. Deflation privileges older favors over doing favors now, which is to say, it privileges existing wealth over the creation of wealth, and savings over labor. Inflation fits with the attitude, what have you done for me lately?

We seem to have accepted that the gradual erosion of the value of favors over time, in that most central banks now target inflation at 2 percent or less. I'm unclear on why this number was chosen, since it puts interest rates perilously close to the zero lower bound, and limits what the central banks can do to respond to a crisis such as we saw in 2008. Probably economists must do more work on how quickly past favors lose their value.

The solution to the shrinkage of China's money supply came when the Spaniards arrived in the Philippines with silver from Central American mines. The Chinese actually began purchasing silver to use as money from the Spaniards with products of their industries and agriculture, and in fact, it was about the only thing the Europeans had that the Chinese wanted until the British introduced opium. In 1743, during the War of Jenkins' ear, George Anson captured just one of the treasure galleons that engaged in this trade, and it was a prize greater in value than any other taken while the prize laws applied to naval warfare.

As it happened, it took Anson a couple years to get into position to intercept the treasure galleon, and peace had broken out in the meantime, so technically, Anson seized the galleon in a time of peace, but the Brits kept the treasure and made Anson Lord of the Admiralty.

It was a British subject, a Scot named John Law, who first argued that paper money was preferable to metallic money, which should be banned. Unfortunately, he had to flee the British Isles after winning a duel. From Wikipedia:

> The wars waged by Louis XIV left the country completely wasted, both economically and financially. The resultant shortage of precious metals led to a shortage of coins in circulation, which in turn limited the production of new coins. It was in this context that the regent, Philippe d'Orléans, appointed John Law as Controller General of Finances.

France really did suffer from a shortage of money, but while working to solve this problem Law created another, the Mississippi Bubble, which resulted in his dismissal from his post. He used his brilliant mind and capacity for quick calculation to support himself by gambling for the rest of his life.

The Grey Lady of Threadneedle Street (AKA the Bank of England) completed the work of inventing the role of the central bank, mitigating the paradox of thrift by acting as a lender of last resort when the financial community panicked, and in general provided a steadying hand on the banking industry which helped England to industrialize.

Much of macroeconomics is concerned with stabilizing the market in talismans representing favors in such a way that people will continue to do each other favors. After all, I would be delighted to give people books without asking for anything in return, but I do ask the grocery store to provide me with food, and if I have no favors to trade to them, why would they, when they don't know me from Adam's off ox?

Marx thought people should do each other favors without the intermediation of money, but no one has managed to make this work on a large scale. Trying to make an economy work without money or property is a bit like banning language because you don't like people shouting. Any powerful system of human organization can be abused, but to ban a useful and ancient institution because it is sometimes abused seems an odd response. Any powerful social institution can be used for good or ill, including property, religion, money, and government.

Sidebar: The Talk, or how penguins are involved in the birth of money

The above explanation of where money comes from seems rather dry, so I've written what I call a Likely Story that explains where money comes from in a manner any parent can use.

It has come to my attention that many people don't know where money comes from, so I think it's time we had The Talk.

You see, gentle reader, when a central bank loves a commercial bank very much, a feeling of great tenderness comes over it and it follows an instinct millions of years old, and slips a loan in that bank's portfolio.

I believe a bird is somehow involved, something that begins with "P," therefore probably a penguin.[*]

So, that loan is new money. It didn't exist before the bank had it, but it exists now. And when that penguin drops the new-born money into the loving arms of J.P. Morgan, he immediately farms it out to work for someone else. Even at a tender age, money can be found working in textile mills, in mines, in steel mills, and on construction sites, 24 hours a day. The riskier the work, the more J.P. Effin' Morgan makes.

Now, as it happens, only about 3% of money is created by government, just enough to control the supply of money. Most of it is created by banks, taking deposits and loaning the money from the deposit to someone else. When you deposit money in a bank, you are loaning it to the bank. It will then loan most of it to some stranger, probably someone you wouldn't trust enough to pick up if they were hitchhiking in the rain.

The theory here is that not everyone will want their money back at once, so you can pay the depositor a small interest, and then loan out their money at a higher interest. The money thus gained is one of the ways banks make profits. But in the process, they make money, in the sense that the depositor and the borrower now have an amount of money equal to the amount deposited and the amount loaned. That's nearly twice as much money, or at least it is until everyone wants their money back at once, which is called a bank run.

The life of money can be long, or it can be short. Many people believe in paying back money, but are unaware that when money is paid back, money is destroyed.

This is why depressions are so depressing. A depression tends to happen when everyone tries to pay back their money at once, thereby destroying the money they pay back. Picture a bunch of blimps on a computer screen quietly dying into darkness as dollar after dollar is paid back and goes to its rest, being paid back and not loaned out again because everyone is afraid to take on the responsibility of bringing new money into such a world.

And not everyone can pay back their loans. Loans that are not paid back are called non-performing. If there are enough of them, banks develop loan performance anxiety, and this results in a slump. With loan performance anxiety causing a slump, banks cannot provide borrowers with the liquidity they so ardently desire. As a result, less money is born.

And a country depopulated of money is a poorer one. If only there were someone who could have the confidence to bring new money into the economy existed, you might be able to do something about the situation. But that would have to be someone who could create money even in the worst circumstances, when most lenders have lost their ability to put loans in borrowers' portfolios, because they are afraid. They are anxious that their next loan may fail to perform.

The reader will have noticed that the commercial bank is acting in both male and female roles, like an earthworm. The phrase "gender fluid" comes to mind. The central bank puts loans into its portfolio, and it puts loans into borrowers' portfolio. So even when the commercial bank's performance anxiety about its loans leaves its ability to loan flaccid, it can still act as a recipient of loans.

If a country has its own currency, its central bank never runs out of money, because it can create an infinite amount. The central bank, seeing its commercial bank compatriot unhappy, will try to restore its ability to loan by creating more money with it. Ah, you say, but if the bank creates lots of new money, won't there be that overpopulation of money that we call inflation?

Well, no, because the reason the central bank is trying to make lending more attractive (think mood lighting, soft music) is because it sees all the money being destroyed as it is paid back, and wants to make sure the economy is not devastated for want of money.

It's a bit like when our soldiers came back from World War II, having seen terrible destruction and loss of life, and created more than enough people to replace the ones they had killed, in what we now call the baby boom.

Central banks cannot always create a boom, because sometimes even an interest rate of zero is not sufficiently low to restore the potency of monetary policy. When that happens, the only thing left is to loan money to the one entity sufficiently stable to invest it, the government. Governments can take advantage of slumps to invest in roads, bridges, and other infrastructure while the price of labor and capital is low, and pay it back in better times. Such fiscal policy can be useful when the economy might otherwise never achieve the escape velocity required to slip the surly bonds of recession and soar to new heights of Gross Domestic Product.

Now, usually, when we talk about money, we think of bills and coins. But those are used to signify money. Money itself can exist with other kinds of signifiers, such as an entry on a ledger or a memory in a computer.

I'm glad we had this talk. If you have any more questions, don't be afraid to ask, it's better to do that than to create unwanted money or destroy money. I admit I'm not an expert, you can always try and get hold of Dr. Yellen, who has brought more money into existence than you or I will ever see.

I know, I know, you're thinking about J.P. Morgan. He's dead, isn't he, so how can he give birth to money? Well, as Mitt Romney was wont to tell us, corporations are people, too. The undead thing we call J.P. Morgan is a corporation, a bloodless thing born at the crossroads of law and commerce for, as the incorporation papers usually say, "any legal purpose." And the money doesn't go to the long-deceased J.P. Morgan, either. It goes to the shareholders. Now, given that corporations are people, and shareholders claim to own corporations, that may look like a peculiar institution to you, but take their claim of ownership with a grain of salt. I'll explain why in Chapter 18.

Expressions of value

The math tends to obscure it, but economics is the study of values. That's why it was invented by a moral philosopher, Adam Smith.

The market is only one form of the expression of values, and it's such an abstract one that most people don't really understand what money is. They reify it, that is, try to take it from the abstract to the real and regard it as something more solid than it is. People who yearn for the gold standard want money to be something that exists outside human values, something by which human values can be judged.

Those who reify money want it to be a sort of value that exists independent of human consciousness, a part of nature to which mankind must accommodate itself. In essence, they want Mammon.

Biblical scholars among my readers will recall that the English-language Bible uses the word mammon, which in Latin means wealth, as if it were personified:

> "No one can serve two masters, for either he will hate the one and love the other; or else he will be devoted to one and despise the other. You can not serve both God and Mammon."
> —Matthew 6:19-21,24

In medieval Christianity, Mammon was sometimes personified as one of the seven princes of Hell. An earlier personification of wealth would be the worship of the golden calf, both gold and cattle being expressions of wealth in the ancient Middle East.

If you own a lot of dollars, you're owed a lot of favors. That's an expression of how people value you; in terms of the structure of language, a signifier that communicates the meaning that you are valued.

It's pretty easy to move from the fact that people often use money to express their values to viewing money as value. And because money is useful only for expressing monetary value, the next step after you've mistaken money as the source of value rather than an expression of it, is to regard monetary value as the only true form of value, and the market as the only true arbiter of value.

This is the flaw in the libertarian project, to consider only the market as a legitimate arbiter of value. It's a handy one, and a great way to distinguish between useful work and work that is not useful, or ugly fashion from delightful fashion, but human society is more complex than just markets. There are other ways of expressing our values. Voting, for example, is an expression of our values, and certainly a better way of expressing how we value leadership in the political sphere than buying candidates. In fact, we are constantly at war between these two ways of expressing value, and concerned with the contamination of politics with money.

Part of the problem here is effective demand. To buy something, you must have money. This is why famine zones have, throughout history, almost always exported food. In a famine, the farmer loses not only the part of the crop which would have fed a family, but also any cash crop remaining. As a result, the family not only does not have food, it also does not have money to buy food. One of the major functions of a government is to correct for such market failures. In the Bible (Genesis 41) the Pharaoh dreamed of seven sleek, fat cows and seven ugly, gaunt cows. The seven gaunt cows ate the seven fat cows. Joseph interpreted the dream for Pharaoh as meaning there would be seven years of abundance followed by seven years of famine, and advised him to store grain from the seven good years to distribute during the famine. This is a form of social insurance against market failure, and is one of the central functions of government. Even defense can be seen as a form of social insurance (against invasion.) Keynesian economics and monetarism, the one with fiscal policy and the other with monetary policy, also are expressions of the idea that in the good times, the government saves, in the bad times, it distributes, to correct for market failures. Mammon worshipers have no use for either system of thought, preferring to deny the existence of market failures.

Here we have an apparent conflict. Hobbes imported the values of the marketplace into politics to show that the leader has value even without religious justification, but the functioning exchanges of the marketplace cannot be a good way of selecting a government when government itself is a form of insurance against market failure.

This is where the logic of the social contract leads to democracy rather than plutocracy, which is the rule of the rich. Each person is given effective demand in the selection of the government by being given exactly the same number of votes, that is, one.

Nor do we wish to see family values expressed through the marketplace.

A society that valued banking highly and children not at all would become extinct. Children were an economic asset when my father was born. His father never got a tractor until the boys went off to war, because the boys meant there was enough labor on the farm to plow with horses, and besides,

Amos Watkins loved his horses.

By the time I was born, my parents didn't expect me to be an economic asset. They had children because they wanted children, because it was an expression of their humanity, and I suppose on some level because the continuation of humanity is worthwhile even if it costs you money. My father's chores had helped keep my grandfather's farm solvent; mine were expected to build my character and teach me how to work. The monetary value of washing the dishes, taking out the garbage, and shoveling snow off the walk (remember, this was in Maine, at least for a while) may have been minimal, but it was an expression of family values.

The curious thing is that people have this desire to worship Mammon or the golden calf, and it keeps happening, from the time of Moses to the time of Jude Wanninski. Wanninski compared family relationships to market relationships, but argued that money is a substitute for trust, and with adequate trust, money becomes redundant.

In one sense this is quite insightful, because it shows a deeper understanding of what money is than most people have. In another, it's appalling, because while family values are often expressed with money, most of the time money is not merely redundant, it's irrelevant. Love is simply better expressed with a hug than a cheque, and expressing some things with money would express entirely the wrong kind of value. How much money expresses "you complete me," or "whatever you've done, you can tell me?" Certainly we value our loved ones, and cherish or forgive them in expression of those values. Much if not most of the things we value cannot be expressed with money.

Yet Mammon remains attractive, because humanity is messy, and the abstract form of value that is money seems less so. To have an outside force that judges our value would mean the messy business of dealing with human emotions could be replaced with simple, solid ledgers. Of course, religion saw this as a threat because priests wanted God to judge you, and that was the major source of power for his earthly representatives. But Mammon worship doesn't just threaten religion, it also threatens to cheapen the rest of our values. For example, trust is an expression of value, and most of us give it sparingly. Can you express it with a substitute for trust?

While it's true that money talks, it is not only incoherent in the areas we've discussed, it falsifies values in some areas. The reason we object to the influence of money in politics and justice is that it counterfeits the values that are supposed to be expressed in these forums. It is legitimate to say, I am owed many favors, and my dollars will redeem them in the form of a nice car; that is a recognized commercial value. It is not legitimate to say, I am owed many favors, and my dollars will redeem them in allowing me to kill my rival without punishment; murder may be a commercial venture, but it is not supposed to be a commercial value. And the values expressed in justice may have a monetary component, but they also transcend the values expressed in money.

The key is to structure society in such a way that these institutions do far more good than harm.

Now, it may seem to you, as you read this, that I've gone a bit off track talking about money instead of democracy, but money is part of our value system, and has a great deal to do with building a country.

Chapter 10: Grexit, the Sinking Fund Act of 1790, and

the construction of a country

A friend from New South Wales asked me, if Europe can't resolve the debt crisis on its periphery by means of the sort of fiscal union that would have a central authority bail out banks, why can the U.S. do so?

I've been following the Grexit controversy (potential Greek exit from the Euro currency zone) with interest, since it has the potential to disrupt one of the great internationalist projects of the last century, the European Union. I think I have the answer to my friend's question.

First, Americans identify with each other culturally much more than Europeans do. Second, we've had real fiscal union since 1790, thanks to the genius of Alexander Hamilton.

After the Revolutionary War, the original 13 colonies had quite a lot of debt, much of it owed to foreign banks and investors (primarily in the Netherlands). Many were in a poor position to pay back the loans, and there was talk of default.

Hamilton pushed through the Sinking Fund Act of 1790,[*] which was somewhat misnamed for political reasons. It didn't really pay down the debt so much as fund it, so it could be turned over periodically and become the basis for a market in securities that would help provide the financing to develop industry in the new nation.

But equally important was its political role. Hamilton saw that if the federal government took over the war debts and financed them through taxes, the states would be dependent on the federal government and the federal taxing authority to pay off their debts. This cemented the nation into one political and financial unit.

Not that this happened without difficulties or entirely peacefully. George Washington led a militia to put down the Whiskey Rebellion (1791-1794), an insurrection against federal taxes on corn whiskey. This happened while George Washington was president, and he became the only president to lead troops in the field while in office.

Economist Jared Bernstein writes that a German economist asked him, "How do you think the people of Manhattan would like bailing out Texas?"

And Paul Krugman points out that they did, big time, during the Savings and Loan crisis.

Bankers were getting convicted of crimes and sentenced to brief incarceration at hard summer camp in low-security prisons, the Resolution Trust Corporation was shutting down S&Ls and the federal government was guaranteeing the deposits, and we never heard a peep out of those parts of the country that contributed money to resolve the situation.

Krugman points out that the resolution of this crisis cost about $125 million "back when that was real money," and about $75 million of that went to Texas. It didn't go in the form of loans, it went in the form of outright transfers from areas like Manhattan that weren't having a banking crisis.

If the powers that be in Europe wanted a United States of Europe, they would act as Hamilton and Washington did to make sure the debts of the weaker states got paid off by a central authority. But they didn't, and they can't, because Europe is not about to become a United States of Europe. German voters won't stand for bailing out Greece, there is no central taxing authority and there is not likely to be one, and a central European authority invading an area that rebelled against a centralized taxing authority is unthinkable.

All of which is why the Euro was a bad idea to start with. There are those in Europe who think that forcing Greece to exit the Euro will make the rest of the Euro area stronger, but actually, it demonstrates why the Euro can't work, and why the project to make a United States of Europe is a doomed enterprise.

America works as a currency area, in part, because large and ongoing transfers of wealth happen between productive states like Massachusetts and New York on the one hand, and low productivity states like Mississippi and Arkansas on the other.

Those wealth transfers go on year after year, in the form of welfare spending, federal unemployment insurance, social security, disability benefits, and other programs. Most of this is so invisible to recipients that they vote for people who want to cut the federal budget.

It had taken a long time for us to evolve our financial system, and there have been some pretty rough patches along the way. Andrew Jackson, one of our worst presidents, set policies in motion that left the country without a central bank from 1836 to 1913. Between the end of the central bank's charter and the beginning of the Civil War, state banks were issuing currency, and how much it was worth depended, among other things, on how close you were to the issuing bank. Repeated financial crises between the 1870s and 1913 convinced the powers that be that we needed a central bank. We didn't get centralized deposit insurance until the bank failures of the 1930s demonstrated how badly that was needed.

But at least we had the basic ingredients for a proper currency union, even when we didn't have a workable currency system thanks to Old Hickory. And the basic principle that we were a nation was settled between 1790 and 1794, with the Sinking Fund Act and the suppression of the Whiskey Rebellion (even if this principle was to be re-litigated on a grand scale in the Civil War).

Europe is currently demonstrating that they do not have the unity the Sinking Fund Act of 1790 represented. Any attempt to set up such a mechanism would probably produce the European equivalent of the Whiskey Rebellion, and there is zero chance that Europe would put up with the military suppression of such a reaction.

Try to imagine German troops marching into Belgium to suppress a tax revolt. It would be déjà vu all over again, and not in a good way. I feel confident that the German people would stand with the Belgians against such an action.

Perhaps there was a gentler path to a fiscal union, one in which the burden was shared without a central authority. For example, the banks that owned most of the Greek debt were Greek, German, French, and Italian. Each country could have bailed out its own banks. Instead, the troika (the European Central Bank, European Commission, and the International Monetary Fund) chose to paper over the issue, pretending that Greece suffered not from insolvency but from a liquidity problem. Some private lenders took a bit of a haircut, then the private debt got converted into ECB and IMF loans to the Greek government. In the end, Greece is on the hook to pay back all the ECB and IMF debt, rather than having defaulted, as logic said they should, and having each country bail out its own banks.

We know that Angela Merkel has been saying privately[*] since at least 2011 that the Greek debt was unsustainable, and that they would, in the end, default. And yet the policy of the German government remained that Greece must pay back every penny with interest. This means that the German government has been pursuing a policy that they knew wouldn't work, so there must be some sort of hidden agenda served by this hypocrisy.

That agenda could be as simple as an unwillingness to face German voters with inconvenient and unpopular truths. The longer Merkel continues to fail to tell the German people the truth, that the Greek crisis will not be resolved by making them pay back every penny, the harder it becomes for her to tell them.

Or it could be that there is some other goal. Yanis Varoufakis, who was the Greek finance minister in charge of negotiating a resolution to the crisis, wrote an op-ed piece in *The Guardian* claiming that Germany wants to scare the bejesus out of France.

"Based on months of negotiation, my conviction is that the German finance minister wants Greece to be pushed out of the single currency to put the fear of God into the French and have them accept his model of a disciplinarian eurozone," he wrote.

Try to imagine the U.S. Federal government punishing Georgia this way to intimidate Virginia. There would have been no United States if that had happened.

No doubt there is more than one reason for the policy of the German and other governments on the Greek debt crisis. Whatever the reasons are, they seem impervious to evidence. Had the initial bailout worked as the troika said it would, the crisis would have been over before Varoufakis got involved.

It's pretty obvious that if the Greek economy were the size the IMF said it would be at the point where Varoufakis was in government – back to what it was before the crisis – they would have far less trouble paying back the debt. But after five years of failure, the troika offered nothing but more of the same policies.

These policies have resulted in the Greek economy shrinking more quickly than the debt is paid back. More of the same can be expected to have more of the same result, which means that the Greek ability to pay back the debt is undermined to the extent that the whole exercise is futile. It also means that since the denominator in the debt/GDP ratio is sinking, a Greek government that started with a debt of 100% of GDP now has a debt of about 170% of GDP, despite paying back billions of dollars.

It's not like the Germans should be unfamiliar with how this works. Debt forgiveness and the Marshall Plan following World War II rebuilt the German economy.

This is covered in a paper by London School of Economics Professor of Economic History Albrecht Ritschl:

In addition, the Marshall Plan injected $17 billion -- equivalent to roughly $160 billion in today's money -- to rebuild the country the allies had spend so much money reducing to rubble.

The debt cancellation, by the way, was supposed to be temporary – only until Germany was unified. But Germany was unified in 1990, and Germany has still not been required to repay the debt.

Having itself relied upon the kindness of foreigners, Germany seems disinclined to pay it forward, and make no mistake, Germany is the driving force in negotiation over the Greek debt.

I can only think that Germany is disenchanted with the European project, and has no wish for a stronger union. It seems they wish to make Greece an example, but what will Greece be an example of?

I think they will be an example of the fact that Europe, despite all the years of the European Union, does not wish to be a true union.

Look more closely at the American currency union, and you see that it was based, in part, on the usefulness of debt.

Alexander Hamilton argued that public debt would be a blessing if it didn't become too large, and so it has been. We've eliminated the national debt once in our history, during Andrew Jackson's administration, and this was followed by an economic disaster.

Now, you can find founding fathers' quotes opposing debt, but they were not talking about capitalism, but about a physiocrat's view of government. However, in practical terms, what they actually did about government debt was based on a mercantilist's point of view, and it's a very good thing that happened.

This country was deep in dept by the time it had won its independence. The physiocrats in Congress were generally in favor of screwing the investors, but Alexander Hamilton realized that the national debt could be a tremendous asset.

From a Sept. 18, 2008 article by historian John Steele Gordon published in U.S. News and World Report:

Hamilton's 1790 *Report on the Public Credit* proposed funding the debt, thereby creating a stable market in bonds in this country that enabled businesses to borrow more cheaply than they could have otherwise.

It is all very well to quote the physiocrats among the founding fathers on the subject of public debt, but their understanding of banking and debt generally was fairly primitive. They were wise enough to follow the advice of a mercantilist on the actual handling of the debt – that "if it is not excessive, will be to us a national blessing."

Now, you might think mercantilists were really capitalists, but you'd be wrong. Mercantilists advocated the development of the nation, and wanted to get as much of the world's wealth in their country as possible. They were empire builders. Cotton grown in India would be shipped to England to be made into cloth, even though the shipping costs and the cost of English labor made the cloth more expensive.

Capitalism broke that bond as well, dooming multinational empires. Once global capital was able to move production to undeveloped countries where the labor was cheap, and avoid paying the taxes that had supported the empire, the feedback loop that supported empires was gone. It is in the nature of capitalism that empires don't pay, and the new world order is one built on alliances within trading blocs.

Chapter 11: Reflections on the Revolutions in France and

America

Reflections on the Revolution in France, published in 1790, is one of the core documents that defines conservatism. Edmund Burke wrote it in response to the chaos he saw happening across the English Channel.

But why did he not write this sort of thing about the American

Revolution, which had happened earlier?

One reason is that the American Revolution was a kinder, gentler, sort of war. In France, anti-clerical and anti-aristocratic feeling was part of the source of the problem. In America, there was no national established church, and no hereditary aristocracy.

In France, the clergy and the aristocrats had so many tax exemptions, most of the taxes fell on everyone else, the merchants, artisans, farmers, and laborers. This was a reflection of the aristocrats and churchmen's power in the country. If you were rich enough, you could buy into this power by purchasing a title. The way this worked was, you bought a position in government that came with a title. The position could not be revoked, and the titles tended to become hereditary. Hard-up French monarchs tended to create such positions and sell them for a high price. As a result, it was the smaller merchants and the peasants and working class that paid the taxes, many of which went to the aristocracy, who were paid for the position they our their ancestors had purchased.

And France was badly in debt, mostly because its kings liked to fight wars. The Seven Years War, known in the United States as the French and Indian War, dragged on from 1756 to 1763, and losing cost France many of its colonies, including Quebec. Louis XV did a lot of the damage, but when he was succeeded by his grandson, Louis XVI, the latter decided to get a bit of France's own back by helping deprive the English of some of their New World possessions.

He backed the American Revolution. Without the rather expensive aid of the French Navy, there might not be a United States of America. It was the French fleet that prevented the British from relieving the troops commanded by Charles Cornwallis at the siege of Yorktown, resulting in his surrender.

But that aid to the colonies had to be paid for. One of the ideas that came to the French regime was a tax on salt. Everyone needs salt to survive, so it was in part a tax on being alive, sort of like a poll tax. But this was worse. The more you sweat, the more salt you need to keep moisture in your body. As a tax on sweat, it was a tax on labor: Those stuck with the hardest physical work would pay the most salt tax. The aristocrat sitting in the shade would pay less than those who labored in his fields.

The American revolution did not involve overthrowing the local power structure. Instead, it relieved them from outside influence.

This is one source of the notion of American exceptionalism. The idea, at least the way the phrase was first used, is that we never had a hereditary aristocracy to rebel against, so some of the more potent sources of working-class resentment that made Communism popular in Europe simply are not here. In fact, American Marxists coined the term in the 1930s to explain their lack of success.

The French Revolution was violent, and not particularly democratic. Their motto was "liberté, égalité, fraternité."

Démocratie wasn't a core value. Interestingly, the most famous liberal philosopher writing in French was a Swiss, Jean-Jacques Rousseau, who argued that even a dictator could represent the will of the people. A country the size of France, he said, should be ruled by an aristocracy. The word aristo is Greek, and means "best." So he wasn't arguing for a hereditary aristocracy, it could be the Committee for Public Safety, if they were the best.

And who would argue the question of whether they *were* the best with those who decided which heads rolled off the guillotine?

The French Revolution eventually produced the Emperor Napoleon Bonaparte. Now, one might think that an emperor would be regarded as an old-fashioned sort of ruler, but Napoleon had replaced the old power structure. Monarchs had relied on force, faith, and custom for their legitimacy. Napoleon had the force, but he was not a hereditary monarch, so he could not rely on custom, and he did not rely on the support of an established church.

For faith and custom, he substituted nationalism and victory in war. This is an unstable formula. First, you stir up the nationalism, and nothing does this better than a good, old-fashioned war. Then you have to win.

But if you fight for long enough, eventually you will lose, as Napoleon did at Waterloo. Nationalism is a dangerous tool for any regime, because the implicit bargain puts the ruler in a position that is difficult to maintain, the position of keeping the people stirred up against other countries but not being defeated and removed from office, either by popular revolt or by victorious enemies.

What made the French Revolution part of the enlightenment project was its reliance on reason to restructure society. The French foot, which was slightly longer than the English foot, found itself in the dustbin of history, replaced by the metric system. Celsius, a more rational system, replaced Fahrenheit. This was a new world, replacing matters which had been adjudicated by custom with reasoned solutions.

Napoleon himself became a symbol of the Superman. In Crime and Punishment, Raskolnikov muses about his notion of the superman:

> "...The real Master to whom all is permitted storms Toulon, makes a massacre in Paris, forgets an army in Egypt, wastes half a million men in the Moscow expedition and gets off with a jest at Vilna. And altars are set up to him after his death, and so all is permitted. No, such people it seems are not of flesh but of bronze!"

In the secular world, God is dead, as Nietzsche would later tell us. This leaves a God-shaped hole in our heads, and who steps forward to claim the plinth on which he loomed over our minds?

The Superman, exemplified by Napoleon, steps up to the plinth. Hobbes, a dedicated materialist, had said that God had to be a material being, simply one of exceptional power. By the time Dostoevsky was writing, people were postulating men of exceptional power to whom ordinary rules did not apply, a sort of God-like man (and it always was a man.)

In a way, this might be seen as a return to the God-king, expected this time to deliver victory rather than rain for the crops.

And we see it still today, when we credit or blame the state of the economy on presidents. Jimmy Carter, for example, presided over some very good economic years in his term in office, but a recession at the end of his four years was one of the reasons for his narrow defeat.

The French went through a series of evolutions and finally settled on a democratic way of governance, but not without such experiments as the reign of Emperor Napoleon III. But the fact that the revolution itself had not been democratic was a warning sign. While the logic of the social contract leads to democracy, not all attempts to replace custom with reason in the ordering of society are democratic in nature.

Karl Marx, for example, tried to come up with a rational way to make society better. But most of the attempts to apply his ideas have been authoritarian. Marxism has replaced the role of faith in these societies, and combined with force to form the governing class. Those societies returned to faith and force as their formula for the legitimacy of their rulers, substituting the Communist Party for the church. It is not an accident that in post-Soviet Russia, Vladimir Putin has come to rely upon the Russian Orthodox Church for support, and stir up nationalism to get the public to rally around him.

The Nazi movement made a cult out of race, claiming it was scientific. The doctrine of blood and soil (blut und boden) emphasized "blood" in the sense of descent (race), and romanticized nationalism and rural living. The link between race and territory was essential to the ideology. Because people were bonded together by race, the social contract Locke and Hobbes postulated was, they said, not needed. And because they preached biological determinism, there was no need for democracy. Certain people were born to lead (this was called the fuhrerprinzip, or leader principle) and the rest were born to follow. Fuhrerprinzip dictated that the fuhrer's word was above all written law, and a leader demanded absolute obedience to those below them. The supreme leader answered to God and the German people, the lesser leaders answered to those above them and demanded complete obedience from those below them. This was rule by will, rather than law.

Nazism was on odd hybrid. It had the trappings of science, but its biology was bogus, merely a disguise for old attitudes. Germany had pogroms in the 1500s and in the 1920s. The Holocaust could be seen as the culmination of attitudes that had been around for centuries, simply carried out on an industrial scale and by the government rather than by mobs. Its "scientific" racism was so lacking in any actual science that German authorities could not detect a number of Jews who went through the war with fake papers claiming they were of "German" descent. And in fact, by any rational standard, they were, since their ancestors had been living in Germany by that time for longer than there had been a German state.

Marxism began with the best of intentions, and spread tyranny and suffering from the purges of the Ukraine to the killing fields of Cambodia. Fascism exploited existing hatreds and a desire for order while adopting the trappings of science. Both demonstrated that attempts to remake society based on reason can be disastrous when reason starts with flawed premises.

Both ideologies lacked a notion of the social contract. For Marx, you were born into your class. For the Nazis, you were born into your race and class. The Nazis thought you should remain in your class, while the Marxist thought you should fight to abolish all but the working class. Neither ideology reasoned its way to a democratic form of government, because each was intent on defeating a demonized enemy, capitalists for Marxists and Jews and other "lesser" races for the Nazis. In war, command and control are far more important than discovering the desires of the people. Nations which adopted these ideologies were not democratic because they did not value democracy, and they did not value it because they had different ideas about the origins and purpose of society.

It seems that those social philosophies that lead to not valuing democracy are those which say that a society that is best led by a single person (the leader principle, or fuhrerprinzip) or by a small group of people (Lenin's intellectual vanguard). Anti-democratic social philosophies also assume that the purpose of society can be known without consulting the people. They have this in common with the old way of ruling through force and faith, in that the monarchs of the middle ages would never have said they were servants of the people. They considered themselves servants of God, and they relied upon God to define the purpose of society (generally saving the souls of those inside the society and spreading the word to, or eliminating, unbelievers.)

One of the early socialists, Henri Saint-Simon, gained quite a following among young intellectuals. They probably would have said it was his ideas they were in love with, but it seems more likely to me that they were in love with Saint-Simon's idea that society should be led by people like them. Lenin picked up on this with his notion of the intellectual vanguard, but the same idea has some currency on the right, where Leo Strauss taught his followers that gentlemen with a sufficiency of wealth, education, and wit should guide the nation. He also believed that the purpose of the United States could be known without consulting the people.

Strauss was known for somewhat eccentric, one might even say perverse, reading of his sources. He called this a method of "close reading," the goal being to understand the author as well as he understood himself. Strauss also assumed that after the trial and execution of Socrates, philosophers learned to write texts that had a surface meaning accessible to any damned fool, and a deeper meaning hidden from all but those able to penetrate the mysteries of the text. One would think that the fact Thomas Hobbes wrote what he meant so clearly that it could have cost him his life twice would be a clue that this is not always the case. Enlightenment thinkers, for the most part, seem to have written with the twin goals of clarity and persuasiveness.

The Poverty of neoconservative philosophy

Neoconservatives, a group which included formerly liberal academics and their younger Reaganite allies, have had a great deal of influence on American foreign policy, especially during the lamentable George W. Bush administration. They envisioned a world in which American dominance would be unquestioned, and opposing regimes would be overthrown and replaced with democratic regimes, as the Bush administration attempted in Iraq.

They tried to portray themselves as the adults in the room, but their program proved impractical, unpopular, and built more on fantasy than reason. There was no economic or any real strategic rationale for the military adventures they championed, and the notion that you can impose democracy by force proved as fanciful as it sounded. Yet they retain influence in conservative foreign policy circles.

How did *that* happen?

Part of the story is about intellectual apprenticeship to a scholar not greatly celebrated in his lifetime, and whose influence may have as much to do with what people thought he meant as with what he actually said and wrote.

The intellectual roots of the movement were sown, as foreshadowed, by Leo Strauss, one of the less coherent political theorists of the 20th century, famously referred to by M.F. Burnyeat as the "*Sphinx without a Secret*," after an Oscar Wilde story in which the subject is a woman who wants to appear mysterious, but has no secrets worth concealing.

Strauss is a peculiar figure in political thought. He wrote nothing I know of about modern public policy, and although his works are widely available in the United Kingdom, he seems to have no great following there or in continental Europe. Although he died in 1973, his influence wasn't celebrated or defended much until his former students began to influence high-level American foreign policy in the 1980s.

Catherine and Michael Zuckert, in *The Truth about Leo Strauss*, considered one of the more balanced books about the man, noted that:

> Many scholars found his books nearly unreadable, and many others considered them so drastically misguided in their substantive readings of the history of philosophy that he was often dismissed by fellow scholars as an eccentric or, worse, as a willful and distortive interpreter of the philosophic tradition.

Burnyeat's takedown, *Sphinx Without a Secret*, published in 1985, was not the work of a political pundit, but of a respected scholar with a great reputation for his studies of the ancient philosophers Strauss taught about. He portrayed an almost cult-like intellectual surrender as part of Strauss's teaching technique:

> Strauss asks—or commands—his students to start by accepting that any inclination they may have to disagree with Hobbes (Plato, Aristotle, Maimonides), any opinion contrary to his, is mistaken. They must suspend their own judgment, suspend even "modern thought as such," until they understand their author "as he understood himself." It is all too clear that this illusory goal will not be achieved by the end of the term. Abandon self all ye who enter here. The question is, to whom is the surrender made: to the text or to the teacher?

This may explain why his followers were his students, not people who had simply read his books and agreed with them. Reading is an interpretive skill, and critical reading is a particularly valuable one. Pleasing the teacher is a social skill, and coming under his spell is a personal transformation.

While liberalism starts with attempts to describe human nature – "man in the state of nature" – and derive from that knowledge what sort of government and society is best suited to mankind, Strauss was more interested in the question of whether the just society was possible (apparently, it isn't, and I've just saved you reading his books).

The best we could do, he said, was for the philosopher to educate the gentleman in how best to manage society.

From *Sphinx Without a Secret:*

> The leading characters in Strauss's writing are "the gentlemen"and "the philosopher." "The gentlemen" come, preferably, from patrician urban backgrounds and have money without having to work too hard for it: They are not the wealthy as such, then, but those who have "had an opportunity to be brought up in the proper manner."[12] Strauss is scornful of mass education.[13] "Liberal education is the necessary endeavor to found an aristocracy within democratic mass society. Liberal education reminds those members of a mass democracy who have ears to hear, of human greatness."[14] Such "gentlemen"are idealistic, devoted to virtuous ends, and sympathetic to philosophy.[15] They are thus ready to be taken in hand by"the philosopher," who will teach them the great lesson they need to

learn before they join the governing elite. The name of this lesson
is "the limits of politics." Its content is that a just society is so
improbable that one can do nothing to bring it about. In the 1960s
this became: a just society is impossible.[16] In either case the
moral is that "the gentlemen" should rule conservatively, knowing
that "the apparently just alternative to aristocracy open or
disguised will be permanent revolution, i.e., permanent chaos in
which life will be not only poor and short but brutish as
well."[17]So who is "the philosopher," and how does he know
that this is the right lesson for "the gentlemen"? He is a wise man,
who does not want to rule because his sights are set on higher
things.[18][*]

Strauss might be called the Saint Simon of conservatism, in that his
popularity among the elite, like that of the socialist Saint Simon, seems to
have had a lot to do with convincing them that society should be run by
people like them, for its own good.

Strauss believed something like what Plato had posited in *The Laws*: A
society must be based on central truths. Plato went further with this: It's all
very well to question those truths in your own mind, but if you publicly do
so, you would, in *The Laws*, be brought before the Nocturnal Council, who
would try to persuade you that you were wrong. If they did not succeed, they
would try to convince you to keep your doubts to yourself, and if you insisted
on publicly questioning the central truths, they would have you killed.

And the central truth, for Strauss's followers, was "American
Exceptionalism," a phrase borrowed from American Marxists, which they
redefined to suit themselves. You can hear the echoes of this belief in their
claims that President Obama did not believe in American exceptionalism.

The phrase was originally a term American Marxists used to explain
the fact that while Marxism had gained many converts in Europe and parts of
Asia, most American workers wanted nothing to do with it. They argued that
America lacked the class structure that enabled European workers to identify
with Marx's thoughts.

Neoconservatives have taken American exceptionalism to mean

America is exceptional, and belief in its greatness became the central truth around which the society was built. That is not necessarily a Straussian view, but one might call it the view of "vulgar Straussians," much as Stalinists came to be viewed by the more refined Marxists of the New Left as "vulgar Marxists."

Strauss repudiated John Locke, whose ideas are by most scholars considered the basis for the philosophy that produced the American Constitution. Strauss regarded Locke as a bridge to modern historicism and nihilism, which he felt led to totalitarian regimes.

The word "totalitarian" was invented by liberals to describe the Fascist regime in Italy, and enthusiastically picked up by the Fascists, who followed Benito Mussolini's dictum, "All within the state, nothing outside the state, nothing against the state."

How that differed from Herrod's Judea, other than the fact that the term had not yet been invented, remains a mystery to me.

Now, it seems strange to anyone who's read Locke that Strauss would think badly of him, since Locke based his philosophy on natural law (now often called human rights,) which at least for one school of Straussians is the central belief on which America was founded.[*] But Locke argued that the social contract that is the basis for any government is formed to protect those rights. Strauss felt that modernism lowered its sights compared to the ancients, having as its goal survival, while the ancients sought truth and justice.

Jefferson, who wrote the Declaration of Independence, considered Locke one of the three greatest men ever to have lived. Clearly, there would appear to have been quite a gulf between the beliefs of the founding fathers and those of Leo Strauss.

Strauss left the University of Chicago in 1969 and died in 1973, so one might think his influence should be waning, if not a thing of the past. But he influenced William Kristol, editor of the influential conservative journal *The Weekly Standard*, and John Podhoretz, editor of another conservative journal, *Commentary*. They, in turn, have influenced a couple generations of conservatives. And while Strauss wrote little or nothing about contemporary American politics, those men have written of little else.

Strauss may have died, but he left behind him Straussians to spread his ideas. Along the way, people who would have been Cold War liberal hawks in the 1960s became attracted to the notion of an armed idealism which would spread the American way through the world by force.

The Straussian understanding of the American project has therefore become thoroughly entrenched in the mindset of many on the right. The problem is, this understanding of America is very much at odds with the basic ideas of liberal democracy as understood by the framers of the Constitution.

The notion of a central dogma all must believe is very much at odds with the freedom of speech and belief enshrined in the First Amendment. We have no nocturnal council, we have instead the flexibility of a republic that can change as minds change.

Now, a philosophy that is as top-down as that of Leo Strauss and his followers might believe we can overthrow opposing regimes and be welcomed as liberators, and they will elect a regime friendly to us. But in practice, any sovereign nation allowed to choose its own government will choose one that reflects the ideas and interests of its people. In Iraq, for example, that was a regime more friendly to Iran than to the United States.

Part of the problem is that neoconservatism is not an economic philosophy, except by association with the supply-siders who were part of the same Republican administrations. They really had no ideas about how their foreign adventures would pay for themselves, and in fact, were not concerned with this. They wanted to spread the influence of American exceptionalism, however they defined it.

The problem is, past empires have been built on an economic basis which modern global finance undermines. You can bring peace to a region and get your nation's companies a chance to exploit foreign markets, but their stateless income will seek the lowest tax regime, not the nation that made that income possible. This means that there is no cycle (virtuous or vicious, depending on your point of view) to support empire.

As a result, it appears the new world order will be built by trading blocs, more like modern versions of the Hanseatic League than like any past empire.

Neoconservatives accused President Obama of "leading from behind," because he tried to form alliances to solve international conflicts rather than going it alone or as a leader of a barely-willing coalition. But his technique seems like a better match to the reality of the modern world system of security. Aggressive nations that assert their individual power tend to generate a backlash against themselves, as China seems to be doing in southeast Asia.

But the failure of neoconservatives in formulating foreign policy that produces desirable results does not seem to keep politicians on the right from listening to them.

In some ways, their notion of the purpose of the United States, their definition of American exceptionalism, is more distressing.

Let's explore further Leo Strauss's idea that totalitarian is a result of the modern nihilism found in the work of John Locke and Thomas Hobbes. Strauss claimed that what is opposed to this is the effort to build the just society.

First of all, we should note that Marxists were all about building a "just" society, by their own standards. They were great believers in the idea that a just society can be achieved by overthrowing capitalism and building a communist society. The fact that they in practice failed to build a just society reveals defects in their thinking. Marxism represented the negation of any need for the political and economic institutions of society. This is what is usually known as political nihilism. Probably this is not what Strauss was talking about. More likely he meant moral nihilism, but let's explore this in terms of the usual meaning of political nihilism.

It's true that Marx made the error of thinking that institutions that cause great harm in society, such as private property and religion, could be eliminated and the harm they caused would stop. He then imagined that the state would wither away, not realizing that when you take away major organizing institutions in society, the gap will be filled by the remaining institutions. In this case, the state filled the gap, which is what has happened wherever Marxism has been tried.

But Marx was not the last Marxist. Lenin stressed the need for a vanguard of intellectuals to push for the revolution and head up the revolutionary government. Totalitarianism could not have come from political nihilism, which denied the need for the state, but only from people who firmly believed that they needed to be in control. To claim that Stalin was a political nihilist who didn't believe in the need for political or economic institutions is utter nonsense and cannot be what Strauss meant. Stalin clearly, based on his actions, believed in a strong, centralized state, firmly in control of the economy, the political life, and even the beliefs of its citizens.

Anyone actually wanting to practice political nihilism in a Stalinist state would have been killed. Marx may have preached a sort of political nihilism, but the lacunae in his own philosophy meant that in practice, all Marxist rulers have been firm believers in a powerful central state.

And what of the fascists? Did they believe in abolishing the political, economic, and social institutions of society?

Hardly. They were big believers in the ideology of nationalism, a strong central state, and strong cooperation between the state and industry.

In short, Marxists were totalitarian in practice because they were not believers in the basic tenets of political nihilism.

But were they moral nihilists, a more familiar sort of nihilist?

Strauss deemed Hobbes a nihilist because his philosophy was based on "mere preservation of life." Hobbes, after all, said that we needed a ruler to enforce laws, so that we would not meet a violent death.

But in saying the ruler has value because he (and the ruler Hobbes had in mind was his pupil, Charles II) does a job of work for the citizen, he was laying the groundwork for democracy. After all, what if the ruler sucks at his job? Shouldn't you be able to fire him? And why should the ruler pass the job on to his first born son? Shouldn't the citizens be able to hire the rulers they want?

But this new basis for the legitimacy of rulers didn't really support the outcome he wanted, which was the absolute monarchy of his friend and pupil.

Was he a moral nihilist? It's a bit hard for me to see him that way. He believed that the injustice of violent death, of theft and banditry, could only be avoided by having a ruler with the authority to enforce the laws we want enforced. In fact, he wanted a society more just than the chaos of the 30-Years War would permit. He had seen what the breakdown of political and social institutions could do, and charted a path away from that.

In Strauss's eyes, this focus on the material matter of remaining alive made Hobbes a nihilist. Since he was arguing in favor of political institutions, he cannot have been a political nihilist, so he must have been indicting Hobbes as a moral nihilist.

If we were to accept that Hobbes was a moral nihilist, should we also accept that this was the sort of modernist approach to ethics that led to the totalitarian philosophies of fascist and Marxist states?

This seems dubious. Marx clearly was motivated by an effort to build a just society, the same goal Strauss admired; he just disagreed with what constitutes a just society. Lenin agreed with Strauss that society would inevitably be ruled by a small group of the "best" people, he just disagreed with Strauss about the nature of the group that should rule and the sort of society that would be just.

Were fascists moral nihilists? I believe that rather, they had a perverted sense of justice. Keep in mind, worse things are done in the name of justice than have ever been contemplated in the name of crime. Mussolini even referred to fascism as a religion.

The Holocaust, the Inquisition, and the killing fields of Cambodia were not carried out by people who believed in the evil of what they were doing. They were carried out by people with a deep conviction in the justice of purifying the world of "bad people," as defined by them. They were following the tenets of their beliefs in building a just world to a horrible conclusion. People without such an ideology, such a central myth, people merely concerned with the preservation of their own lives, would not have acted in these despicable ways.

This may explain why the Nocturnal Council in Plato's *The Laws* bears more than a passing resemblance to the Inquisition. Plato considered central truths, that is, a central myth of society, to be necessary for building a just society, and a body to enforce that belief to be essential. But when it was put into practice, this notion produced a system that was notoriously unjust.

This makes it rather odd that Strauss would place such emphasis on belief in a central myth as being necessary for building a just society.

Neoconservatives seem to think that central myth of American exceptionalism is not what those who coined the term meant by it, but something more in the sense of John Winthrop's 1630 sermon, *"A Model of Christian Charity"* which is often referred to as *"A City Upon a Hill,"* indicating the notion that America is a model of what the world should be. This is interpreted as a claim of national greatness, not so very different, in fact, from the claims of national greatness made by fascists in Germany and Italy in the 1930s.

Certainly I prefer Winthrop's vision of Christian love and charity to Hitler's vision of a triumphant Aryan race. But it is not the central idea of America. Winthrop wrote his sermon in 1630 for a Puritan audience. Most American settlers were not Puritan. Many were Anglican, or Baptist, or Methodist, or Quaker, or Catholic, or Jewish. To say that the Puritan project was the project of America is to vastly overstate their importance. Many of my ancestors were Quaker, and became so after one of them was kicked out of the Puritan church for giving aid and comfort to Quakers during a storm. Being the descendant of those who where kicked out of the church Winthrop belonged to for being too inclusive in their associations makes me skeptical of the notion that a Puritan in 1630 defined the essence of America.

The essential nature of the American experiment has much more to do with the thought of the outlaw John Locke than the Reverend John Winthrop.

Winthrop did not believe in religious tolerance or democracy. He presided over the trial of Anne Hutchinson, who did not agree with the Puritan credo that it took both faith and good works to get into heaven. Like many modern-day Christians, she believed that faith alone was enough. For this she was labeled a heretic and banished from the colony, and Winthrop called her an "American Jezebel."

Nor was Winthrop an admirer of democracy, saying:

> "If we should change from a mixed aristocracy to mere democracy, first we should have no warrant in scripture for it: For there was no such government in Israel ... A democracy is, amongst civil nations, accounted the meanest and worst of all forms of government. [To allow it would be] a manifest breach of the 5th Commandment."

To my Catholic and Lutheran readers I should explain that Winthrop was using the Calvinist system for numbering the commandments, so he was referring to "honor they father and mother," not "thou shall not kill."

Thomas Jefferson, author of the Bill of Rights, thought very highly of John Locke and did not approve of the intolerance of the Puritans.

James Madison, who had as much to do with the framing of the Constitution as anyone, argued in Federalist Paper #10 that religion was one of the major sources of faction in a country, and this tendency to faction could only be controlled in a large and diverse republic. Madison was also a major supporter of the Bill of Rights, in which the rule against the establishment of religion ensures that no one can be punished for not believing what people like John Winthrop might think they should.

The vision of America that Jefferson and Madison proposed was one that varies greatly with the vision neoconservatives insist upon. The open society they wanted did not rely on perverse readings of ancient texts, but on easily understood concepts embodied in the Constitution. Straussian readings tend to seek the hidden meaning of texts, but Jefferson and Madison and the other founding fathers were doing their best to make their meaning clear and persuasive. I don't think they would have seen the point of hiding their meaning, and I suspect any hidden meaning found is one made up by the reader.

In practice, the neoconservative notion of American exceptionalism amounts to an assertion of national greatness. In foreign policy terms, the neoconservative idea seems to be that America can lick any man in the house, and should fight anyone who looks at us funny. Their American exceptionalism amounts to nothing more than Amerika über alles, hardly a slogan for a democratic country.

Chapter 12: The End of History

History ended on a Tuesday afternoon, October 14, 1806. We know this because Georg Wilhelm Friedrich Hegel told us so.

It was about 1 p.m. that Napoleon made the decisive move that defeated the forces of the Prussian monarchy at the Battle of Jena. To Hegel, that meant that the ideas of the French Revolution had triumphed in the world, by which he apparently meant the German-speaking part of northern Europe, and we would henceforth take as our standard of good government liberty and equality, rather than the custom, faith and force that had legitimized the Prussian monarchy.

Never mind that the French Revolution had devolved into the Terror and reformed itself into a despotic and aggressive empire, Napoleon never the less represented the triumph of *liberte, egalite, fraternite* and that meant that man's long evolution from stone-age tribe through its various eras was at an end.

Sure, history as it is usually understood, (people doing stuff and people writing about it in an effort to shape how people remember that stuff) would continue to occur, but history as envisioned by Hegel, a dialectic that worked to a definite end, had reached that end.

Hegel was a dialectical idealist. He is unfortunately largely remembered as the precursor to Karl Marx's dialectical materialism, but he is actually part of the liberal tradition rather than the Marxist one. Marx used his idea of thesis meeting antithesis, and the conflict producing a synthesis that became the new thesis, but he used it to advocate for a quite different system than Hegel admired.

However, unlike Hobbes, Locke and Rousseau, Hegel saw mankind not as the product of a fixed nature, but as an evolution of history. As a result, instead of the sort of thought experiment about what sort of government was natural to man, his philosophy was teleological, one in which man aspired to greater perfection and worked through the dialectic of history to the goal of the perfect form of government.

Oh, sure, there were still monarchs, "Oriental despots," dictators and aristocrats in the world, but they were atavistic after the Battle of Jena. Edmund Burke fought a gallant rear-guard action with *Reflections on the Revolution in France*, maintaining that custom and prejudice were the organic wisdom of society, but he could not claim history was on his side, and one of his intellectual heirs, William F. Buckley, in 1955 wrote of his own publication, "….if NATIONAL REVIEW is superfluous, it is so for very different reasons: It stands athwart history, yelling Stop, at a time when no one is inclined to do so, or to have much patience with those who so urge it."

Conservatives have defined themselves as backward-looking, even those who follow the radical logic of Ayn Rand or libertarian thinkers.

With the fall of the Soviet Union, Frances Fukuyama wrote his famous essay analyzing the delegitimation of Communism as *The End of History*, published in the summer, 1989 issue of *The National Interest*. He later expanded this into a book.

The 2011 Arab Spring saw history ending again in another part of the world, and the efforts of the Green movement in Iran showed that the theocratic state could be challenged. In China, a Communist Party that no longer practices Communism is clinging to power and trying to justify one-party rule through solid economic growth and nationalism, which is certainly more stable than Napoleon's attempt to justify his rule through military victory and chauvinism. But this may not be as enduring as a form of government that has the relief valve of letting the people peacefully choose a new leader.

Even the worst dictators often seem to feel a need to hold rigged elections, because if they cannot make even the most implausible claim to be chosen by the people, they have no other claim to legitimacy. Why is this? Why do other forms of legitimacy fail, when for most of history, mankind has been ruled by force and faith?

I maintain that this represents a change in our dominant mode of thought. Much of the wisdom of ancient civilizations was transmitted in a mytho-poetic manner, explaining the world through the actions of capricious gods and spirits, coordinating civilization through religion and custom.

The weird, wonderful word of symbolic thought that we live in with our minds and our culture while our bodies inhabit the animal world of food, sleep and sex brought awe to the human mind before it brought reductionist logic. The mythic world of beauty, grace and terror has a pull on our minds that appeals no matter how logical we attempt to be. At a time when our practical, problem solving abilities were primarily aimed at making better tools and growing crops or hunting game, our minds were exploring the virtual reality of the imagination, and the ancients were organizing their lives around symbols of power, beauty, strength, and fear.

We will, I hope, never be free of this world of songs, poetry, faith and art, nor should we aspire to be. But as wealth increased, and our problem-solving selves were evidently the reason for it, reason itself became recognized as an increasingly potent source of power. And if reason could solve the problem of how to build better ships, could it not also solve the problem of building better ships of state?

As we discussed in the first chapter, the religious conflicts of Enlightenment Europe made continued reliance on mythic justifications an untenable source of legitimacy for governments. If half your people belong to one religion and half to another, neither will stand for being ruled by an apostate, and the wars will be without end, or at least for thirty years.

Reason was on the rise outside the realm of government already. The Black Plague had killed off a third of Europe, and since arable land was the main source of wealth, this meant that the survivors were wealthier. It also meant that there was plenty of used clothing to make rag paper. Earlier generations had engaged in palimpsest, erasing ancient texts because they needed the velum to make a new Psalter or such, but Johannes Gutenberg found plenty of paper on which to use his movable type.

In addition, wealth had begun to feed on wealth, and Europe had begun its great era of exploration, which resulted in the European settlement of much of the rest of the world, including the conquest (or, if you like, theft) of three continents. Reason increased our wealth, not just through business, but through the instruments of navigation and improved ships of exploration and improved weapons of conquest. Europeans gained material benefits, it seemed, wherever reason was applied, and reason began to dominate the way we organized our societies, making myth and custom seem old-fashioned.

We called the rise of reason as an organizing social force the Enlightenment. But of course, the light shined brightest in European culture, and the light cast some strong shadows as well.

Those who were not enlightened by European culture were viewed as benighted. That included the first peoples of the conquered continents, who were viewed as a lower order of human, and could only be "enlightened" by giving up their old culture and adopting the new one, even if this had to be forced upon them by removing children from their homes and punishing them any time they spoke their native tongue.

In addition, while reason can be used to solve problems, it can also be used to justify what you want to believe, which is how the Fascist movement gave a scientific sheen to its racism (although really, they were about tribalism, and the doctrine of blood and soil). And it can be used to take a false premise and logically move from there to a wrong conclusion, which I maintain is pretty much the story of the Communist project as well.

David Hume, the most powerful thinker of the Scottish Enlightenment, said that "Reason is, and ought only to be the slave of the passions." After all, my computer doesn't think about anything I don't tell it to, because it lacks passion. My car does not drive itself, because it has no destination. If it had appetites, it might be as fractious as a mule when I run the gas tank low, but it doesn't care if the engine is starved for fuel because it lacks the capacity for caring.

This capacity for caring is the main restraint on those powerful ways of organizing our world, faith and reason. Marx saw that the faith of religion sometimes produced injustice, and concluded that religion should be done away with, saw that the logic of property sometimes produced injustice, and concluded that private property (except for personal effects) should be done away with. The results were disastrous, as the main organizing principles of society were abandoned and the only remaining organizing principle were force and faith in Marxist ideology. Marx would not have objected to the goals as the French Revolution, *liberte, egalite, fraternite*, but his philosophy brought on even more spectacular Terrors. Such is the nightmare of reason.

Liberalism is a term that usually is taken to mean a belief that society should be organized around liberty, free markets, and free and fair election of government representatives. But the way the word is used in American politics has another element. Conservatives advocate traditional religious views and somewhat radical free market functioning, with the claim that these produce just outcomes.

Liberalism has come to mean that the capacity for caring, an empathy with one's fellow citizens, acts as a restraint on the excesses of markets and religious doctrines. Burke thought the ascendance of reason and the excesses displayed in the Terror could only be restrained by clinging to tradition and custom, maintaining that they were the organic wisdom of a civilization.

But there are reasons no one today offers the forthright defense of "prejudice" Burke did, because prejudice itself is in need of restraint. You don't have to know the sad history of lynching in America or the struggles of the civil rights movement to understand this. You need only have a little empathy for the kid who gets beat up for being a "queer," or the customer treated badly because of race.

It is this very empathy that modern conservatism disdains in modern liberalism, yet in the end it is the main restraint on the excesses of faith, the cruelty of prejudice and the nightmare of reason.

But is liberalism the end of history? It is hard to imagine a new force organizing society with greater legitimacy, but the old forces remain potent. New mythologies are arising, such as the Rapture of the Geeks (the notion that an all-knowing computer can give the Elect an eternal life in the Cloud). At one point during the 2012 election, the Republican candidate leading the polls in the selection of a nominee to run for president was Rick Santorum, a sort of pre-Vatican II Catholic who has trouble imagining any governing idea not based on religion.

In a campaign stop in Ohio Feb. 18, 2012, Santorum said Barack Obama based his rule on the wrong theology. From the New York Times:[*]

> "It's about some phony ideal, some phony theology. Oh, not a theology based on the
> Bible, a different theology," he said. "But no less a theology."

This is a sort of paleo-conservative view that finds it impossible to imagine any source of legitimacy other than religion, and it appeals to conservatives who share that view. There may at some point be enough of them to nominate a presidential candidate, and probably there are more of them now than there were when John F. Kennedy ran for president. During that campaign, he found it necessary to give the following reassurance:[*]

> "...These are the real issues which should decide this campaign. And they are not
> religious issues — for war and hunger and ignorance and despair know no religious
> barriers.

> "But because I am a Catholic, and no Catholic has ever been elected president, the real
> issues in this campaign have been obscured — perhaps deliberately, in some quarters
> less responsible than this. So it is apparently necessary for me to state once again not
> what kind of church I believe in — for that should be important only to me — but what
> kind of America I believe in.

> "I believe in an America where the separation of church and state is absolute, where no
> Catholic prelate would tell the president (should he be Catholic) how to act, and no
> Protestant minister would tell his parishioners for whom to vote; where no church or

church school is granted any public funds or political preference; and where no man is denied public office merely because his religion differs from the president who might appoint him or the people who might elect him.

"I believe in an America that is officially neither Catholic, Protestant nor Jewish; where no public official either requests or accepts instructions on public policy from the Pope, the National Council of Churches or any other ecclesiastical source; where no religious body seeks to impose its will directly or indirectly upon the general populace or the public acts of its officials; and where religious liberty is so indivisible that an act against one church is treated as an act against all."

Barack Obama had to give a speech demonstrating that he also would not shape his rule to suit his pastor, Jeremiah Wright. But Santorum represents a kind of tribalism, and for him his faith is the right one to be a part of the tribe. He portrays President Obama as the Other, because he sees faith and tribe as the sources of legitimacy for the presidency.

And the election of Donald Trump in 2016 involved many Evangelical Christians voting for a thrice-married former casino owner who talked about grabbing women "by the pussy." Even faith had disappeared from the conversation, replaced by a feeling that what was needed was a strong man who appealed to the tribalism of his followers.

This means that history has not ended. It has, perhaps, instead entered a recursive loop, in which we must choose time and again between tribe and faith on the one hand and reason and empathy on the other. The first can fall prey to the doctrine of blood and soil, the second to the nightmare of reason based on bad premises, so the loop serves a purpose.

Francis Fukuyama in 1992 extended his essay into a book, like the essay titled *The End of History and the Last Man*. In it, he said that:

What we may be witnessing is not just the end of the Cold War, or the passing of a particular period of post-war history, but the end of history as such: that is, the end point of mankind's ideological evolution and the universalization of Western liberal democracy as the final form of human government.

He failed to anticipate the resiliency of authoritarianism, and in some cases, its transmutation into illiberal democracy. They still hold elections in Zimbabwe, Russia, and Iran, but not just anyone is allowed to run and not just anyone is allowed to publish opinions about who people should vote for.

Elections, the press, and the judiciary are subjugated to a strong leader or oligarchy. Russia, for example, now has a record of not just silencing its critics, but of killing them, even if they live abroad. People following the path of Russia's Vladimir Putin, Venezuela's Hugo Chavez, or Zimbabwe's Robert Mugabe may think they need the trappings of democracy to have legitimacy as a ruler, but they do not tolerate its substance.

One of the marks of such regimes is that they silence the press or find ways to bend it to their will. A tactic often used is to set people against each other, Mugabe, for example, instigated genocide against the Ndebele people, killing about 20,000 people. Claiming there was an internal threat enabled him to consolidate one-party rule.

An internal threat can be used to silence critics, as Turkey's Recep Erdogan did in Turkey, detaining lawmakers from the opposition party based on claims that they were associated with Kurdish militarists and arresting the editor and about a dozen journalists from a left-of-center newspaper which had embarrassed him. He claimed the newspaper had ties to a cleric living in exile in the United States, who he supposed had been the inspiration for a failed coup attempt.

It has long bothered me that some on the far right seem to regard the constitution as a rough draft, constantly wanting to change it to comply with their agenda on issues like same-sex marriage and the balanced budget (legislators could, of course, simply pass balanced budgets if that's what they want.) Would-be strongmen take this approach as well, for example when Erdogan decided the Turkish constitution needed to give the Turkish president more power, or when Chavez, at the peak of his popularity, held a referendum to revise Venezuela's constitution to give him more power.

The problem is, when you vote in someone who does not really believe in democracy, it's hard to get rid of him. And it usually is a "him." When the same party controls both the legislature and the executive branch, and allows only its own picks to get on the courts, only the leader's own party can control a drift to authoritarianism. And, if they are getting their agenda passed by the strongman, why would they?

Only a strong commitment to democratic principles on the part of all powerful parties in a system can stem the authoritarian drift. The question for our nation is, do we have that?

A further question is, can a multi-ethnic democracy work? Nation-states evolved in the dissolution of multi-ethnic empires, evolving as ethnically homogeneous entities. Some of the worst disruptions within nation states have come from trying to make them still more homogeneous.

But that was in a time when most people would spend their lives in one village. Or, if you were part of the European takeover of the New World or Australia, you might build a new village, welcoming to people like yourself. Not, by nature, welcoming to people unlike yourself. So, you fight some with the people unlike yourself. Afterwards you say, you go over there, I'll go over here, we leave each other alone, okay? Until you need more space, anyhow.

But now, things are different. The whole world is in communication, and everybody is going everywhere. The Great Wall of China was a useful system of fortification at least as recently as the 14th century, when they were still building it, but it is now merely historic and ornamental. Physical boundaries can be easily breached now.

That means that only rigorous social controls can keep a nation ethnically homogeneous. To see the cost of that, we need only look at Japan, where the economy has plenty of problems, one of them being that a stagnant population makes it difficult to grow the economy. And Japanese culture, admirable as it may be, does not have a history of welcoming immigrants.

Who knows if the world will ever be ready for a world government, but navigating in this new world where physical boundaries mean less than ever before, the ability to absorb new culture and new labor is essential for the survival of nations.

What's needed is national identity not connected to religion or ethnicity. The United States has a major advantage there, in that we have a concept of what the nation is to be that is not connected to race or religion.

America was founded to do more than exist as an ethnic entity, as other nation-states did. It was founded as a place where people could worship as they wished and speak their opinions as they wished. It was formed as a place where the people could shape their will through free speech and express it through democratically elected representatives.

Men like Thomas Jefferson and Alexander Hamilton disagreed about a great many things, but they did agree that they wanted to build a country that was free, fair, and tolerant. There were problems with the way they lived their lives (such as Jefferson keeping slaves, some of whom were his own offspring) but they had a worthy vision that was an inspiration to the rest of the world.

We cannot retreat from this vision to become an ethnically and religiously homogeneous state. I say this not because I do not wish us to do so, although that is the case, but because we are already too diverse to ever return to such an imagined state. Besides, if, as some wish us to do, we define ourselves as a Christian nation, we must then define who is a Christian, a trap this nation's founders were all too familiar with.

Chapter 13: Burning the booksellers: Religious freedom

and the secular state

My copy of *Foxe's Book of Christian Martyrs* has a woodcut illustrating a particularly odious form of book burning – a bookseller being burned with his books.

Not that the punishment was without an internal logic. The booksellers had been selling Holy Scripture in English. The Catholic Church objected to this, and any Protestant heresy that involved removing the priest's mediation of scripture. The Bible, the Church decreed, was meant to be in Latin, a language taught mainly to the clergy.

The booksellers were therefore heretics, spreading the false gospel of a personal relationship with God. Once people began reading the Bible themselves, they came to conclusions about its meaning that varied from Church orthodoxy. They and their booksellers had to be punished, and not just their vile bodies. At the time, most Christians believed that to be resurrected on Judgment Day, your body needed to be buried more or less intact.

The booksellers were burned so that they could not be resurrected on Judgment Day.

This dispute was part of the genesis of liberalism, of the separation of church and state, and of free speech. It also relates to the belief in the literal interpretation of the Bible.

The Anglo-Saxons had translated the Bible into their language, no problem. But the Norman French did not speak Anglo-Saxon, and the Catholic Church was trying to assert more control over peoples' religious lives. The Norman invasion brought with it the Latin Bible.

The Church cracked down on the (mainly French) Goliard poets in the late 13th century and early 14th, labeling them "Bohemians" in an effort to link them to the gypsies, who they called by that name. John Wycliffe, an Oxford don, translated the Vulgate Bible into English, and while he was allowed to die of natural causes in 1384, his body was burned to prevent his resurrection (ironically, the Vulgate Bible was translated from Hebrew and Greek into Latin so that citizens of Rome could read the Bible in their own language).

William Tyndale, a scholar born about a century after Wycliffe's body was burned, went back to the Hebrew and Greek text to produce a better translation into English. He did much of this while hiding in the Netherlands, but the Church caught up with him in 1535, and in 1536 he was sentenced to death by strangulation and his body was burned at the stake.

Two years later, Henry VIII broke with the Catholic Church and decreed that the Bible should be published in English, resulting in the Great Bible, partly based on Tyndale's work.

Henry VIII (I suppose Twitter would abbreviate that to Hank8) did not intend to separate church and state. He intended for the state to take over the church. Thomas More, that martyr of conscience, died for the principle that the Pope should be able to tell monarchs whether they could have their marriages annulled, thereby ruling on who was a legitimate heir (Elizabeth I would not have been legitimate based on the Catholic Church's ruling).

English kings continued to rely on religion for the legitimacy of their rule. James I wrote *The True Law of Free Monarchies* and *Basilikon Doron* (*Royal Gift*), both asserting the divine right of kings. There had been a time when kings did not need to assert such things, because they were taken for granted, but James kept having run-ins with parliament, which asserted that his right to rule was not absolute.

Following the Gunpowder Plot in 1605,[*] he required Catholics to sign an oath of allegiance denying the Pope's authority over the king.

But he married a French princess who was Catholic, and his son, Charles I, was a believer in the divine right of kings.

And that's where it gets interesting.

If you are of any given religion in a nation that is divided between Catholics, Anglicans, and non-conformist protestants such as Puritans, Quakers, Ranters, Anabaptists, Diggers, Muggletonians and other more obscure groups, whose God gives you the right to rule?

Charles I was an arrogant and high-handed ruler who was inclined to ignore parliament, based on his claim of divine right. In the end, he rather lost his head. On a chopping block. Charles I was, in fact, the first head of state to be impeached. The idea here was essentially that of the king's two bodies. Charles Stuart, the corporeal man, was charged with abusing the power of Charles I, king of England and the 'body politic' of said king. When America's founding fathers were looking for a way to replace a bad ruler without the necessity of a revolution, they came up with two methods, election and impeachment. And to make impeachment less painful, they made the penalty removal from office, rather than removal of the ruler's head.

The beheading of Charles I

The need for a secular government was created by a crisis in faith, the splintering of the Church into a dizzying array of churches. The blossoming of the Protestant churches could only encourage the formation of a secular state, because freedom of religion requires that you be free from the religions of others.

We tend to forget what the establishment of religion means. Here's an example. The 1599 Act of Uniformity made it illegal not to attend official Church of England services, providing for a fine of one shilling for each missed Sunday and Holy Day. If you conducted unofficial services, as many dissenters were inclined to do, you were subject to a larger fine or even imprisonment. Two dissenters were executed for holding unofficial services in 1593, so the 1599 Act may have been more merciful.

The Pilgrims came to America in 1620, a generation before the English Civil War, to be free of the state religion of England, free to practice their religion as they saw fit. Not that they wanted a secular state; they wanted to set up their own colony with their own state religion.

For different groups to share the new land with freedom to practice religion as they saw fit, they needed to be free of each other's religion. I've noticed that deeply religious people sometimes have trouble wrapping their brains around this. They tend to focus on the practice of their religion, and, not having been forced to practice the religion of others, not think about what establishment of religion could mean.

After all, it was back in England that people were executed for conducting unofficial services, and that was a long time ago. And no one has been executed for blasphemy in the United Kingdom since 1697, nor has anyone been executed for it here.

But those were real penalties for holding the wrong religious beliefs under an established church. We still see them today in places like Iran where religious authorities reign supreme.

John Locke wrote *A Letter concerning Toleration* (1689) to argue that the state should not dictate belief. He pointed out that while the state can compel people to practice a religion, it cannot compel them to believe in it. That had been enough for Hobbes, who thought that as long as everyone practiced the state religion, the state would function properly. But Locke argued that religious conflict happened not because people believed different things, but because the state tried to make them all believe the same thing. Given that the state had no special competence in determining true religion, and attempts to enforce uniform religion led to unrest, why should the state be in the religion business at all?

America's founding fathers knew what it was like to live under an established church. Quite a few American colonies had established churches. The Puritans, for example, managed to establish the Congregational Church in New Hampshire, Connecticut, and Massachusetts, leaving many of the functions we now expect of the state to churchmen, such as running the school system. This was not good if you were not a congregationalist. In addition, Puritans for quite some time denied citizenship in these colonies to Quakers and Roman Catholics. Maryland, which started with a religious toleration law, soon saw that law repealed and control seesaw between Catholics and Protestants. In 1718, Catholics in Maryland lost their right to vote. In many states, the Anglican Church was the established religion.

There were historical reasons for establishment of religion. After

British officers of the Catholic faith turned their positions over to their Catholic co-religionists during the war for the Netherlands' independence from Spain,[*] Queen Elizabeth decreed that only Anglicans could be officers in the military or practice law or hold public office. But the American colonies were in many cases founded by dissenters, so its army was far more diverse.

In the American revolutionary army, you could be of any faith. Colonel Mordecai Sheftall, for example, was Jewish. But how did our founding fathers feel about the role of religion after they got independence?

Well, the first amendment to the constitution decrees that Congress shall make no law regarding establishment of religion. That seems clear enough. And in 1797, congress unanimously passed the Treaty of Tripoli, the English-language version of which decreed that:

> As the Government of the United States of America is not, in any sense, founded on the Christian religion,—as it has in itself no character of enmity against the laws, religion, or tranquility, of Mussulmen [Muslims],—and as the said States never entered into any war or act of hostility against any Mahometan [Mohammedan] nation, it is declared by the parties that no pretext arising from religious opinions shall ever produce an interruption of the harmony existing between the two countries.

That seems clear enough.

However, not everyone respects history or the original intent of the founders. For example, *World Net Daily* confronts us with the headline, *America: A Christian Nation, Like it or Not*. Reading the story, we learn that an Evangelical group points to some 19th century Supreme Court decisions that indicated that at the time, a majority of justices viewed America as a Christian nation.

Just as kings never had to make the argument that they possessed their power by divine right until that was in doubt, conservative Christians seldom had to make their argument until an increasingly large proportion of the population were either unchurched or belonged to non-Christian faiths. The percentage of the population professing no religion in 1953 was 1 percent; the number in 2013 was 15 percent. In the same period, the percentage of the population identifying as Protestant declined from 70 percent to 41 percent. Non-specified Christian, a group not counted in 1953, is now 9 percent, and Catholic has held steady at 24 percent.

The percent Jewish has declined from 4 percent to 2 percent, and the percentage "other" has risen from 1-2 percent to 5 percent. Not only are Protestants no longer a majority, nearly a quarter of the population does not claim to be Christian at all.

This has accompanied a radical change in our nation's ethnic makeup. The reason Catholics have held up as a percentage of the population is the vast number who have immigrated from Latin America. The reason "other" keeps increasing is that we have so many immigrants from areas where Christianity is a minority religion, in Asia, the Middle East, and Africa.

The drive to define this country as a Christian nation is not led by traditionally black denominations. It is led by traditionally white denominations who are concerned about how America is changing.

Most people would say that after WW II, America came into its own as the most powerful nation in the world, supplanting the battered British Empire. Yet to those who wish to define America as a Christian nation, this appears to be a period of decline, starting with a 1947 ruling:

> From the time of Everson until today, decisions by the U.S. Supreme Court have helped to bring about the greatest decline in American civilization. It was as if the Supreme Court had declared a bloodless revolution in America -- a revolution more subtle than yet just as destructive as the Russian revolution under Lenin. Over the next three decades, we witnessed a stream of liberal court rulings that gradually reshaped who we are as a nation.[*]

The author quotes Alexis de Tocqueville saying that America's greatness is connected with America's goodness, which the author claims is lost when we don't regard America as a Christian nation. This ignores Tocqueville's own views on religion, as revealed in an interview he did with an American newspaper:

> Q. In your opinion, what would be the best way to render to religion its natural empire?
>
> A. I believe the Catholic religion less apt than the reformed to accord with ideas of liberty. However, if the clergy were entirely separated from all temporal power, I cannot but believe that with time it would regain the intellectual influence which naturally belongs to it. I think that to appear to forget the church, without being unfriendly to it, is the best way and even the only way to serve it. Pursuing this policy you will see public education little by little falling into its hands, and the youth will with time adopt a different attitude....

It seems he was right. The European nations that had established churches are not typically as religious as America. Separating the church from all temporal power may well be what's made it so influential in our culture.

But there does seem to be a group of people who really want to define America as a Christian nation, and in effect, establish Christianity as the national religion. First, there are the Dominionists, relatively few in number, who believe that God gave Christians dominion over the earth, so they should rule. Then, there is the broader public of the Christian right, which *World Net Daily* appeals to. This is a larger, and in fact, vast group, though far from a majority in the country.

This is the group that supported Rick Santorum for president, and he provided them with a suitably Dominionist critique of President Obama, which I've mentioned before:

> Obama's agenda is "...not about you. It's not about your quality of life. It's not about your jobs. It's about some phony ideal. Some phony theology. Oh, not a theology based on the Bible. A different theology," Santorum told supporters of the conservative Tea Party movement at a Columbus hotel.

> He enlarged on the theme when talking about environmentalism:

> "When you have a worldview that elevates the Earth above man and says we can't take those resources because we're going to harm the Earth ... it's just all an attempt to centralize power, to give more power to the government."

Santorum's supporters, in addition to wanting Christianity to dominate our government, have shown themselves intent on ridding the Republican Party of people they consider RINOs -- Republicans In Name Only. Put them in charge, give them their wish of a theocratic state, and soon you'd see them suppressing those they consider CINO -- Christian In Name Only. This would doubtless apply to the church my mother has attended for about half a century, which has a female preacher and is happy to accommodate gay marriage.

There is a reason the people who want to define America as a Christian nation don't want to include churches like hers.

First, you must understand that while pundits tend to talk about evangelical churches as if they were a unified group, they are anything but. Black evangelical church attendees tend to belong to an entirely different political coalition than white evangelicals. And even among white evangelicals, there are historical divisions that go back to before the Civil War.

For example, in the area where I live, the Independent Evangelical Church is active. It was formed by a merger of the Swedish Evangelical Church and the Danish Evangelical Church. Southern Baptist evangelism has a different history. Most historians trace the Baptist Church back to 1609, and whatever your view, the first Baptist church in America was founded in 1639. From the First Great Awakening, a time of Christian fervor and major growth for the Baptist church in the 1730s and 1740s, Baptists became anti-slavery. About a century later, in 1845, the Home Mission Society of the church refused to allow slave holders to be missionaries if they insisted on taking their slaves with them on missions. It was over this that the Southern Baptist Church separated from the rest of the Baptist Church. As a result, there are northern and southern evangelists who believe many of the same things, but have a history of different cultures. They do hold some important values in common, and as the Republican Party began to craft its message to appeal to certain evangelical sects, it began to appeal to most evangelicals. However, the alliance started with a subset of southern white evangelical churches.

Evangelical churches didn't become politically very active until the IRS started cracking down on "white academies" – private schools, often associated with a historically white church, which sprang up in the South after school integration began to spread to the region. The Christian right has long been tainted by an association with this effort to revive segregation. In short, the problem isn't just a desire to see Christianity dominant, it is also an element of ethnic panic, a fear that the identity of their nation will no longer be associated with their ethnicity.

That's why the more tolerant Christian sects are anathema to those who want to see America defined as a Christian nation. As a political matter, these sects tend to belong to different parties. Stanley Greenberg, a pollster, has described the Democratic coalition as "diverse America and the whites who are comfortable with diverse America."

And the Republican Party, because of its reliance on a conservative Christian movement associated with the white academies, consists in part of whites who are not comfortable with diverse America.

I should note that there are many white evangelicals who don't have a problem with diverse America, or with sending their kids to public schools. They remain culturally conservative, and generally fall in the Republican camp politically. But then, most of them aren't big on gaining temporal power for religion. As conservative politicians found them to be reliable allies, they tailored their message to appeal to evangelicals of all types.

To establish Christianity as the national religion puts the state in a position of defining who is Christian. Who would actually want that?

Perhaps the advocates of this idea should remember where the freedom to start their churches came from, and what could happen to that freedom.

Chapter 14: The Way West, individualism, and the

marginal revolution

Hegel may have thought history ended with the supremacy of liberal ideas in 1806, but the term "liberal" had not entered the language in its current sense at that point. This is because liberalism was still being invented, and key concepts had not yet entered the fray. The word entered the English language more or less officially in 1815 to describe a political movement that had already brought on two revolutions.

Not coincidentally, one of the leading liberals of the 19th century also brought attention to a system of value based on utility.

Liberalism started as a way to explain why government was needed in a time when governments were facing a crisis in legitimacy. Now, we have people arguing that "government is the problem, not the solution," a motto which directly contradicts the thinking of the founders of liberal thought and the framers of the U.S. constitution. The motto can only be true if they are thinking of a different problem than Thomas Hobbes was thinking of when he wrote *Leviathan*.

The reason for this change is a tendency, as liberalism has developed, to place increasing emphasis on the rights of the individual, and less on the social contract.

The term liberal has quite a few meanings, and the most important founding thinkers of liberalism were dead by the time the word started being used to describe their system of thought. In the sense of tending to favor freedom and democracy, its use began in France in 1801, and it started to be used in England by its critics during the excesses of the French Revolution. Prior to that, it had been used in 16th and 17th century England as a term of reproach, referring to a lack of restraint on speech and action, a sense that is retained in the word.

In our earlier ruminations on liberalism, we discussed its roots in social contract theory. Hobbes and Locke both tended to emphasize how individuals made a contract with each other to form a society, because to live in a society is far better than the war of each against all.

The rights of the individual could only exist in the context of the social contract, because without the sovereign to protect them, there was no guarantee that the individual could enjoy life itself, let alone the rights Locke insisted we were born with and could not sell, or in his quaint turn of phrase, alienate.

In modern day America, it seems that the right and left have a conversation that has traditionally stayed largely within the bounds of liberalism. In matters related to property, conservatives emphasize the rights of the individual and progressives emphasize the social contract, while in the sphere of criminal law conservatives emphasize the social contract and liberals emphasize individual rights. Both stay within the bounds of liberalism. Socialism, in the sense of the state (representing the People) owning the means of production, is a discredited economic philosophy,[*] and fascism has been a discredited political philosophy for even longer. Indeed, Ambrose Bierce, in *The Devil's Dictionary*, made this distinction:

> **Conservative**, n. A statesman who is enamored of existing evils, as distinguished from the **Liberal**, who wishes to replace them with others. [Ambrose Bierce, The Devil's Dictionary, 1911]

Perhaps this is what the end of history, in Hegel's sense, looks like: Brothers battling over small differences in their interpretations of a doctrine they both accept, in which mankind has a natural right to liberty and the state exists to serve the governed. Terms like "fascist" and "socialist" are still thrown about, but not with their original meaning, instead referring to the poles of this smaller universe of acceptable debate.

The individual looms larger in this debate than it did for Hobbes and Locke, and the values of the marketplace have become such a powerful force in our model of how the world works that there are people – certain libertarians – who regard government's only legitimate role as being to protect property rights. The U.S. Constitution states that congress shall provide for the common defense and general welfare of the United States, but there's a virulent strain of thought that says that while defense is a legitimate role for government, the welfare of its citizens is not.

How did we get from a philosophy based on the need for people to come together to one that insists, in some cases literally, on the sovereignty of the individual? Certainly the term "sovereign citizen" would have seemed incoherent to Hobbes; the sovereign in his view was needed by the people to govern the society they had formed, so an individual could only be a sovereign by ruling other people.

It can be difficult to put ourselves in the minds of people who did not work with the same concepts we do. It used to be that economics, then called "political economy," was done not based on notions of how individuals would act, but based on the way classes of people would act. Markets were understood by reference to how landowners as a class would act and how workers as a class would act, regardless of whether the economist was a liberal, a conservative, or a communist. This changed with the notion of marginal utility.

But before we could have a marginal revolution, we had to have a concept of utility as it related to a system of values. That was developed by the utilitarians, notably Jeremy Bentham and John Stuart Mill. Just as Adam Smith became interested in markets because, as a moral philosopher, he was interested in values, the utilitarians started with a system of moral values.

Utilitarianism maintains that to act ethically, we should consider the consequences of our actions, and the moral worth of an act can be calculated by how much happiness and how little pain results from it. It is a logical and reductionist theory that would allow someone with no moral sense – a term which as used here means an emotional feeling about what is right – to calculate what action is morally acceptable. Psychologists relying on ethics tests based on utilitarian ethics have found that psychopaths do better on them than normal people. Presumably this is because psychopaths lack empathy, and that makes normal ethical responses inaccessible to them, so to function as normal they learn to make the logical calculation utilitarianism calls for.

It is the very calculating nature of utilitarianism that makes it attractive to economists. It means that you can do math related to what people value. The utility of a thing can be measured in dollars and cents, and because you can infer the value from the financial figures, you can apply mathematics to a science of human values.

The marginalists made this concept more powerful by noting that there is such a thing as diminishing marginal utility. If I am hungry, enough food to satisfy my hunger has a certain value, and more food has a lesser value because I know it's going right to parts of my anatomy I wish were smaller, and at the extreme, if I eat too much I'll puke. You can actually chart the extent of my value for food on a supply and demand curve to arrive at the proper price. Suddenly, an area of thought that was interesting to philosophers became essential to bankers and businessmen. And since there was no unit of value called the Util, they applied the value of money to the problem of turning this into mathematical equations.[*]

And it didn't need to regard how classes interacted. You could make calculations about how people would decide to spend their money while regarding them as an aggregation of individuals rather than as members of a class.

While this was happening in the intellectual world of liberalism, geographic mobility was rapidly increasing for people in general and Americans in particular. In all of pre-modern Europe, as in most of the world, the vast majority of people lived and died in a community, often going no more than 50 miles from the center of that world in their lifetime. The opening of the American West meant that people left their communities in order to -- well, Firesign Theatre puts it better than I can:

> **WAGON BOSS:** My fellow settlers! We stand here at the Edge O' Civilization, on the banks of the Mississippi River, lookin' West, at Our Destiny!
>
> **PIONEER:** You can say that again!
>
> **WAGON BOSS:** What may appear to the fainthearted as a limitless expanse of Godforsaken wilderness...
>
> **THIRD PIONEER:** Sure is!
>
> **WAGON BOSS:** ...is, in reality, a Golden Opportunity for humble, God-fearin' people like ourselves, an' our families, an' our children, an' the generations a-comin', to carve a new life – outta the American Indian!

Of course, they could only do this with the support of the U.S. Cavalry (and the Buffalo soldiers) but in leaving their communities behind, they felt as if they were doing this as individuals rather than relying on the community they had grown up in. The conquest of a continent (some would say theft, but the words mean much the same) was an enterprise that only a powerful community could accomplish, but the satisfaction was quite often individual, and people therefore tended to assign credit to themselves.

The feeling of individualism in this country therefore tends to relate to our history, but the philosophy of individualism owes much to the way the values of the market have become more dominant in our society as time has gone on. As a philosophical stance, libertarian and Objectivist ideas of how the world should work are attempts to find a rational basis for society, which sounds fine to us children of the Enlightenment, until you consider that the French Revolution produced the Terror, and the Marxist revolutions that also attempted to find a rational basis for society produced worse nightmares of reason. Bierce had excellent reasons for his cynical observations of the difference between conservatives and liberals.

The irony of our present situation is that two sorts of extremists have made common cause, as conservatives who want to see the domination of traditional beliefs, social institutions and prejudices have joined with libertarians whose dream is a rational, individualist, disenchanted world that a psychopath might understand better than Edmund Burke.

There is additional irony in the fact that Hobbes first applied the values of the marketplace to restore legitimacy to government, and now, some people prefer to think that only the market is legitimate. The ultimate expression of this is libertarian anarchism, in which the claim is that the state is a forced monopoly, so the social contract is invalid. Rodrick Long makes the argument. It strikes me that he gives short shrift to Hobbe's claim that a social contract was needed to protect the individual.

Libertarian anarchists are as utopian as Marxists. But whereas Marxists proposed abolishing two of society's main ways of organizing itself, property and religion, leaving only the state as an organizing principle, libertarian anarchists would remove the state, leaving the market as the only organizing principle. It is as much based on reason to the exclusion of experience as Marxism, and if attempted, would probably produce its own evils. The notion of the social contract and the necessity of the state impose a logic that leads to democratic representation, but the U.S. also has a history of undemocratic representation, oddly enough.

Chapter 15: Thoughts on undemocratic representation

When the founding fathers wrote the constitution of the United States, one of their models was the Roman republic. Another source of information for them was Aristotle's *Politics*, which advocated the republic over pure democracy.

But here's the problem. The Roman senate was, for the most part, not democratically elected. It was more like England's House of Lords than the House of Commons.

And the story of the evolution of American government has been one of the battle between those who want to restrict who chooses representatives and those who want to widen the voting franchise.

Qualifications for voting are largely left up to the states, or were, until after the Civil War. Women could not vote, and in many states, felons still cannot vote.

But the thing is, women and felons were counted in the census, and contributed to the number of representatives states had in the House and how many electoral college votes states had for electing a president.

The founders supposed that we would elect wise men to gather and decide who the president should be. As far as I can tell, the electoral college system never actually worked that way. And even if it had, many people who were counted in determining the number of electoral college votes a state had were not allowed to vote themselves.

Slaves could not vote, but were counted for census purposes as three-fifths of a human being, so they increased the leverage of slave-state legislators and electoral college representatives, who represented them by opposing the abolition of slavery.

Following the Civil War, federal troops during Reconstruction enforced the right of former slaves to vote. But when Reconstruction ended,[*] Jim Crow laws ensured that blacks could be denied the vote.

This led to a long period when blacks were counted for census purposes as full human beings, but were not allowed to vote as such in many states. The result was a Southern congressional delegation strengthened by the number of black citizens in their districts, but elected to work against their interests.

The civil rights movement sought to end this, and with the 1965 Voting

Rights Act, it looked as if the Justice Department was back in the business of defending the right of African Americans to vote.

That sparked anger in the South, and when Richard Nixon set out to remake the Republican Party in his image, his genius for exploiting resentment and setting people against each other came to the fore. The Republican Party now dominates the South, and the South dominates the Republican Party.

So, it is not too surprising that the Republican Party is now in the forefront of trying to limit the voting franchise, just as Southern Democrats used to. Their anti-government message isn't what the Republican Party has always represented. Most of the rhetoric about small government started with the 1964 Civil Rights Act and the presidential campaign of Barry Goldwater, who opposed it.

Republicans worked for years to get enough conservative Supreme Court justices to pull the teeth of the Voting Rights Act of 1965. Their most notable success to date was the 2013 Shelby County, Alabama, decision which removed the provision requiring districts and states with a history of racial discrimination in voting to get prior approval from the Justice Department for changes in their voting laws.

Texas immediately went forward with a voter identification law which experts said would mainly make it harder for African American and Hispanic voters, and to some extent students, to exercise their vote.

Texas was allowed to use this law in the 2014 election, but as of this writing, it is still going through a long process of legal challenges. The law has plenty of imitators, particularly in the South.

The rapid population growth in Texas is something its government brags about, but the problem is, its government is dominated by a party that is not the choice of the main group of people driving this increase – Hispanics. So, they attempt to gain that tempting goal, representing people who aren't allowed to vote.

Voter ID laws are sold on the thin premise that there is a plague of vote fraud in the form that this would address, but those pushing such legislation have not produced evidence of anything of the sort. The intent is clearly to get back the old advantage the South had when the Three-Fifths Compromise gave them disproportionate clout in proportion to the number of voters they had.

Garry Wills, writing in his 2005 book, *"Negro President": Jefferson and the Slave Power*, said without the Three-Fifths Compromise,

> ...slavery would have been excluded from Missouri ... Jackson's Indian removal policy would have failed ... the Wilmot Proviso would have banned slavery in territories won from Mexico ... the Kansas-Nebraska bill would have failed.

In addition to the slavery issue, men were expected to represent women when the nation was founded. The notion that women should be allowed to vote, as well as being counted in the census for purposes of deciding how many House representatives and electoral college votes a state would have, gained some ground by the late 19th Century, with several Western states allowing them the franchise. But the 19th Amendment, which gave all women in America the vote, did not become law until 1920.

The cultural context is that men were considered to represent their households. Under the doctrine of feme covert, women were considered for property purposes to be one with the man's household, and subordinate to him. The wife therefore had no property of her own, and if she divorced, all property of the household, even that which she brought to it, would stay with the husband.

Husbands representing households was about property and subordination. When the nation was founded, only holders of sufficient property could vote. The property qualification for voting did not entirely disappear until 1856 in the U.S. It does not seem like any sort of accident that women got their property rights before they got the vote. Some things are deeply embedded in the culture.

In general, the policy of assuming that some classes of people, such as slave owners or husbands, should represent other people has run aground on the simple fact that they represent their own interests, not those of their slaves or wives.

But that's the point of restricting the franchise. Those who wish to limit the voting franchise usually want to do so in order to use the legislative power granted by the numbers of a population against those who are counted for purposes of determining political power, but not allowed to vote.

Chapter 16: The industrialization of Democracy

For most of human history, we have been ruled by force, faith, and custom. Enlightenment thinkers thought they could do better, by coming up with a form of society that would be better suited to humanity. One might think that as our way of life has changed, our form of government would need to change, and it has.

At the time when Enlightenment thinkers were inventing liberalism, one of the few examples around of a democratic society was Switzerland.

The Swiss cantons were predominantly occupied by people who owned small farms. During the middle ages, they were famous for producing pikemen who could stand up well to cavalry. Jean-Jacques Rousseau, who was Swiss, considered the Swiss way of life ideal for democracy. There was an equality of means between the farmers, and the technology that they employed in warfare did not require the investment in armor that tended to result in rule by aristocracy elsewhere in Europe.

This is part of the reason the founders of the United States designed a democratic republic, rather than a direct democracy. The economy of the U.S. varied from Maine fishermen who caught lobster from a small boat to planters like George Washington and Thomas Jefferson, who owned large estates worked by slave labor. Everything they read from the great thinkers of their day and the ancient Greek philosophers said that a large and varied country needed to be guided by the wise men.

However, they chose to have those wise men selected by the voters. They left it up to the states to decide who could vote, and in the beginning it was mainly men with property. (Not women, and not men who *were* property.)

But our country has become more democratic over time. Where the constitution originally said that state legislatures would select U.S. senators, that system was found all to easy to corrupt. In 1899, William A. Clark simply paid Montana state senators to vote him into office as a U.S. senator. The senate refused to seat him after the scandal broke, This resulted in the 17th Amendment, which provided for direct election of U.S. senators.

In 1800, 83% of Americans were engaged in agriculture. Currently, about 2% of the American population work on farms. Capitalism, a term not invented until 1850, has transformed our way of life, yet we still manage under the same old constitution. How is this possible?

The answer is that we have marvelously flexible institutions which have managed to change as society changed.

Not everyone has been happy with that. Andrew Jackson, president from 1829 to 1837, was a great believer in democracy, and the extension of the voting franchise to the common man -- that is, all white men. He envisioned a country of yeoman farmers, provided with land by removing Indians and colonizing their land.

This went with a version of values favored by the physiocrats, claiming all real value came from working the land. He feared moneyed interests would undermine republican values. It's all too easy to connect the term "republican values" with the values of the Republican Party, but that's a very different thing.

Republican values, to a person of Jackson's day, were the values of a virtuous citizen. Such a citizen exemplified civic virtue and patriotism above greed and power. John Adams, the second American president, said the following in a 1776 letter to Mercy Warren:

> "The Spirit of Commerce, Madam, which even insinuates itself into Families, and influences holy Matrimony, and thereby corrupts the morals of families as well as destroys their Happiness, it is much to be feared is incompatible with that purity of Heart and Greatness of soul which is necessary for an happy Republic."

Adams ended that letter with the following:

> "Every man must seriously set himself to root out his Passions, Prejudices and Attachments, and to get the better of his private Interest. The only reputable Principle and Doctrine must be that all Things must give Way to the public."

Good luck with that, Mr. Adams.

Jackson worried so much about the monied interests that he took some steps, such as not renewing the charter for the Bank of the United States, and requiring that payments made for government land had to be made with silver or gold coins, and eliminating the U.S. government debt, that sent the nation into an economic crisis. We didn't have a proper central bank again until 1913, by which time it was evident that we needed some means of dealing with financial panics.

The fact is, our democratic republic has had to adapt to enormous changes in the way we live, and has also changed the way we think about ourselves. More and more people have had their humanity recognized, in the form of the ownership of their own souls and the equality of all people before the law in such areas as voting, holding property, and marriage.

Groups who once counted toward the distribution of power, but were not allowed to vote, have gained the ability to have a say in who governs them and how.

Representation had to become more democratic, because our ideas about humanity changed. When John Locke was writing, society in general accepted the notion that the head of the household should represent the household. Now our ideas are in accord with the reality that women have strong minds and strong opinions, and wish to speak for themselves. We stopped accepting slavery as an institution, because Locke's philosophy permeated our society with the notion that we each own ourselves.

We quite rightly worry that our current way of life leads to great inequality, but what could be more unequal than slavery? We have had undemocratic representation from the first. What we have now are huge differences in the wealth of voting-eligible members of society, and a far more urban way of life than the founders could have envisioned.

The urbanization of society tends to warp the issue of representation, because apportioning districts tends to favor rural populations. Those whose concerns are urban are, by the very nature of cities, concentrated in a smaller space than those with rural concerns.

Another issue is that the vision of a nation of yeoman farmers people like Andrew Jackson wanted is long gone. Most people work for wages, which goes against the old tradition of American individualism.

In the 19th Century, there were radical individualists who believed that working for wages was no better than slavery, and invented the term "wage slave" to make their point. This was the theory of liberty that Canadian political scientist C.B. McPherson called possessive individualism, the idea that liberty consists of freedom from dependence on the will of other people. We still hear echoes of this in, for example, former President George W. Bush's use of the term "ownership society."

Tom Palmer at the Cato Institute, an advocate of Bush's policies, put it this way:

> As the American Founders knew and as generations of serious students of society have long known, an ownership society is a society of responsibility, liberty, and prosperity. A number of policy initiatives - including creation of personal retirement accounts, expansion of medical savings accounts, and school choice - have been

proposed recently that seek to strengthen an "ownership society." Such initiatives build on a long and deep tradition.

Part of what Palmer was referring to was Bush's poorly-received plan to remake Social Security. Social Security Insurance has always acted as insurance – those who can work pay into the fund from which those who can no longer work are paid. Bush proposed to turn it into sort of a saving program, which would have meant that somehow, we would have to pay Social Security benefits for retirees while working people would be paying into retirement savings plans. As it happened, there already was a program for retirement savings plans called 401(K) accounts, and the plan was financially unworkable in any case.

Palmer attributed the "ownership society" tradition to the founders, but as we've seen from what John Adams wrote, some of them were big believers in personal sacrifice and public service. Adams was also a big advocate of strong central government. Adams even pushed through the Alien and Sedition Acts, a horrible law which, among other things, resulted in the arrest of 20 newspaper editors who opposed Adams. When Jefferson became president, he pardoned those serving time under the law and made sure their fines were repaid. The law is now considered unconstitutional.

The sort of possessive individualism that Palmer and Bush admired had more to do with the tradition of Adams' opponents, among them Thomas Jefferson. Jefferson, and later Andrew Jackson, advocated a different sort of country with the ownership of property the key to liberty.

This fit with the notion of manifest destiny, in that people could have land by homesteading the land formerly occupied by Indians.

There were a couple of problems with this. The Indians did not willingly give up their land, so the U.S. military had to take it from them by force, a public investment to make this possessive individualism possible. Homesteaders may have felt they were building a new life for themselves by the sweat of their brow, but the thing that made that possible was a major government initiative to conquer the land they homesteaded. And the logistics that made the settlement possible started with clipper ships and Conestoga wagons, but getting their crops and cattle to the cities of the East required the construction of railroads.

Some of the more important railways were built with government loans and on land grants given to them by state and federal governments. About 9.5 percent of all federal land was granted to the railroads between 1850 and

1870. The railroads then sold off much of the land to help defray the cost of building the railroads. Once the main lines were in, private capital built the rest of the railroads, so that only about 8% of American railroads were built with government loans and land grants -- but they tended to be the most important ones.

All this was in aid of a vision of America as a country of small farms. And it was such a country. It wasn't until about 1920 that more people lived in and around cities than lived in the countryside. Now, about 80% of Americans live in urban areas.

One major problem with the 19th century version of radical individualism was that most people working for wages don't feel that they are slaves. People often quit their jobs if they don't like them. As a book store owner, some of my best and most loyal employees have been people I hired after they left their previous jobs in disgust. For an employer competing for smart, honest, hard-working people, treating people well turns out to be a competitive advantage.

The other problem with this idea is that it doesn't fit with capitalism. One of the distinguishing features of capitalism is that it produces large enterprises which invest funds in the means of production, and hire people to do the work. Jacksonian democracy would have seen this as inevitably undermining the virtues of the republic and its citizens.

One answer to that was to get the workers representation through organizing unions. And, when unions were strong, they produced a society with greater equality of incomes than America had before or since then.

Part of the reason this could happen was a moral climate that opposed an economic aristocracy. In a reaction to the inequality and abuse of workers seen in the Gilded Age, top tax rates were raised so that a tiny number of very rich people were subject to a 90% tax rate, and inheritance taxes aimed to make it harder for families to accumulate great wealth and power. It didn't take William Clark buying a seat in the U.S. Senate to convince people that wealth equaled power, there were plenty of other examples.

But since 1970, there has been a political movement to increase inequality.

Chapter 17: The political movement to increase inequality

6. Productivity and real hourly compensation, manufacturing sector, first quarter 1949-

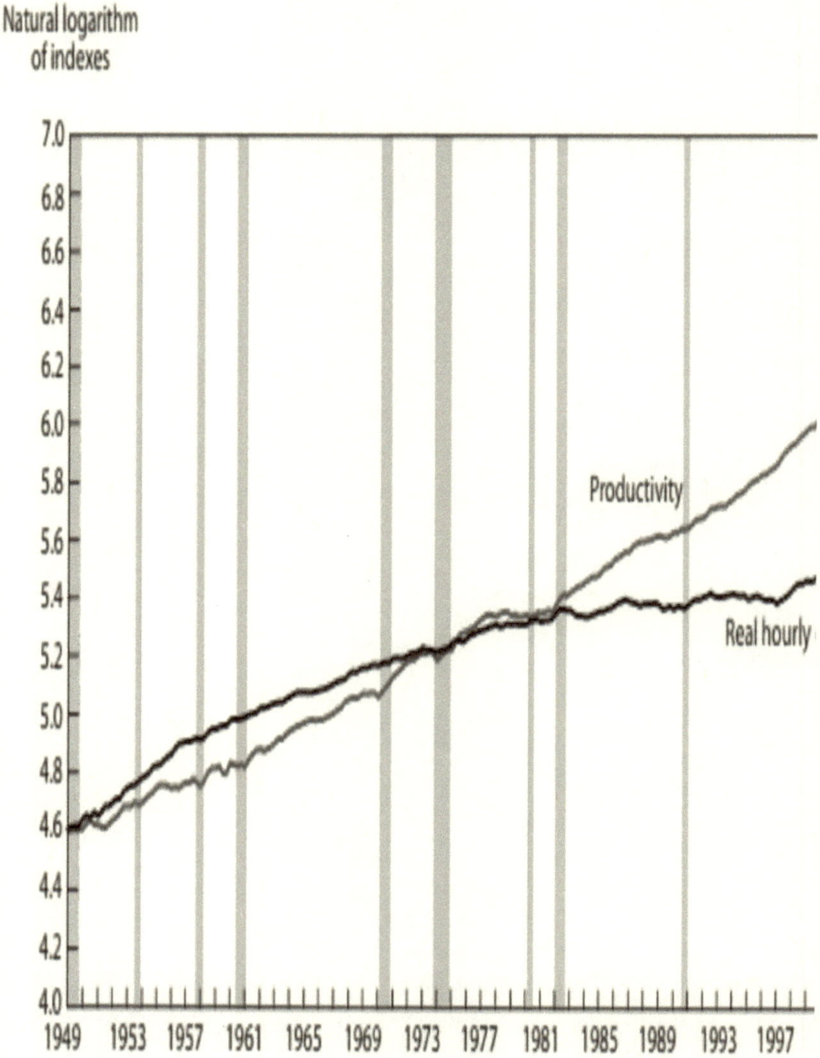

NOTE: The shaded bars denote National Bureau of Economic Research (NBER)-designated recessions.

From "The Compensation-Productivity Gap: A Visual Essay," by Susan Fleck, John Glaser, and Shawn Sprague, Bureau of Labor Statistics

By now, I suppose we've all seen the graph that demonstrates the decoupling of productivity and median income growth. It looks even worse expressed as hourly wage growth. Productivity has increased 254% since 1945 and inflation-adjusted hourly wages have increased 113% since 1945 – but almost all of that increase came before 1980, according to the Bureau of Labor Statistics.

Essentially, hourly wages have not gown since about 1980, while productivity has roughly doubled.

Communism promised 'from each according to their ability, to each, according to their needs.' Capitalism, in practice, operates on the axiom, 'from each according to their ability, to each according to their pricing power.' The way to change the distribution of wealth in a society is to change the pricing power of actors in that society. Starting in the 1970s, a political movement sought to move pricing power from people who worked for wages to people who made their living by owning things.

One of the levers used to move society in the desired direction was property rights. After all, our constitution was founded by people who admired the thought of John Locke, and one of the natural rights Locke argued we all possess is the right to our property. Property, in Locke's view, was produced when people applied their labor to nature.

Now, it seems obvious that a philosophy that says property should be a natural right should favor the owners of property over those who aspire to own property, but that's not what Locke said. All of our rights have limits, because we cannot exercise any of our rights without the compromise inherent in the social contract. The basic limit set by the social contract is that our rights cannot interfere with the rights of others.

There is a saying in law, that "your liberty to swing your fist ends just where my nose begins," often attributed to Oliver Wendell Holmes Jr., although it seems to have originated in the temperance movement. Locke made it clear that this applied to property just as it applied to other natural rights.

In Chapter V of the Second Treatise of Government, Locke argued as follows:

...Nor was this appropriation of any parcel of land, by improving it, any prejudice to any

other man, since there was still enough and as good left, and more than the yet
unprovided could use. So that, in effect, there was never the less left for others because
of his enclosure for himself. For he that leaves as much as another can make use of, does
as good as take nothing at all. Nobody could think himself injured by the drinking of
another man, though he took a good draught, who had a whole river of the same water
left him to quench his thirst. And the case of land and water, where there is enough of
both, is perfectly the same.

So, it's fine, you can acquire all the property you want, whether land, buildings, machinery or patents, provided it does not interfere with other people's ability to acquire property. I wonder if such a condition has ever existed. When the ability to keep others from acquiring property or even making a living becomes too egregious, we have acted in the past to prevent such injustices. The Sherman Anti-Trust Act was the best example of this, although few people realize that the theoretical basis for this as a moral policy goes back to Locke. Politics is the process by which our personal moral judgments are adjudicated and transformed into the rules we all must live by. Politics was the basis for trust-busting, and politics had to be the mechanism by which the movement to increase inequality triumphed.

Several things had to happen to make things turn out this way. I think the best way to understand it is as a political movement in which the well-off waged a war of words, money, and organization to wrest control of public discourse and political power from working people. The foot soldiers were cultural conservatives who provided the votes, the generals were economic elites who dictated the economic agenda.

The culture war was an important part of the economic war on working people. The same urge to define society by religious, cultural, and racial ethnicity that is creating so much trouble internationally has also fueled conflict within our society. Those who felt there was danger of white, Anglo-Saxon protestants losing their dominant role in society were vulnerable to a sort of bait-and-switch scheme in which they gave their votes to people who made war on their economic interests while paying lip service to their cultural agenda. This proved to be a powerful and durable coalition that is only now showing signs of strain.

One of the first shots in this war was the Powell Memo, a document the United States Chamber of Commerce solicited in 1971 from Lewis Powell, a corporate lawyer for the tobacco industry who would eventually be appointed to the Supreme Court.[*]

Powell responded with a memo that told businesses that they were losing to the left, and needed to build institutions that would push for their interests. Looking at the charts of the increase in wages and productivity, it would appear that they were not losing – wages were growing no faster than productivity, allowing business to make a decent profit. But this was a time when the New Left had not yet fallen by the wayside.

Powell told his readers that they were under attack, and were unable to exercise power in the political arena.
Lewis Powell wrote:

> "...as every business executive knows, few elements of American society today have as little influence in government as the American businessman, the corporation, or even the millions of corporate stockholders. If one doubts this, let him undertake the role of "lobbyist" for the business point of view before Congressional committees. The same situation obtains in the legislative halls of most states and major cities. One does not exaggerate to say that, in terms of political influence with respect to the course of legislation and government action, the American business executive is truly the 'forgotten man.'

> "Current examples of the impotency of business, and of the near-contempt with which businessmen's views are held, are the stampedes by politicians to support almost any legislation related to 'consumerism' or to the 'environment.'"

Powell wrote that they could gain power through the courts, through persuasion of the public with television and radio, through rewarding a "faculty of scholars" to publish work in support of their views, and through direct political lobbying:

> Business must learn the lesson, long ago learned by labor and other self-interest groups. This is the lesson that political power is necessary; that such power must be assidously (sic) cultivated; and that when necessary, it must be used aggressively and with determination — without embarrassment and without the reluctance which has been so characteristic of American business.

> He also suggested that shareholder could use their power to sway politicians:

> "The question which merits the most thorough examination is how can the weight and influence of stockholders — 20 million voters — be mobilized to support (i) an educational program and (ii) a political action program.

> "Individual corporations are now required to make numerous reports to shareholders.

Many corporations also have expensive "news" magazines which go to employees and stockholders. These opportunities to communicate can be used far more effectively as educational media."

A large part of what he proposed was propaganda. Whether because of his memo or because they were going to anyway, business interests have founded think tanks like The Heritage Foundation and helped publicize the work of people like Arthur Laffer, built funding mechanisms for political campaigns and supported model legislation by ALEC (the American Legislative Exchange Council) for state legislators to introduce in support of business aims.

But the business aims supported here are not those of the people working in non-supervisory jobs at businesses. In fact, those are defined as the enemy pretty much explicitly in Powell's memo. That's Labor, union bosses and strikers, malcontents all.

In fact, the aims supported by this political movement are those of top-level management and owners of large blocks of stock. They are the aims of the people Christopher Lasch was referring to in his 1996 book, *The Revolt of the Elites and the Betrayal of Democracy.*
From that book:

> Today it is the elites, however - those who control the international flow of money and information, preside over philanthropic foundations and institutions of higher learning, manage the instruments of cultural production and thus set the terms of public debate – that have lost faith in the values, or what remains of them, of the West.

As Daron Acemoglu and James A. Robinson demonstrated in their book, *Why Nations Fail,* an arrogant and grasping elite can destroy the economy of a nation in order to retain their positional status. They argued that the success of a nation depends to a great degree on the inclusiveness of its economic and political institutions. Once you shut down entry into the elite, the rot sets in.

Not that this is the only thing a nation needs to succeed. They note the disparity in wealth between the Arizona side of the border and the Mexican side, and suggest one of the problems has been the weak and corrupt Mexican state, which has never been an effective guarantor of life and property.

Which makes the nature of the alliances formed by the elite Powell was addressing in order to have the votes to control the country all the more alarming.

The Republican Party had long been allied with business elites, but faced with the New Deal alliance of the Democrats, they were a minority party. One of the pivotal figures of 20th century politics, Richard Nixon, attacked the problem by rebuilding the Republican coalition after his own image -- resentful, conservative, obsessed with enemies, and a bit racist.

The Democrats had been strong in the South, essentially from the passage of the Posse Commitatus Act in 1878, which allowed whites to elect the government even where there were black majorities, until the Democrats re-started the work of Reconstruction with the passage of the 1964 Civil Rights Act and the 1965 Voting Rights Act.

The Posse Commitatus Act ended the role of federal troops in the South in enforcing the voting rights and civil rights of the black citizens of the former Confederate states. It freed state and local authorities to deprive blacks of their voting rights and civil rights. Congressional seats are distributed by population,and electoral college votes are allocated one per congressman and one per senator for each state. Because senate, congressional, and electoral votes are not distributed by number of voters, this gave racists a disproportionate influence in our politics. Their power was given based on their population, and under Jim Crow laws, only the white population was voting.

In 1964, Barry Goldwater was the Republican nominee for president, and he opposed the Civil Rights Act. Nixon seized on Southern resentment to rebuild the party around disgruntled white voters.

George Packer wrote a brilliant account of this in *The New Yorker*, an article titled somewhat prematurely *The Fall of Conservatism*. From that article:

> The Southerners were the kind of men whom Nixon whipped into a frenzy one night in the fall of 1966, at the Wade Hampton Hotel, in Columbia, South Carolina. Nixon, who was then a partner in a New York law firm, had traveled there with Buchanan on behalf of Republican congressional candidates. Buchanan recalls that the room was full of sweat, cigar smoke, and rage; the rhetoric, which was about patriotism and law and order, "burned the paint off the walls." As they left the hotel, Nixon said, "This is the future of this Party, right here in the South."

Law and order? The South was the home of one of the most notorious extra-legal customs in America, the lynching, and home to one of the most notorious organizations to engage in extra-legal activities, the Ku Klux Klan. The Klan existed to terrorize blacks and whites who sympathized with them.

Ronald Reagan gave a speech on the topic of states rights during his 1980 run for the presidency at the Neshoba County Fair, a few miles from Philadelphia, Mississippi, site of the 1964 murder of civil rights workers. I'm sure the symbolism wasn't wasted on his audience. States' rights during the run-up to the Civil War had meant the right to hold slaves, states' rights after the war ended meant the right to discriminate without federal interference.

Moderate Republicans of the sort who voted for the Civil Rights Act in 1964 are now called RINO – Republican In Name Only. They've largely been ridden out of the party at this point, much to the disappointment of voters like me who have historically voted a split ticket.

Tapping into the South's deep well of resentment to support an agenda really set by the economic elite was deeply cynical. When Southern churches began setting up "white academies" – private schools intended to preserve segregation – they ran afoul of the IRS, which was in charge of enforcing laws that said a non-profit could not discriminate. The IRS started examining whether tax-exempt schools were discriminating during the Nixon administration, and a Supreme Court decision during the Ford administration (Jan. 19, 1976) the IRS terminated the tax-exempt status of Bob Jones University, an evangelical stronghold that had a history of discrimination. The school dropped its rule against interracial dating in 2000, and has since regained its tax-exempt status, but at the time, Evangelical leaders such as Jerry Falwell were furious.

The late Paul Weyrich, a religious conservative, political activist, and co-founder of the conservative Heritage Foundation, realized that segregation was not a great issue for conservatives to campaign on. He'd tried to interest conservative Christians in abortion as an issue after the 1973 Roe vs. Wade decision, but had met with little enthusiasm. Following the IRS decisions on the tax status of segregated private schools, he was able to interest more of them in the issue, and it made natural allies of conservative Catholics.[*]

They found a welcoming ally in business interests that wanted to do down the Internal Revenue Service. The result was a lot of rhetoric in support of the cultural agenda of the churches, and a lot of tax cuts and relaxed regulation on their business allies.

The churches got some of what they wanted. But for the most part, the votes were coming from segments of the population that harbored racial resentment against the policies of the Democrats, and the benefits were going to the business elites. What was said to get the votes was just the prolefeed, a term George Orwell invented in his novel, *1984*, in which the Ministry of Truth manufactures a sort of literature that is designed to keep the proletariat content and not too knowledgeable.

The propaganda arm of the movement harnessed agnotology, the science of creating ignorance, which had been pioneered by the tobacco industry. If scientists say you are harming people, pay some other scientists to say you aren't. The truth doesn't matter, just the bottom line.

And if your pundit is continually wrong, as Arthur Laffer has been, that doesn't matter. Just keep quoting him as if he were a reliable source of information.

Not that all were obviously wrong. One of the great controversies of the 1970s was about the viability of Keynesian economics in general and the Phillips curve in particular. The Phillips curve describes how higher inflation tends to be related to lower unemployment, but was challenged in the 1970s by a period of high inflation and high unemployment, called stagflation.

Milton Friedman, the great monetarist, claimed that the unemployment rate could not fall below a certain level without sparking a wage-price spiral, which he called the "natural rate" of unemployment. The Modigliani–Papademos paper of 1975 introduced it as the non-inflationary rate of unemployment.

There are other contributing factors, but it's probably not entirely coincidental that real hourly wages for non-supervisory jobs have not increased since the Federal Reserve Board started using the non-accelerating inflation rate of unemployment (NAIRU) as a tool in setting monetary policy.

The movement Powell was associated with paid attention to many things most people don't, like who gets appointed to the Federal Reserve Board. They backed, with cash, candidates who drank the Kool-Aid about low taxes on rich people stimulating the economy and generating more tax revenues, and the idea that regulations could be eliminated with no harm and a stimulating effect on the economy.

Robert Bork wrote a book published in 1978 titled *The Antitrust Paradox*, in which is said, sometimes you get lower prices with one large company than with several competing companies, so why penalize predatory pricing? With the election of Ronald Reagan in 1980, this became the official policy of the Justice Department, and still is. Walmart used tactics that were illegal up until then to become the largest employer in America.

(In 1967, the Safeway grocery store chain, then the second largest in the country, signed a consent decree with the Justice Department in which they agreed to stop engaging in predatory pricing – selling below cost in order to drive the competition out of business. A generation later, in 1983, Safeway correctly perceived that the Reagan Justice Department would take a different view of their activities, and asked to be released from the consent decree, and was freed of its restrictions.)

One result of this is that predatory pricing, which is hard on small business and only possible for large businesses, has, as one might expect, resulted in many small businesses closing. Another is that Walmart exercises enormous power over wages of their workforce and of prices for their suppliers. This redistributes power in ways that destroys workers' and suppliers' negotiating power.

Another theory that got a lot of support at about that time was managing corporations for shareholder value. Strangely enough, given our current beliefs, this is not how corporations were usually managed prior to the 1970s. Public corporations had been managed on the theory that they were persons, and their chief purpose was to survive and thrive. Shareholders did not have the rights of partnership property, they only had a claim on future earnings should the board decide to issue a dividend. One might compare this to 'owning' a fighter, in which you own part of the fighter's future winnings. You can't actually take the fighter apart and eat the bit you own if you get peckish.

Under this system of managing corporations, shareholders had an important stake in the company, as did bondholder, customers, and employees. The public corporation was a sort of gestalt being, made up of many other beings occupying its metaphorical body.

When Milton Friedman and others began promoting the idea that the shareholders were owners more in the sense that partners are owners, they found ready support for this view among people who could make money on it. Changes in the banking industry made it possible for corporate raiders to raise money to buy up companies. What they did then was described in a paper by Larry Summers and Andrei Schleiferwere titled *Breach of Trust in Hostile Takeovers*.

From that paper:

> One striking fact militating in favor of the importance of wealth transfers as

Now, consider the reason companies exist. Ronald Coase explored this question in a highly influential 1937 paper, *The Nature of the Firm*. Coase noted that you could hire individuals to do everything you need done, no matter how big the job, so why have companies in which the employer has obligations to long-term employees instead?

The answer, he said, is that contracting individually for each person needed to perform the tasks of the firm would require exorbitant transaction costs to negotiate and enforce the contracts. Much better to gather a group of people to work for a common goal, such as making better and cheaper widgets to make a profit in the widget business. This effectively replaced individual contracts with implicit contracts binding the employee and the firm together.

Summers and Schleiferwere argued that what Icahn and others were doing was appropriating money by violating those implicit contracts.

This is not one of their examples, but consider the case of the Boeing aircraft corporation. In the late 1960s, management bet the company on the first jumbo jet, the 747. Engineers worked so enthusiastically that they came to be called 'the incredibles.' Management would tell people to go home, only to have them drive around the block and come back to work when management wasn't looking.

Their devotion paid off. The company dominated the commercial airliner market to the point where Lockheed withdrew from the market and Boeing took over McDonnell Douglas and canceled all but one their airliners (the one they didn't cancel was sold as the Boeing 717.)

However, McDonnell Douglas executives proved more adept at corporate infighting, and gained considerable influence over the company, resulting in some big changes.

In July 2014, Boeing CEO Jim McNerney created a controversy by saying he wouldn't retire at 65 because, "The heart will still be beating, the employees will still be cowering, I'll be working hard."

This is a major change in attitude. Boeing was not subject to a hostile takeover, it is simply that public corporations are run differently than they were in the past.

Summers and Schleiferwere noted that employees in companies that had been subject to a takeover found that the company had no loyalty to its employees. They cite a number of employee reactions, but the one that put the issue most clearly to me was, "How can you go to another company now and give 100 percent of your effort?"

Leeham Co. LLC, which describes its business as "intelligence for the aviation industry," examined the Boeing situation on their blog in a Nov. 2013 post titled *Loyalty is a One-Way Street at Boeing:*

> ... when the unions see record profits, billions of dollars going into stock buybacks that benefit the McDonnell family and Harry Stonecipher among other shareholders–which for a long time starved research and development of funding in favor of derivative models rather than new designs–union members are less willing to give back benefits previously hard won. Executive pensions have reached the obscene level ($265,000 a month for Jim McNerney) while McNerney advocates taking traditional pensions away from Boeing employees and changing Social Security for the nation's citizens.

> Still, it was the members of IAM 751 and SPEEA that toiled to work through the 787 and 747-8 program debacles. It was the 751 members who cranked up production on the 737 and 777 lines to keep the cash flow coming to support the billions of dollars in cost overruns of the 787 and 747 programs.

> Members of both unions feel disrespected and unappreciated by Boeing.

The problem is, if a company is not "managed for shareholder value," it becomes a target for takeover. As a consequence, companies that invest their profits in the business instead of starving research to pay stockholders are the companies that become a target for takeovers unless they are taken private.

Would Boeing in its current position benefit from the fierce loyalty and enthusiasm of "the incredibles" on a project launched today? It seems unlikely the employees still feel that way.

The new, more extractive model used by Boeing under McNerney is the rule rather than the exception today. Once the banking business changed in ways that encouraged takeovers, the very nature of the publicly traded corporation changed. And when money is changing things, it can call out the justifications for what it is doing. In an earlier time, when the question was whether such corporations existed to serve the shareholders or if the shareholders were just one of the stakeholders in the company, the latter view had won out.

In fact, people in the business world today overwhelmingly believe that corporations have a fiduciary duty to maximize shareholder value, even though the case law doesn't support this, and the case most often cited in support of this is an odd one.

The case usually cited is Dodge Brother vs. Ford. In 1916, Henry Ford owned 58% of the company, the Dodge brothers owned 10%, and five other individuals owned the rest. Prior to WW I the Dodge Brothers were both a major investor in the company and a major supplier of engines, transmissions, and chassis. Ford was planning to build a factory that would make him no longer dependent on the Dodge Brothers for his manufacturing, and trying to drive down the price of the stock so he could buy the brothers out.

As chairman, president, and the majority stockholder, he was in a great position to do this. He decided to withhold a dividend that the brothers would need to complete their own plant in which they planned to start building their own line of cars.

Now, if Gordon Gekko's golden rule – "he who has the gold makes the rules" – were applied, Ford as majority stockholder should have been able to decide what dividend, if any, the company paid out. This was not a publicly traded company, it was a closely held corporation which Ford owned most of. The Michigan Supreme Court, which is not usually considered an authority on corporate law, ruled that Ford had an obligation to pay out a substantial dividend.

Lynn Stout, a Columbia law professor and author of *The Shareholder Value Myth*, argues rather credibly that Dodge vs. Ford is about a majority shareholder's obligation to minority shareholders, not about the obligations of publicly traded corporations. She also raises the question of why this case is cited rather than later cases from more expert courts (such as Delaware's Supreme Court, which rules in the state most large corporations choose to incorporate in.)

The answer, I'm afraid, is that intellectuals can serve more than one purpose. They can seek truth, or they can manufacture justifications for actions influential players want to take. Even when they do not view themselves as doing the latter, they may take a view that is picked up by those players and used as a justification.

In some cases, it is hard to assume altruism on the part of the intellectual involved. Arthur Laffer may once have believed that cutting taxes on the richest people would spur the economy and generate higher tax revenues, but it strains belief to think that he continues to hold this opinion for purely altruistic reasons. Saying exactly what the rich wanted to hear was the making of him. Admitting he was mistaken would be the unmaking of him.

Laffer first described the "Laffer curve" to Dick Cheney and Don Rumsfeld at a lunch meeting in 1974. The curve shows that at some point between 0% and 100% tax rates, there is a rate that maximizes revenue. This was first proposed by an Arab philosopher and historian, Ibn Khaldun (he lived 1332-1406 AD, and he is considered by some to be the father of modern economics, demography, sociology, and historiography.) Laffer's innovation appears to have been to propose that we are always at a higher point than optimum on the curve whenever he is asked, and we can therefore increase revenue by cutting taxes.

However, research since 1974 has shown that cutting top marginal rates does not increase gross domestic product above the rate that would have occurred without the cuts. And research on the rate at which tax revenues are maximized seem to show that it is about a 70% top marginal rate, which it was in 1974, before Laffer's theory was applied. (Economists Peter Diamond and Emmanuel Saez calculated in a 2011 paper that the revenue maximizing top marginal rate is 73%.)

Laffer wasn't bothered when the Reagan administration increased payroll taxes, because he was more concerned with top marginal rates. By the end of Reagan's term in office, it was evident that Laffer was wrong, but he still reliably said what his audience wanted to hear, and he has been rewarded with several directorships at large corporations.

Lowering the top rate from 70% to 28% didn't quite stick, but the top marginal rate of 35% on ordinary income and 28% on capital gains is still far below where it was when the U.S. economy was growing more rapidly, and the 28% rate applies to the way rich people tend to make money. Lower taxes on high earners and higher payroll taxes represented a large shift in wealth to the high earners.

One consequence of lower tax revenues was a reduction in investment in things that benefit us all, such as roads and bridges. Federal infrastructure investment has fallen from a peak of about 1.2 percent of GDP in 1950 to about .2 percent, or about 1/6th.

The result is a loss of productivity and international competitiveness. A truck waiting for a train to pass rather than driving on an overpass is a job lost for someone. Corporations have no national loyalty, and move their income around to the countries that allow them to minimize taxes. If America becomes less competitive, that's fine, they can always invest in some other country. The stateless income of international corporations does not support the well being, let alone the greatness, of countries.

These companies lobby for lower taxes, lobby for the freedom to flee to tax havens, and donate money to politicians. Public investment only interests them if it benefits them and they don't have to pay for it. The case of Citizens United v. Federal Election Commission, decided by the U.S. Supreme Court in 2010, ruled that prohibiting expenditures by corporations or unions violated the First Amendment guarantee of free speech, which means that although a corporation is not a voting citizen, it is sufficiently a person to finance a campaign for or against a candidate.

In his last book, *The Revolt of the Elites and the Betrayal of Democracy*, Christopher Lasch in 1995 argued that the privileged class had managed to isolate themselves from the crumbling social structure and decaying cities around them. In becoming international in their outlook, "citizens of the world," they have given up on the responsibilities of citizenship in their own countries and communities, and pursue only the interest of their class.

Lasch had no clear solution to this problem, nor do I. We seem to have developed an Ayn Rand elite, narcissistic and self-serving, who have the wealth and the connections to run things. They do not seem restrained by empathy for the less fortunate or a sense of duty to their nation or community. As inequality increases, there are reasons to think that the wealthy become less empathetic.

Studies of the effects of wealth on compassion and fairness have shown, as a report in Scientific American put it, that "as people climb the social ladder, their compassionate feelings towards other people decline."

And given the psychological effects of wealth, it is not surprising that the justifications for these attitudes are often couched in terms of freedom. Berkeley psychologists Paul Piff and Dacher Keltner suggest that, "The less we have to rely on others, the less we may care about their feelings. This leads us towards being more self-focused."

We are living in a world built by a political movement driven by these people -- people alienated from community and nation, and from any but their own class of wealthy cohorts. They are able to remain in power because of the alliance they formed with others, who are alienated from nation and community by prejudice and resentment. Both sides of this alliance wrap themselves in the flag while displaying contempt for the very notion of the national government.

It seems odd to me that we keep hearing about national greatness from people who support policies that make America poorer and weaker.

The political movement to create inequality has a lot to answer for. It has prevented the majority of Americans from participating in the increases in wealth driven by their own increasing productivity. It has created economic elites who seem to care more for their class than their country. And it has created an environment where we can't seem to have a good economy without risking asset bubbles.

Dr. Englebert Stockhammer of Kingston University in London, in the inimitable style of an academic, puts it this way in a 2012 paper titled *Rising Inequality as a Cause of the Current Crisis:*

> First, rising inequality creates a downward pressure on aggregate demand, since it is poorer income groups that have high marginal propensities to consume. Second, international financial deregulation has allowed countries to run larger current account deficits and for longer time periods. Thus, in reaction to potentially stagnant demand, two growth models have emerged; a debt led model and an export led model. Third, (in the debt led growth models) higher inequality has led to higher household debt, as working class families have tried to keep up with social consumption norms despite stagnating or falling real wages. Fourth, rising inequality has increased the propensity to speculate as richer households tend hold riskier financial assets than other groups. The rise of hedge funds and of subprime derivatives in particular has been linked to the rise of the superrich.

Essentially, this means that people trying to continue as members of the middle class are having to borrow more, and the very rich have plenty of money to throw at risky investments.

In fact, it looks like we have too many investment dollars looking for places to invest in the private sector and make money, and too little money in the hands of consumers to create the needed investment opportunities.

China, which has even worse inequality than the United States, is trying to transition from an export-led economy to a consumption-led economy. It is difficult to see how they can make that transition until they are able to put more money in the hands of consumers rather than investors. With no social insurance worth the name, Chinese workers are well advised to save their income for their old age rather than spend it, and with most of the money going to a small percentage of the people, even the most spendthrift among the wealthy can't consume enough to provide a healthy basis for the transition.

In the U.S., unlike China, public investment has been starved as well, leaving us with aging bridges, roads, and water systems, while private investment produces a series of asset bubbles.

We have long been told that letting the rich keep more of their money would cause them to invest it, making us all richer. Now we see why that is not true. According to a 2013 report by the American Society of Civil Engineers, "...the average age of the nation's 607,380 bridges is currently 42 years."

Their report further states:

> The Federal Highway Administration (FHWA) estimates that to eliminate the nation's bridge deficient backlog by 2028, we would need to invest $20.5 billion annually, while only $12.8 billion is being spent currently. The challenge for federal, state, and local governments is to increase bridge investments by $8 billion annually to address the identified $76 billion in needs for deficient bridges across the United States.

Instead, we're keeping taxes low so that investors can keep money they use to chase whatever the most recent fad is and bid up the price of that asset.

This is not a formula for national greatness. Worse, it appears the trend reinforces the inequality that causes it.

Justin Fox, at the time the economics columnist for Time magazine, wrote in an April 15, 2009 column:

> The rise in income inequality over the past 30 years has to a significant extent been the product of a series of asset-price bubbles. Whenever the market (be it the market in stocks, junk bonds, real estate, whatever) booms, the share of income going to those at the very top increases. When the boom goes bust, that share drops somewhat, but then it comes roaring back even higher with the next asset bubble. It's not the same people raking it in every time—there's lots of turnover in the top 400—but skimming the top off of asset bubbles appears to have become the leading way to get rich in these United States in the past three decades.

Fox is, as of this writing, the editorial director of the Harvard Business Review Group.

The consequences of inequality are an unhealthy private investment market, infrastructure starved for investment, and a middle class that isn't participating in the economic gains made by the nation. Inequality produces more financial shocks that tend to slow growth. We are a less wealthy and less stable country because of it.

It also has political consequences. Having lots of money means that you can buy lots of influence. Political campaigns often live on the money they can raise from supporters, and what political action committees can spend on their behalf. Those in a position to spend large amounts of money on behalf of a candidate can often influence what policies that politician will pursue, and as a result, wealthy donors may get such money as they spend back when the tax code is up for revision.

As Lasch pointed out in *The Revolt of the Elites and the Betrayal of Democracy*, many of the rich are displaying signs of a decay of those republican values men with views as different as John Adams and Andrew Jackson felt were needed to allow the nation to flourish. Wealth has insulated them from the needs of the nation, and selfishness has caused them to show a lack of care for the needs of their fellow citizens.

Another problem with inequality is that it creates unrest. Hourly wage earners working full time in 2004 had a lower real income than wage earners working full time in 1973, and the situation hasn't improved since.[*] This is going to create resentment, and people striking out at those they hold responsible. Right now, the target seems to be women and minorities, at least for blue-collar white men. Pe

Real Average Hourly Earnings:
January 1964-October 2005

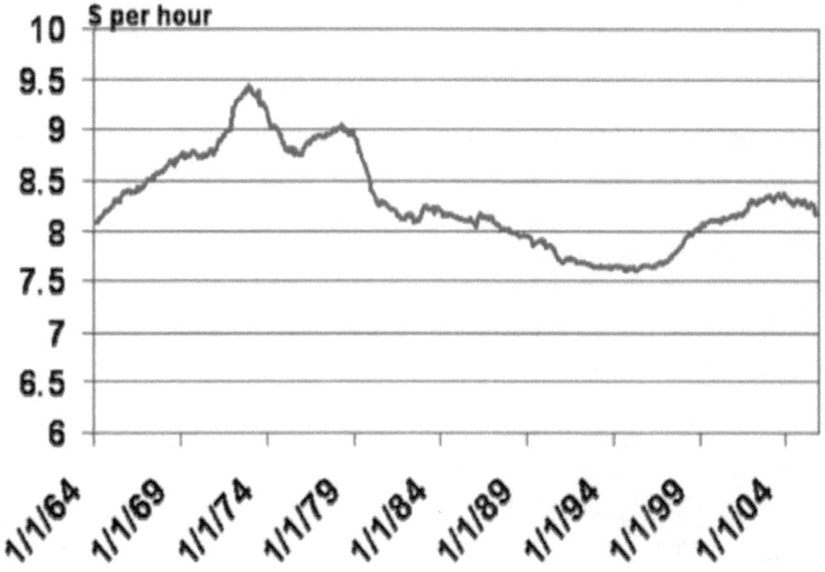

rhaps the next shift will be to add those who have actually been getting the money to the list of those resented.

Or perhaps they will be able to continue to shift the blame. In reality, shifting income share away from people working for wages has made the nation poorer, but the policies that have achieved this have been sold as having the opposite effect.

It is a curious thing, but the American economy, like those of other developed nations, does not appear to be managed to maximize national wealth.

Rather, it is managed to maximize profits, and to steer the distribution of wealth toward the already wealthy.

How does this work? For one thing, the most profitable situation for many companies is to have just enough slack in the labor market to suppress wages. The nation as a whole might be richer if wages were higher, leading to higher demand, but if more money goes to people working for wages, the people at the top benefit less.

From the 1940s through the 1960s, this was not in their control. That has changed, due to the political movement described above.

An example is the decision by the Federal Reserve Bank to increase the federal funds rate by 25 basis points in December 2015. The Fed is supposedly shooting for an inflation rate of 2%, and yet with the core Consumer Price Index running at 1/10 of that, .2%, they decided to raise interest rates, something the Fed usually does to tamp down inflation.

The reasoning was that with unemployment down to 5%, inflation lurked on the horizon. Wages were increasing at a rate of 2.3%, making up some ground lost during the recession.

And wages have a special place in the Fed's deliberations. Since Milton Friedman proposed it in the 1970s, the Fed has considered the non-accelerating inflation rate of unemployment as part of their deliberations. Since they accepted the idea, median wages have barely increased in real terms, while productivity has increased vastly.[*]

The NAIRU also accompanied a concerted effort to reduce employee leverage in wage negotiations by undercutting unions, for example, by passing "right to work" legislation state by state, which basically makes it impossible to have a union shop.

Now, there is a way to restore employee leverage over wages -- allow the unemployment rate to fall below NAIRU. After all, "non-accelerating inflation rate of unemployment" translated into plain English is "the rate of unemployment at which real wages do not rise."

The result of such a policy, in retrospect, is that the additional wealth produced by increased productivity does not go to the increasingly productive workers, but to people who do not work for hourly wages. That would be top management and shareholders. If wages had continued to track productivity, inflation adjusted wages would be about twice what they were in the early 1970s.

Imagine how much more wealth this country would have if this were the case. More money would be in the hands of people inclined to spend it, and the increased demand would cause industry to expand to fill it. Concentrating wealth in the hands of the top .1% leads to a lot of money looking for profitable investments that aren't there because of a lack of demand, resulting in bubbles. But that doubling of wages hasn't happened, because the economic elites have rigged the system to increase their positional status at the cost of making the country as a whole poorer.

What happens when unemployment falls below the NAIRU? What we saw in the late 1990s was that the labor participation rate increased, as people who had been out of the labor force discovered they could get jobs, and real wages started to rise.

Now, one would think that would be a shining example of what can be accomplished, and one to be followed.

But instead, we keep suppressing real wages, while demagogues work up anger among the white working class against immigrants and others they compete with for a piece of a pie that isn't growing. In fact, as a percentage of the economy, wages have been falling. In 1970, wages and salaries amounted to almost 54% of GDP. By 2010, they had fallen below 44%.

If the average wage were twice what it is now, I submit that riling up white working class voters against those they compete with would not be possible. Right now, people who work for wages see top managers getting richer while they don't, meaning their positional status is declining. The know that there's a lot more wealth in the country, and someone is to blame for not letting them have a piece of the action.

White male wages peaked in 1973. Women's wages have increased since then, so there is a loss of positional status here, as well, for white male workers. If the wages of both genders were growing, I doubt it would make much difference that women's wages are growing faster, but when you keep reducing the share of the economy paid for wages, there's plenty of room for resentment.

Not only are wages falling for white males, but labor participation is falling, so fewer are working for wages. While the male labor force participation rate has been falling since the mid 1950s, the female labor force participation rate was climbing until 2000. I strongly suspect we could create a lot more jobs without seeing much decline in the unemployment rate, because more people would come off the sidelines if they could.

A side note on this is that the way we raise revenues has an impact on things like our trade deficit. We did not typically run large trade deficits until the 1970s. Part of what changed is a long-term trend toward the U.S. getting more of its revenue from payroll taxes and less from corporate taxes. (Revenues from individual income taxes have remained fairly steady as a share of revenues, because much of the reduction in corporate revenue comes from the use of pass-through corporations to get revenue out of corporations without paying the corporate income tax, and have it taxed at the lower individual tax rate.)

This redistribution of the tax code means that the cost of hiring workers in the U.S. has increased, while taxes paid by people who own things for a living have decreased. And why would those owners hire people who are expensive to pay?

The result is a world where it is easy to set one group against the other, and this is a handy way to distract people from the issue of who is actually getting the money that isn't going to working men.

When you've rigged the system, it's nice to have someone else to blame.

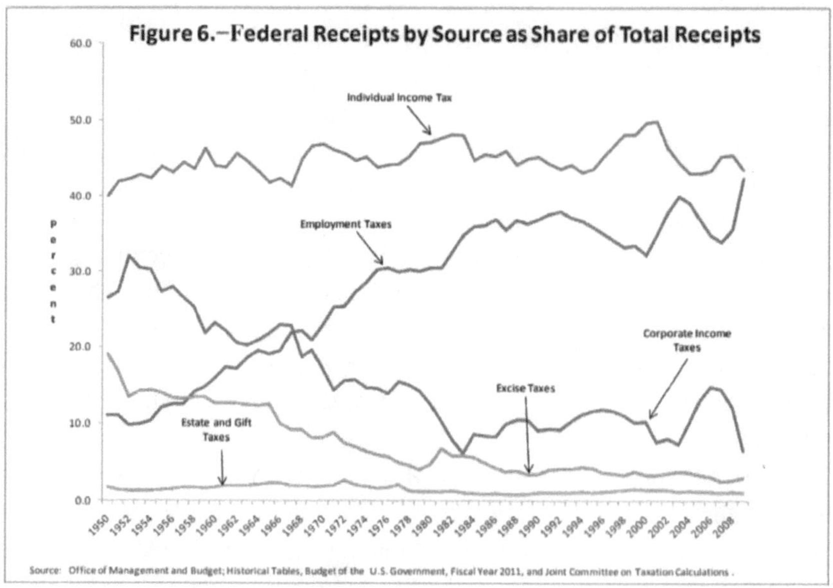

Suppose we tackled the problem directly, and tried some corrective action to reduce inequality, what would the policies look like?

A plan to reduce inequality

Everyone talks about inequity, but no one does anything about it. I propose to examine how we got where we are, and what we should do to reverse the situation. It seems to me that on both left and right, there is a longing for a time when the economy worked better for the average Joe, and I mean to find out how we lost it and how to get it back.

I am now well stricken in years. I remember the time conservatives long for, when a man could call his home his own, his wife would be waiting with a martini when he got home, everyone smoked cigarettes, even your doctor, and if you worked hard and remembered to be white and male, the world was your oyster or some similar mollusk. One feature of this world was that the middle class had a decent income. A one-income family could afford to own a house, run a couple of cars, and even send the kids to college.

Things have changed. Median income for male workers has been declining since 1973, while women are more likely to be working and are making better money (but still less than men.) For a while, two-income households managed to keep the median household income rising (until 2000.) Now, median household income has fallen to the level of about 1979

Most of the increases in income have gone to those at the higher end of the income scale, while the poor haven't gained much since the mid-1980s, and the median have gained some, then lost some. As society as a whole has become more prosperous, the gains have mostly gone to those at the higher end of the scale. How did that happen? Let's review:

Part of the story is taxes. During World War II, congress imposed a 94% top tax bracket. Few people paid it, but it was a way of saying, we're all making sacrifices, we're all in this together. Now, say what you will about Arthur Laffer, the Laffer Curve, which he did not invent (that honor belongs to an Arab thinker about 800 years ago) if you have high enough taxes, it does apply. Recent research indicates it applies to rates above 70%,[*] which means that Jack Kennedy took care of that problem in the 1964.

Attempts to apply the Laffer Curve after the problem was already solved did nothing but help increase the share of national income the richest people got to keep. It did not stimulate the economy so much that tax revenues actually increased, as Laffer promised. It just resulted in more debt.

During the Reagan Administration, we lowered the top marginal tax rate from 70% to, eventually, 28%. But some taxes were increased. When Reagan entered office, payroll taxes (Social Security and Medicare) were 9.9%. By the time George H. W. Bush left office, they were 12.4%.

Now, something that occasionally makes the rounds is the idea of a flat tax, as if calculating our tax rate were particularly difficult after we'd worked out all our deductions. Usually, the idea is to not tax incomes below a certain level, so that it's fairer for the poor. The payroll tax is a flat tax turned upside down: It applies to the first dollar you make, but any amount you make above the base wage ($128,400 for 2018) isn't taxed.

Since payroll taxes are part of the unified budget, this amounted to cutting the top tax rate while increasing the regressive inverted flat rate of the payroll tax. Meanwhile, the capital gains tax, which peaked above 40% during the Ford Administration, is now 15%, the lowest it has been since shortly after Herbert Hoover left office.

People who make a living by owning things, which used to be called the rentier class, tend to be the ones paying the capital gains tax rather than the payroll tax or ordinary income tax. The system can also be manipulated to turning what looks like ordinary income into "capital gains" for tax purposes. Greg Mankiw provides an example of that in what I suppose was intended to be a defense of capital gains taxation of, for example, hedge fund managers.

Here are some of Mankiw's examples:[*]

> • Carl is a real estate investor and a carpenter. He buys a dilapidated house for $800,000. After spending his weekends fixing it up, he sells it a couple of years later for $1 million. Once again, the profit is $200,000
>
> • Dan is a real estate investor and a carpenter, but he is short of capital. He approaches his friend, Ms. Moneybags, and they become partners. Together, they buy a dilapidated house for $800,000 and sell it later for $1 million. She puts up the money, and he spends his weekends fixing up the house. They divide the $200,000 profit equally.
>
> • Earl is a carpenter. Ms. Moneybags buys a dilapidated house for $800,000 and hires Earl to fix it up. After paying Earl $100,000 for his services, Ms. Moneybags sells the home for $1 million, for a profit of $100,000....Earl's $100,000 is ordinary income.
>
> ...(snip)...
>
> This brings us to Dan and his partnership with Ms. Moneybags. The tax law treats this partnership as exactly equivalent to Carl's situation. In this case, however, the $200,000 capital gain is divided into halves: some of it goes to Ms. Moneybags, who provided the cash, and some goes to Dan, who provided the sweat equity. Once again, nothing is treated as ordinary income.
>
> In some ways, this treatment makes sense. After all, Dan is doing half of what Carl did, so why should he have to pay a higher tax rate than Carl did on that half of his income? On the other hand, it seems that Dan is getting off easy. Dan does not seem very different from Earl, because both are getting $100,000 for fixing up the house.

Now, here's a question. If it's hard to say which tax applies, why are

we charging different rates? It appears we have decided to reward owning
over working, and reward tax dodges designed to make it look like we're
owning over admitting that we're working.

In fact, we're so sure owning is better than working, we have a top
marginal rate of 39.6% on "ordinary" earned income, the kind of income Earl
got, and a top long-term capital gains tax rate of 20%[*] on the kind of income
Dan, in the example above, got. We are so in love with the virtues of owning,
we reward it by charging a lower tax rate for it than for those misguided saps
who work for a living. In pricing various activities, our tax system says that
flipping houses is more socially desirable than building them, provided you
keep them for at least a year.

I can understand why we might want a lower rate for someone who
has spent 30 years building up equity in a home, but why someone who has
spent a year and a day? Perhaps we could divide the capital gain by the
number of years it's been held to determine the marginal rate to tax it at, since
other taxes on income have their marginal rate determined on an annual basis.

Another sort of income people get from owning is dividends. Most of
us don't see much of that, but for a small and quite wealthy group of
Americans, it is a substantial source of income. While the top marginal rate
for earned income is 39.5%, the top marginal rate for dividends is 23.8%.
Once again, our tax system sends the message that owning is more socially
useful than working, provided you've owned the stock that paid the dividend
for more than 60 days.[*]

Well, what makes owning better than working? The oft-repeated theory
is that if we encourage investment, the economy will be better and we'll all be
better off. Another version of the argument is that we should use
consumption taxes to encourage savings, because saving is better than
consuming. This is an odd argument, because encouraging saving is also
encouraging borrowing, and when you think about it, the whole point of
having an economy is consuming. In national income accounting, savings has
to equal investment – government borrowing and private borrowing have to
equal private savings and foreign capital inflows or outflows. This isn't
controversial, it's how the savings accounting identity is defined.

So when you complain about the financialization of the economy,
remember, all that investment income is savings, and when you have a giant
pool of money, it has to be loaned in order to make it grow. One reason that
the pool of money in the 2000s was so giant was that China was operating its

economy much the way America was in the 1920s. They were exporting mightily, and when you earn a lot of money this way, it usually means that lots of money comes into your country and that causes inflation, so that the low wages that made you a super-competitive exporter increase, and you lose your advantage. It also pushes the value of your currency up.

The people running China didn't want that to happen. So, they didn't keep the money in China. They "sterilized" their export income by buying securities in countries they wanted to export to. America and France did something similar in the 1920s, and it ultimately undermined international trade and contributed to the financial collapse that led to the Depression. The problem is, these actions produce a giant pool of money – excess savings – chasing good investments in the country targeted for sterilization. And that produces financial bubbles.

A model that says savings and investment are better than working and consuming will tend toward this sort of thing. And surely, the whole point of an economy is to produce things and consume them. So why have we valorized owning things over making and consuming them?

Well, one way of justifying this view is to say that if we encourage people to invest and realize capital gains instead of working for a living, we'll have a more prosperous society in the end, and a rising tide ~~sinks~~ raises all boats. A low capital gains tax will encourage this sort of prosperity, we're told.

Only there's no actual evidence this is so. Len Burman, a professor of economics at Syracuse University's Maxwell School, has run the numbers on all the natural experiments we've had in this regard as the capital gains tax has gone up and down. Here's what he found:

> If low capital gains tax rates catalyzed economic growth, you'd expect to see a negative relationship–high gains rates, low growth, and vice versa–but there is no apparent relationship between the two time series. The correlation is 0.12, the wrong sign and not statistically different from zero. I've tried lags up to five years and also looking at moving averages of the tax rates and growth. There is never a statistically significant relationship.
>
> Does this prove that capital gains taxes are unrelated to economic growth? Of course not. Many other things have changed at the same time as gains rates and many other factors affect economic growth. But the graph should dispel the silver bullet theory of capital gains taxes. Cutting capital gains taxes will not turbocharge the economy and raising them would not usher in a depression.[*]

At a minimum, Leonard Burman has shown that raising or lowering the capital gains tax doesn't seem all that influential. So why penalize earning money as wages relative to making money on investments?

Well, it may have something to do with power. People who make the bulk of their money as capital gains tend to be wealthier and better connected. And they tend, more than wage earners do, to be U.S. senators.

Less than 10% of Americans have a net worth of $1 million or more. In the U.S. Senate, 66 of 100, or two-thirds, are millionaires as of this writing. High net worth individuals, by definition, own a lot of stuff, so capital gains taxes are important to them. Both your senator and his or her biggest campaign donors and bundlers tend to care a lot about capital gains. So if you expect them to be treated no better than people working for a living, you're starting in hard luck. The people writing the laws are rich, the people writing the checks to the people writing the laws are rich, and most of the the rich get most of their income from capital gains.

We've had enough experience to know Burman is right, so the only possible explanation for the continued coddling of the rich is that the tax laws are written for and by them. The way to change that is to bring it front and center in our national conversation, so that they can stop lying about their reasons for treating their investments better than your wages.

If we're going to value work as much as owning, we need to do something about the upside-down flat tax on wages. We ought not to be charging any payroll taxes on people's earnings below the poverty line. We can make up for that by raising the base wage, and by taxing all income the same for social insurance purposes. If you are making less than $11,490 and you are a single person, why should you pay 12.4 percent tax, when the Koch brothers, when they sell off a $100 million block of stock, pay hardly any more tax on it, if their accountants haven't found a way to make sure they pay no tax at all?

Now, suppose they paid $90 million for that stock, and their profit is $10 million. Should they pay less tax on that $10 million than a basketball player with a $10 million salary? I can't see why they should. They didn't work any harder, and even if they didn't make a dime on that stock, they'd still have $90 million. We could broaden the base for Social Security and Medicare taxes by taxing interest and dividend income for SSI taxes, not including retirement accounts or such income for those above retirement age. And taxing these sources of income at the same rate as earned income would allow us to lower taxes on people who work for wages.

And why should there be no payroll tax on earned income above $128,400 a year, or whatever the basis wage is in a given year? Why not $500,000 a year? The higher the base wage, the lower the rate needs to be. We can make up for the payroll taxes lost by not taxing the poor by taxing the affluent a bit more. Reagan sold an increase in the tax rate on payrolls as needed to keep the Social Security Fund solvent, but raising the base wage would have worked as well. For that matter, when the Highway Trust Fund became insolvent, congress didn't increase taxes, they just topped it up from the general fund. Keep this in mind when you hear people hyperventilating about the Social Security trust fund.

In effect, Reagan raised taxes on working families and lowered taxes on the rich, with the revenues from tax increase on workers making the lost revenue of his tax cuts on the rich look less like an invitation to bankrupting the country.

This represented a major transfer of wealth from people who make less than the maximum basis wage to those who make a whole lot of money. And since then, we've lowered taxes on the way the rich tend to make money – capital gains – while keeping that higher payroll tax in place on people working for wages.

George W. Bush pushed for what he called an "ownership society," in which, for example, we'd all own investments in a retirement account instead of having a guaranteed benefit through Social Security. But as we've seen, one man's savings is another man's debt, unless, like Smaug, you choose to sleep on a bed of gold. And by taking his wealth out of circulation (and by flame-broiling anyone who tried to work the land) Smaug made the world poorer.

The alternative to owning investments and building up debt is the "pay as you go society." That's how Social Security is designed, so that it works as a compact between the generations. People of working age are taking care of old people, knowing that the next generation will take care of them.

While savings and debt certainly have a place, no one has yet explained to me why a pyramid of savings and debt is better than paying your way, which makes our treatment of investing as contributing more to wealth than working all the more puzzling.

Wealth tax:

Redistributing earnings from the middle class and the poor to high earners is one way of increasing inequity. We might redress some of this with a tax on wealth.

Henry George, a 19th century political economist, advocated a "single tax," a tax on land value (not including improvements such as buildings), which he argued would go some way to solving the problem of inequity.

George argued that the reason increasing poverty accompanied increasing wealth was that as population increased, land values increased, so that working men had to pay more for the privilege of working the land.

There are some problems with this idea. Study after study has shown that property tax valuations are essentially regressive. When properties sell, you can compare their valuation to their selling prices. High-value properties are consistently under valued by this standard, and low-value properties are typically over valued.

The only place something like this has been made to work was Hong Kong, where the colony leased the land from China and subleased it to businesses and homeowners. Leases went for market rates, and by all accounts, the system worked very well. Without those special circumstances, I doubt the single tax is really workable.

Other than property taxes, the wealth tax we have now is the estate tax, which has been under assault by certain politicians and their paymasters for years. In 2001, it applied to estates above $675,000 in value, and the top rate was 55%. As of this writing, it applies to estates of more than $5.25 million, and the top rate is 40%. This has had a predictable effect on the number of estates to which the estate tax applies.

The number of estates affected by the tax went down dramatically during the Reagan and George W. Bush (Bush the lesser) administrations, up during the George H.W. Bush and Clinton administrations. Reagan and Bush II both exploded the national debt, while Bush I and Clinton worked to reduce it.

We have, in effect, reduced taxes on high incomes, investment incomes, and large estates, while increasing taxes on low and ordinary incomes and on wages.

And we wonder why inequity increases.

A Plan

So, to start with, let's lower taxes on working and on low wages, by exempting wages below the poverty line from the payroll tax. We can make up for this by applying payroll taxes to higher incomes than we do now and, (I can dream) on investment income.

Let's stop privileging owning over working. Tax capital gains like earned income. Face it, creating giant pools of money leads to financial bubbles, and in a mature economy, to have investment opportunities, you need consumption. That means you need people working and paying as they go, not just saving and lending. We've got the balance wrong right now, and we need to move it back toward working and paying as you go.

When we're in recession or not fully recovered from one, we have too much unemployment because of a lack of aggregate demand in the economy. But there is such a thing as a "natural rate" of unemployment, defined as the rate at which lowering interest rates produces more inflation without producing more jobs. To a great extent, this means workers' skills don't match the remaining work that needs doing. We can reduce the natural rate of unemployment by increasing worker skills.

Unfortunately, we've been moving in the other direction, defunding schools and forcing people to go deeply into debt to acquire the skills they need to develop a career, while bureaucratic entrepreneurs increase the number of administrators while relying on adjunct (that is, temporary) faculty to do more and more of the teaching.

We need to provide funds for educating our workforce. Public universities can't push tuition up indefinitely and students can't take on unlimited debt. A skilled workforce works and pays taxes. We seem to have forgotten the public benefit of helping people get better skills.

There's been some speculation that we are entering a period of stagnation. Bullshit. If we didn't invest in our factories, we'd enter a period of stagnation. We've greatly slowed our investment in public goods, and that's producing stagnation. Dwight Eisenhower thought the greatest achievement of his presidency was the Interstate Highway System. He understood that to mobilize a great nation, you need to get the logistics right, and building the highways would make the country more productive.

But since the late 1960s, we've spent too little on public goods. Democrats cared more about programs like Social Security, Republicans cared more about defense spending and cutting taxes. The result? The age of our public capital stock, things like roads and bridges, went from an average of about 17 years old in 1969 to 23 years old in 2009, and as mentioned previously, the bridges are especially old.

President Obama had the right idea with his notion of an infrastructure bank, but the loyal opposition seems to think that only private investment increases productivity. Next time you're stuck in a traffic jam, think of all the hours being lost for the want of some transportation spending. Another problem is that we don't get as much per dollar for our infrastructure spending as other developed countries, so we should take a good hard look at the way they do this and learn what we can.

It's always easier to divvy up a growing pie, and we can grow the pie. In doing so, we can put the country back to work.

And if we're to get back to an economy where we work and pay our way, growth and greater equality will have to go hand in hand. As economist Walter Frick noted, "given the diminishing marginal utility of income, it's hugely wasteful for the super rich to have so much income."[*]

Chapter 18: Getting your "share"

ADP, the company that does my payroll, includes in its promotional material a common bromide – that automation "can cut costs dramatically and free up time for higher-value work."

And that has generally been the argument for productivity growth. It means more wealth, therefore it will make you wealthier.

Except, of course, that whether this is true depends very much on who you are, and what your prospects for participating in the new wealth are. Andrew Carnegie became one of the richest men in America by always making sure his steel mills had the best technology. Carnegie had seen the effects of falling behind first-person. His father was a weaver in Dunfermline, Scotland, who lost his profession when the handweavers were put out of business by the big weaving mills. The family had to borrow money to move to America, where Andrew's first job was as a "bobbin boy" at a textile mill in Pennsylvania at age 13.

He worked 12 hour days, six days a week, changing spools of thread for $1.20 a week. But he was a man of great ability. Fortunately, through a family connection, he was able to get a job as a telegraph messenger boy, and his energy, ability to learn, and hard work brought him to the attention of his superiors. He was more a self-made man than any other I can think of, but he never lost sight of the things that helped him. And he never forgot that his father had been a skilled man and a hard worker, yet had been ruined.

That's the trouble with disruptive technologies. Our society gives us time in our youth to learn a profession, and expects us to make our way based on those skills for the rest of our lives. But when skills become obsolete, it tosses people aside, with little chance to ride the new wave.

And as to the higher-value work, was the elder Carnegie doing work that called on his human abilities to a greater extent as a weaver in Scotland or as a textile mill worker in Pennsylvania? Was the work less routine, more challenging, requiring more of his judgment?

Perhaps for the term "higher-value work" we should substitute "harder to automate work." Higher-value is a term that makes us think of getting a promotion, of using our judgment more. Yet the jobs created when others are destroyed are not necessarily of that nature.

Janitorial work is hard to automate. So is sex work, the ultimate "high-touch" profession. We've seen a decline in workforce participation as productivity has soared. And it has soared. In 1820, GDP per person was $1,257, now it is close to $30,000.

The other problem is one unique to capitalism. The distinguishing characteristic of a capitalist system is that a major source of wealth is the investment of capital in the means of production, rather than, say, conquering more land or enslaving more people.

As a result, there is a tendency for wealth to concentrate in the hands of those who own a lot of capital. And with wealth, comes influence, and with influence, comes the temptation to rig the game in your favor.

Rising inequity creates unrest, seen in the late 19th and early 20th centuries in the form of the Grange movement, labor strife, and extremist movements.

Part of the problem here is that the distribution of wealth depends in part on politics. In the U.S., decisions at the federal level have moved the tax burden from those who make their money by owning things to those who make their money working for wages. Wages were already declining as a percentage of the GDP, from about the time corporate raiders started changing the way companies do business in the 1970s.

The new orientation justified making war on a company's own employees to produce higher profits to benefit shareholders, stripping assets to pay off the debt contracted in a takeover, and other tactics that would in an earlier age have been considered bad for the company. Private equity companies, such as Mitt Romney's old company, Bain Capital, raised money from investors to do similar work.

I have a book to recommend on this subject, one I've mentioned before, *The Shareholder Value Myth*, by Lynn Stout, Distinguished Professor of Corporate and Business Law at Cornell Law School. Professor Stout makes a compelling argument that the pursuit of "shareholder value" – a term with difficulties of its own – has been bad for investors, corporations, and the public.

The problem is that we've seen this movie before. It was a bit more direct when federal troops killed 30 strikers during the Pullman Strike of 1894, but the basic idea of making war on the workers for the benefit of owners is a time-honored one in American history.

Now, it's done through legal maneuvering, outsourcing, or moving work to right-to-work states (where a worker has a right to not belong to a union in a workplace where unions have won the right to represent the workers).

In an unequal society, as wealth goes from being widely distributed to being held mainly by a smaller and smaller group, the kind of work available changes. What is happening as companies have reoriented from serving a variety of stakeholders to serving mainly the shareholders has been a bit like the Inclosure Acts that drove many people off the land during the British industrial revolution.

The reader will recall, there used to be something called the Commons in many British communities, land on which anyone in the community could graze their livestock, and which was sometimes farmed by landless peasants. The Inclosure Acts privatized that land, giving what had been a source of income to a large number of people to the local lord, who now gained ownership of it. Property is not objects or land, after all, it is the system of rights affecting how people use them, and when those rights are changed, ownership changes.

The result was that people who had worked the land were now "free labor," that is, they had been freed from their previous source of income and were now free to alienate their labor in any way they wished, as the outlaw John Locke noted in his *Second Treatise of Government*.

The rhetoric of freedom is again being employed, along with a change in the nature of property rights, to redistribute property from those doing the work to the most fortunate and wealthy. As Stout noted in *The Shareholder Value Myth*, a shareholder has never been an owner in the sense that a partner is. A partner can direct that the company sell assets to buy out that partner's equity on the company, while a shareholder can only sell whatever shares of stock they own. This, in fact, is one of the major reasons for starting a public stock company. Such demands have ruined many a business started as a partnership, while public companies have been able to take the long view.

No more. As shareholders have acted more like owners, they have forced companies to take the short view, which is why more and more companies are being taken private. The number of public corporations declined 39% between 1997 and 2013. (Pass-through corporations, which are not publicly traded, have increased in number. They are used to pass earnings from a corporation to the owners without paying the corporate income tax.)

This trend has accompanied another, the trend toward cutting taxes on inherited wealth and capital gains. Payroll taxes, which are charged only on income below the income level of the 1%, were raised in the 1980s.

It seems to me that shareholder value ideology, supply-side economics, and a shift from Keynesian economic modeling have one thing in common. They abandoned empiricism (such as how well the Phillips Curve[*] was actually working) and a reliance on knowing history (such as the legal history of the purpose of corporations) in favor of plausible-sounding logic that appealed to moneyed interests.

And those interests are not always about the money. Sometimes, they are about positional status, and about making sure "the employees will still be cowering."

This interest fit very well with shareholder value ideology, and the war on companies' own workers. It also fit well with the snake oil of supply-side economics, which promised wealth for all if we'd just let the rich keep more of their money.

Keynesian economics did nothing for the positional status of the rich. It argued the government could create full employment, and while a full-employment economy may make everyone richer, it gives workers more leverage when it comes to negotiating wages -- they can stop cowering.

So the new classical economics promoted by Robert Lucas, Jr., and Thomas Sargent, which claimed that the government can't do much about employment, was bound to attract wealthy sponsors. For different reasons, it had a certain appeal to academic economists, as Simon Wren-Lewis notes on his blog, *Mainly Macro*:

> If mainstream academic macroeconomists were seduced by anything, it was a methodology – a way of doing the subject which appeared closer to what at least some of their microeconomic colleagues were doing at the time, and which was very different to the methodology of macroeconomics before the NCCR. The old methodology was eclectic and messy, juggling the competing claims of data and theory. The new methodology was rigorous!

In short, Wren-Lewis argues, it allowed economists to leave behind a history of the dismal science as a messy social science and act more "scientific" -- even though the new method did not provide better empirical results. My own interpretation is, once mathematical proofs substituted for empirical proofs, the logic of economics was freed from reality.

Shareholder value ideology had a similar appeal for the purity of its logic. The "managerialist" view of corporations said that just as you can buy a "share" in a prizefighter, but you can't own him, a shareholder was but one of the stakeholders in a corporation. Economists, in particular, preferred the purity of the owner-agent model to the messy business of the traditional legal status and purpose of corporations.

But I cannot imagine this having as much impact as it did, if it had not suited the purposes of the corporate raiders and private equity companies that were becoming prominent at the time. If you say things that give rich people justifications for what might otherwise be viewed as pretty dodgy behavior, you won't lack for people willing to promote your views.

Natural rights and the corporate person

What is a person, and who has natural rights, such as free speech?

In Citizens United vs. FEC, the Supreme Court ruled that corporations and labor unions cannot be prevented from spending money on "electioneering communication." They did so based on the idea that neither citizens nor associations of citizens may be prevented from the exercise of free speech.

The majority ruling was that the first amendment to the constitution protects free speech regardless of the identity of the speaker, and therefore rules could not make distinctions between, say, for-profit companies and other kinds of associations.

The dissent, written by Justice John Paul Stevens, argued that the form of the corporation has certain inherent dangers to the political system. He quoted the Austin vs. Michigan Chamber of Commerce case in which the court noted that corporations have "'special advantages – such as limited liability, perpetual life, and favorable treatment of the accumulation and distribution of assets,' 494 U. S., at 658–659 – that allow them to spend prodigious general treasury sums on campaign messages that have 'little or no correlation' with the beliefs held by actual persons..."

He argued that these legal entities were not the "people" for whom the constitution was written, and for whom such rights were preserved.

There is a great deal more to the argument on both sides, but I'm not a legal scholar, and what really interests me here is the question in political theory of whether a corporation is a person who must be allowed to exercise free speech.

First, while there is some dispute about John Locke's influence on the people who wrote the constitution, to my way of thinking, it was decisive. So it's worth looking at his version of natural law and inalienable rights.

Inalienable rights are those that cannot be sold, or alienated, and assigned to someone else. The computer I'm writing this on does not have inalienable rights. I can own it, sell it, and it will never raise an objection, because it has no use for rights. If someone were to claim to own me and sell me, and use me in ways I do not like, I could not help but have feelings about it. That's why my right to freedom of conscience and freedom of speech are inalienable, and why it is immoral to treat people like things that can be bought and sold.

From Locke's Second Treatise of Government:

> The state of nature has a law of nature to govern it, which obliges every one: and reason, which is that law, teaches all mankind, who will but consult it, that being all equal and independent, no one ought to harm another in his life, health, liberty, or possessions: for men being all the workmanship of one omnipotent, and infinitely wise maker; all the servants of one sovereign master, sent into the world by his order, and about his business; they are his property, whose workmanship they are, made to last during his, not one another's pleasure: and being furnished with like faculties, sharing all in one community of nature, there cannot be supposed any such subordination among us, that may authorize us to destroy one another, as if we were made for one another's uses, as the inferior ranks of creatures are for ours.

In Locke's view, all of nature was created by God, and the sort of people who had natural rights were natural people. Such people, he wrote, are born owning themselves, and the rights they possess as their own master are inalienable: They cannot be assigned to another.

The two sides in Citizens United argued very different things. The majority argued that corporations have freedom of speech as associations of people. The dissent argued that corporations do not have free speech rights *as* people.

Stevens' view is the easier to argue. Corporations are not their own masters. They must do as their board of directors decides, and have no opinion of how they are used. They can be bought, sold, merged or dissolved and the corporation itself has no feelings about any of these things, because it is a legal entity, not a natural person.

The majority view is harder to argue. Certainly there are legal entities that are allowed to be political actors. Political parties are the most obvious case. But does that mean that all associations *should* be political actors?

Political parties are voluntary associations for the purpose of political action. So are political action committees. You do not have to belong to them for any purpose other than to act politically, so the legitimacy of any political action they might take seems unambiguous.

But what about, say, ExxonMobil? First of all, its nature as a person is somewhat contested. Shareholders don't own it in the way that partners do, in that they cannot demand their share of the assets and force the company to sell assets to pay them. Sometimes they manage to get the company to sell assets in order to finance a dividend, but the process is nothing like what happens when a partner wants to sell out its share. Shareholders own a claim on the company's future earnings, but they do not directly own a share of its assets. They are stakeholders, as are bondholders, banks that have loaned the corporation money, employees, and customers.

None of these stakeholders have associated with ExxonMobil for the purpose of political action. Some of the shareholders are pension funds, some are mutual funds. To claim that the corporation's political speech represents a sort of speech the people who have associated in the corporation want to express requires a vast leap of faith.

One of the major political issues ExxonMobil is involved in is climate change, and there is turmoil among its shareholders on the issue. From PR Newswire, May 11, 2000:

> Jane Dale Owen, the granddaughter of a founder of Humble Oil (which became Exxon's largest domestic asset) contributed to the solicitation packet. "I believe that ExxonMobil's recalcitrant position on global warming, held in the face of widely accepted scientific facts and growing acceptance by the rest of the industrial sector, now casts serious doubt on the integrity of the company and its leadership," said Owen. "As a long-term shareholder, I would like for ExxonMobil to take account of these issues, both by reflecting the [global warming] liability risks in shareholder reports and accounting, and by taking immediate action to redirect the company to minimize these liabilities."

Yet the company continues to donate money to politicians who deny the danger of climate change. At a minimum, we can say with some certainty that ExxonMobil's political speech does not represent all of its shareholders. And many of the people whose money is invested by pension funds and mutual funds don't even know their money owns shares in a company that is a major political actor, let alone have any influence over how it spends its money. While the law considers shareholders only one of the stakeholders in a corporation, even if we only consider shareholders, the corporation is not competent to engage in political speech on their behalf.

For one thing, the corporation may not be revealing all it knows to the shareholders. Owen mentions that ExxonMobil has not included climate change liability assessments in reports. But the problem is bigger than that. In the late 1970s and early 1980s, Exxon's own scientists were telling it about the problem of climate change. From *Newsweek*:

> "Present thinking," wrote Exxon senior scientist James Black in 1978, "holds that man has a time window of five to ten years before the need for hard decisions regarding changes in energy strategies might become critical." And in 1982, Edward David, Exxon's head of research, echoed that sentiment, saying "few people doubt that the world has entered an energy transition away from dependence upon fossil fuels and toward some mix of renewable resources that will not pose problems of CO_2 accumulation."

In short, the company had pretty good data on climate change, but instead of using this in a way that might benefit those whose pensions were invested in the company by pioneering a move away from fossil fuels, it chose to invest in another direction; political action to prevent any move away from fossil fuels.

As a for-profit company, its incentives were clear. However, they conflicted with the political interests of many of the people who either directly or indirectly held the shares. They were not allowed to know that the company had researched climate change and discovered it was real long before the public became aware of that fact, until *Inside Climate News* did a series of reports[*] on the topic.

This is why we cannot take for-profit companies formed for non-political purposes as representing the collective political will of those who associated with them. In part, this might be described as an owner/agent problem. The interests of the managers of the company may be to gain a short-term advantage in their careers that conflicts with the interests of long-term shareholders, such as the generations of shareholders represented by Owen.

Now, it may be that a non-profit like Citizens United is sufficiently closely held that its representation of its associates' views is not a problem. We then must deal with the fact that an artificial "person" has been granted natural rights.

It seems to me that any corporation may publish a book with a political point of view, as long as there is a natural person to take responsibility for its content. Michael Moore, for example, directed a propaganda film aimed at George W. Bush. But Moore was there to take responsibility for his views. Citizens United was attempting to air a film about Hillary Clinton. I think as long as the prime mover of the film was clearly identified and that natural person was personally liable for the content of the film, that should be allowed. Citizens United planned to show the film on a pay-per-view basis, so it is not as if it insisted that its shareholders contribute out of their own pockets, the project seems to have been intended to pay for itself. But the ruling in the Citizens United case seems to have gone far beyond this, claiming that corporations could spend company money for political speech that was not clearly a commercial venture and was not necessarily representative of its shareholders' or other stakeholders' views.

I don't think we have to overturn corporate "personhood" or "money = speech" to fix the problems posed by Citizens United. I do think if a corporation engages in political speech, it should be clear that it does in fact represent the views of those associated in it, and/or it should be clear that a natural person takes responsibility for that speech. The corporate person itself should not be able to make political contributions larger than a natural person is allowed. After all, the persons associated in the corporate person are all capable of acting on their own behalf, why allow the corporation to out-shout them?

A corporate person is incapable of action without actions taken by natural persons. They make the speeches, write the checks, push the buttons, and write the algorithms. If we should shield these people too much from the actions they take while working for a corporations, the responsibilities of citizenship disappear.

It seems quite reasonable that regulators should be able to make some distinction between organizations that are formed for the purpose of political speech and corporations formed for other purposes that engage in political speech. After all, it is possible that a corporation could act in the political sphere in a manner that is in the interests of the managers making the decisions about political spending, but inimical to the interests of all other stakeholders in the corporation and even the corporation's own continued survival.

Chapter 19: Stateless income and the fall of empires

Empires have come in several varieties. Old-fashioned empires like the Roman Empire tended to conquer territory and extract wealth in the form of the agricultural surplus and any natural resources that happened to be laying around. Mercantilist empires such at the British Empire tended to extract resources to feed their home industries.

In general, empires may be defined as one geographically defined group of people dominating other such groups of people for the benefit of the dominant group.

Now, it's a curious fact, but when the United States tried to set up an empire, we sucked at it. We were extremely successful at conquering territory and settling it with our own people, but leaving the original people on the land and extracting wealth from them while ruling them with an iron fist does not seem to be in our skill set. To mix Star Trek and Star Wars metaphors, we were successful as the Borg, taking new territory and peoples into our own society, but we failed as the Empire, attempting to rule other people without absorbing them.

We conquered the East Coast, we bought the Louisiana Purchase and Alaska, we took half of Mexico and lots of Indian land by force, but the United States made a total mess of the remnants of the Spanish empire that it acquired in the Spanish-American War in 1898.

Some say our democratic traditions make us lousy at empire, but what if the real problem was capitalism?

I have learned of the delightful term, "stateless income." It is a product of global capital, and one reason for the parlous condition of the international system. And it is tied to the tax system.

No one *really* seems to want tax simplification. That's because of the old, old story of those who want tax favors being the ones who can afford the lobbying muscle to actually affect the tax code. The more complex the code, the harder it is to see who's bought a favor.

Stateless income is certainly a part of this particularly annoying bit of corruption, but it's also a part of a larger trend.

The American Revolution started in 1776, the same year Adam Smith's *The Wealth of Nations* was published. Capitalism was in its gestation, not even its infancy. Most politicians were either physiocrats or mercantilists.

The physiocrats tended to be planters, who valued that philosophy for two of its major tenets: That all value came from the soil, and the laissez faire idea that government should leave business alone. The latter was attractive to planters whose wealth was built on slave labor, because even at the time of the revolution, people like George Mason were saying that slavery was immoral.

Mercantilists, on the other hand, were natural empire builders. They believed that the state should work with business to increase the wealth of the nation, and in many cases, that meant getting colonies to supply raw materials for manufacture in the home country. India could grow cotton, for example, but it was shipped to the British textile mills. Gandhi rebelled against this, telling Indian men that they should spin and weave their own fabric.

Of course, it would be far more profitable for the cotton mills to be in India, where the labor was cheaper and the transport costs of the raw material less. And had the mills been in India, the people who lived there might have been better able to afford the fabric.

But under the mercantilist system, the most profitable parts of the process were to be in the home country. The result was that the taxes needed to support the very expensive business of maintaining an empire were paid by the companies that benefited from the empire.

But the most envied positions in business are monopolies and free riders. If you can't swing the monopoly -- and starting with the Grange movement after the Civil War and culminating in anti-trust legislation, societies became increasingly hostile to monopolies -- the next best thing is to be a free rider.

This is inherent in the nature of public goods. For example, the most frequently used example of a public good is the lighthouse.

The problem became evident when private industry tried to supply the crying need for lighthouses. They were a benefit to all mariners, but who would pay for the use of a lighthouse? It's lit or it isn't, and if someone else pays for the lighthouse, it is impossible to exclude anyone from the use of a lighthouse.

So, governments granted lighthouse owners the right to collect fees, and ended up enforcing that right. Essentially, it took the government to collect the fees to support a private lighthouse.

That solved the free rider problem, but then it became evident that the incentive for lighthouses was to crank up the fees and spend as little on maintenance as possible, an example of rent-seeking by a monopoly. This led to public demand for the state to provide better lighthouses. A lighthouse is a natural public good, and so is an army.

Think about this in terms of public order. The British Empire, at tremendous cost in lives and treasure, maintained a relatively peaceful and lawful place to do business in India, and its merchant class brought profitable business to Britain that paid taxes to support the empire. But you can no more exclude someone from peace than from the spinning ray from the Fresnel lens of a lighthouse.

Ford was probably not the first, but in 1926 the company built plants to produce the Model T in India for the Indian market. Given how much help America had been in WW I ("Damned yanks, late to every war...") it was not politically practical to tell Ford to take a hike, and in any case, the age of empires was ending.

Ford was a harbinger of the age of global capital. It is an age in which companies have no loyalty to country. As Mitt Romney told us, "corporations are people, too," but they are people without empathy, loyalty or conscience.

In short, a corporation is a sociopath. Unless, as with some small corporations like Twice Sold Enterprises, Inc., all the officers are one person (me), it cannot have the character traits we value in people. Lacking loyalty, patriotism is just one more emotion a large corporation cannot feel.

It is the perfect free rider, not caring about the unfairness of it taking advantage of a system it undermines by dodging payment for the service it enjoys.

At present, nearly half the world's military expenditure is spent by the good ol' U.S. of A., a country that comprises close to 25% of the world economy. The Pax Americana is partially defrayed by the money paid by some other countries for the protection we offer. Japan, for example, pays about $2 billion a year to help maintain American bases on Japanese soil. (Well, mostly on Okinawan soil, which is a bit of a sore point with the people of the Ryuku Islands, annexed by Japan in 1872 and still treated as a somewhat separate people for matters such as who marries who.)

But it is becoming increasingly evident that America, like the empires before her, cannot maintain the world system. The expense is simply not paid by those who benefit. The feedback loop that provided the British Empire with funds to maintain the empire simply isn't there, because stateless income seeks tax havens, and does not pay for the maintenance of empires.

The United States, in any case, is not a traditional empire. We have trading alliances and defense alliances, generally defined by the same regions. The fact that after 1898 we stopped invading other countries in order to annex their territory encourages our allies to trust us.

There was much to despise in the old imperial system. The Sepoy Mutiny[*] would hardly have happened in a harmonious nation where people actually liked being ruled by foreigners. The competition between countries that had empires, such as Spain and Britain, and those who desired them, such as Germany and Japan, led to horrendous wars with enormous loss of life.

The systems that have replaced it – the competition of the Cold War and the resented hegemony of the Pax Americana – isn't necessarily any better. Granted, when a country asks America to leave, we do. (My father flew as a navigator/bombardier on B-57s, and we had to leave Laon in 1958 because Charles de Gaulle did not want any American nuclear delivery aircraft on French bases. Yep, it's as easy as that to get rid of us, if you're an ally. Tell us to leave, and we go.)

But is the world as safe as it was before governments of powerful countries started to realize that all that money spent on wars was never coming back?

Presumably, stateless income and free riders on the international system will at some point undermine the safety of overseas investments to the point where they are not profitable. At the same time, if wars are not profitable, there may be fewer wars. Or some other form of order must be found.

But what sort of order is possible in a world of global finance, corporate capitalism, and stateless income?

In areas where total peace is breaking out, such as western Europe, tribalism is reasserting itself. Catalonia, Venice, and Scotland once again contemplate independence within the European Union, confident that they will not have to defend themselves from rogue state actors. Their expectation is that matters such as currency and central banking can be left to the EU, and perhaps they can either enjoy the protection of NATO as free riders or even as participants.

Ethnically diverse states outside of such organizations are in trouble. Breakaway groups can make alliances with predatory states, as South Ossetia did with Russia in the Russo-Georgian War.

Vladimir Putin attempted to swing the Ukraine into the Russian orbit with soft power, offering money and cheap natural gas to the elected government as a reward for turning economically away from Western Europe and toward Russia.

In exchange for $15 billion and a 33% discount on natural gas, Putin got Ukrainian President Viktor Yanukovych to agree not to sign the E.U. Association Agreement that was on offer. This led to riots that eventually caused Yanukovych to flee the country, leaving behind documents that showed how much he'd stolen from the citizens he was elected to represent.

Faced with the fact that no one seems to want to link themselves with Russia except at gunpoint, Putin brought out the guns, which like the uniforms, trucks and armored vehicles of the Crimean invasion force, were not marked with their nationality.

This is making association with a larger protective association essential for countries with bumptious neighbors.

The emerging order relies on organizations like the EU, NATO, ASEAN, SEATO and the African Union, some economic and some security related, to keep regional order. This represents a continuation of the trend for the replacement of a system of empires with one based on hegemony, of the soft power of voluntary association replacing the hard power of conquest. It also represents an end to empires based on conquest.

Economic associations tend to grow more rapidly than security associations, but the need for the latter becomes evident after the establishment of the former. Just as empires relied on economic feedback to support their military adventures, and economies relied on empires to protect their interests, economic unions lead to a need to protect trading partners. Putin understood that a Ukraine economically enmeshed with Western Europe would eventually want the protection of NATO.

Only the largest countries, such as China the United States, can afford to operate independent of such associations, and the U.S. has found it wisest to act within them. Russia, with an economy smaller than the United Kingdom or Brazil, is clearly trying to punch above its weight, but with an economy about the size of Italy's, it is not clear that it can afford to sustain its aggressive posture over time. The use of *maskirovka*, or masked warfare, may be cheaper than an out-and-out invasion, but even such tactics won't keep costs down if there is sustained resistance.

One of the lessons of the Soviet war in Afghanistan is that a Russia dependent on hydrocarbons for income it spends on imported food is economically vulnerable. Russian farming is not quite the disaster Soviet farming was, and the nation now provides itself with grain, but it still imports more food than it sells.

Russian interference with the Ukraine and Chinese assertiveness in the South China Sea are going to test this new system. I don't know how willing voluntary associations will be to defend the Parcel Islands, but populated areas that are part of security organizations are probably going to be safe. Areas not part of such associations, not so much.

Voluntary economic associations are related to liberal ideas. They may include autocratic states such as Myanmar, but they then become a source of pressure on such states to institute liberal reforms.

Chapter 20: Globalization and its discontents

One of the villains of the conspiracy buffs is the Bilderberg Group, a bunch of influential people who meet together to discuss an agenda to "bolster a consensus around free market Western capitalism and its interests around the globe."

Denis Healey, one of the group's founders, said of it, "Those of us in Bilderberg felt we couldn't go on forever fighting one another for nothing and killing people and rendering millions homeless. So we felt that a single community throughout the world would be a good thing."

Now, that sounds reasonable, doesn't it? So why are they villains? I mean, aside from the fact they ignore, which is that only people who interact with each other fight (World War I happened at a peak in international trade and travel, so the notion that you can achieve world peace through trade and internationalism is suspect to start with.)

Well, a lot of people are not comfortable with the idea of a single community throughout the entire world. It would, after all, make existing groups obsolete. For example, if you are British, and consider Britishness inexorably linked to being white and speaking English with a certain range of accents, you might be uncomfortable with the open borders policy of the European Union, and vote to exit it.

Or, if you are American and consider whiteness and Christianity to be essential to Americanism, you might be uncomfortable with Muslims, or with allowing people from Latin America to immigrate, or having someone with African ancestry being president.

There are other issues, of course. You may oppose free trade because you see too much of what you buy being made in other countries. You may oppose immigration because you think your wages are suppressed by competing with immigrants for jobs.

But the biggest problem might just be that you feel your identity is threatened, what it means to be a part of your tribe. I think of this as ethnic panic, a psychological reaction similar to homosexual panic, in which someone snaps because a homosexual makes an advance to them and they respond violently because they are faced with their own suppressed homosexual desires.[*]

As in homosexual panic, the person suffering from ethnic panic is faced with an identity they are uncomfortable with, for example, an identity in which you can be American, gay, brown, and Muslim. The more America looks like the world, the more the identity of America as being white and Christian is lost: It's tribalism is being lost.

I say good riddance to it, but then, I lived abroad as a child, and have a different relationship to identity than many Americans.

Now, consider this idea in the context of Sigmund Freud's *Civilization and its Discontents*. Freud argued that there is a natural tension between the individual and civilization.

He said that the development of the ego consists of differentiating one's self from the world around us, toward an erotic interaction with the world in which we seek to maximize the pleasure principle, doing that which nature intended by doing what feels good, which puts us in conflict with society. This is because we must suppress our desires in order to have a stable, working society. We cannot, for example, have sex with whomever we please, because it might not please them (or their mate.)

We sublimate our desires because we have a need for order and protection. Infants, after all, need the father's protection as much as the mother's nurturing, in the Freudian (somewhat dated) scheme of things.

Compare this to liberal theory: Humanity in the state of nature is free, but cannot exercise freedom because of all those other assholes trying to exercise their freedom on the food you wish to eat and the mate you wish to seduce. The only way to resolve this is with a social contract that reigns in the individual so that they may have freedom from the war of each against all, and to enforce that social contract, they need the leviathan, who has the power to enforce laws.

In short, Freud's theory is liberalism plus psychology, which gives us a way to look at the issue of identity within civilizations.

Most of the progress in civilization has consisted of a broadening definition of who belongs to our group. To a hunter-gatherer from 10,000 years ago, the notion that there could be 325 million people in the world would have been unimaginable, let alone there being 325 million people in a tribe called "American." Rome became immensely powerful in its day in part because you didn't have to be from the seven hills of Rome to be a Roman citizen. Allowing those who joined them to become Roman soon meant that Rome had more people and larger armies than their enemies.

But progress can leave people feeling dislocated. Foreigners joining the tribe can make people wonder what defines the tribe. And if the new members are very different, people can suffer from unease. They can feel that the tribe is changing, and their own definition of the identity "American" (or, for that matter, Iraqi) is being left behind. Even well short of a violent reaction to ethnic panic, they may suffer a discontent with the changing face of their nation.

Of course, there are other aspects of the current discontent in our nation. Part of the reaction to immigrants is connected with the fact that white men in this country haven't seen wages rise in real terms since about 1973. And those who have actually been getting the money – the very rich – have managed to avert a rebellion against themselves by blaming the "other" – all those people who do not meet the definition of what it means to be American that so many people have in their minds.

The real reason real wages haven't risen has more to do with the political movement to create inequality. The grievance is real, and seeing manufacturing go to other countries enforces the idea that globalism is the problem, but solving the problem of more and more money going to the people at the top of the income stream does not necessarily mean getting rid of globalization, and getting rid of it won't solve the problem of inequality. Getting real wages to rise is a separate question.

Both the economic grievance and the discontent over the changing identity of the nation are real problems, not just excuses for bigotry, as some liberals suppose. Granted, bigots may find common cause with people suffering from this discontent and grievance.

Discontent over such matters can make a democracy vulnerable to demagogues willing to exploit these discontents. It has been said that private property can guarantee freedom, but history does not bear this out.

Chapter 21: Liberalism and capitalism

Successful industrialization requires capitalism, not democracy. F.A. Hayek said in *The Road to Serfdom* that "...the system of private property is the most important guarantee of freedom. It is only because the control of the means of production is divided among many people acting independently that we as individuals can decide what to do with ourselves."

And yet, business interests supported the totalitarian regimes of Adolf Hitler and Benito Mussolini. The German *mittelstadt*, the medium-sized companies that form the backbone of German industry, continued to flourish in this environment. Capitalism has managed to thrive in a number of nations that have been ruled by dictators. Capitalism no more guarantees liberal freedoms than any other market-oriented economic system has throughout history.

But liberalism has provided a more welcoming environment to the creative energies that can be released by capitalism than dictatorships, and in any case, dictatorships tend to produce rent-seeking by officials whose power cannot be questioned. The resulting corruption interferes with commerce, as those with power siphon off wealth.

Hayek had it backwards. Property is not a guarantor of freedom, but freedom is a guarantor of just property claims, because in a dictatorship you are under the rule of the leader's will, not the rule of law. To have freedom, you must have the rule of law. That was the point of social contract theory; you could not exercise your freedom during the war of each against all. After all, as Hobbes observed:

> ...wherein men live without other security, than what their own strength, and their own invention shall furnish them withall. In such condition, there is no place for Industry; because the fruit thereof is uncertain; and consequently no Culture of the Earth; no Navigation, nor use of the commodities that may be imported by Sea; no commodious Building; no Instruments of moving, and removing such things as require much force; no Knowledge of the face of the Earth; no account of Time; no Arts; no Letters; no Society; and which is worst of all, continuall feare, and danger of violent death; And the life of man, solitary, poore, nasty, brutish, and short.

Rousseau defined freedom as being subject to a law of your own making, that is, a socially agreed upon set of rules in which those subject to the law have a say in the making of the law.

Totalitarian states do not consider the state to be serving the individual citizen. They consider themselves, instead, to be one with the people. In the case of Marxist states, the state is meant to represent the victory of the working class, therefore the imposition of a classless society. In the case of fascist states, the individual is considered weak unless a member of the state. Consider the flag of the Partito Nazionale Fascista, Mussolini's national Fascist party. It is a black field with, on it, a fasci, a bundle of sticks with an ax head sticking out, the metaphor being that the individual rods are weak, but together they are strong. This represents the unity of the people.

Mussolini believed that nationalism had replaced class as the cause that really mattered to the common man. And because the nation was what mattered, individual rights did not. Fascist states had some support from convention, because their biological determinism caused them to think that people should remain in the status they were born to. If your father was a laborer, you were genetically fit to be a laborer. Some were born to lead, some were born to follow. At each level, the leader demanded complete obedience from those below, and gave complete obedience to those above. The people were at one with the state, which was led by one born to lead. There was no need to consult the individual, because the individual was nothing except as part of the state.

Consider what Benito Mussolini & Giovanni Gentile said in *Doctrine of Fascism* (1932)

> Fascism is for the only liberty which can be a serious thing, the liberty of the state and of the individual in the state. Therefore for the fascist, everything is in the state, and no human or spiritual thing exists, or has any sort of value, outside the state. In this sense fascism is totalitarian, and the fascist state which is the synthesis and unity of every value, interprets, develops and strengthens the entire life of the people.

Totalitarian states were not democratic because they did not value democracy. They could accommodate capitalism if, as with the fascists, their ideology did not have a problem with private property and markets.

But the fascists failed for the same reason Napoleon did. They depended for their legitimacy on nationalism, and stirring up the people against the nation's neighbors. This in the end called for war, and if you keep fighting long enough, you will eventually lose.

Marxism, by contrast, claimed to represent the worker against the oppressive capitalist. One problem with building a Marxist society was that

Marx did not produce a workable system of value. It is all very well to say that labor creates value, but how do we know that a person is doing labor *of* value? Liberalism's subjective version of value tells us that it is dependent on the need and judgment of another. Marx did not show how society would reward labor on what needed doing in contrast to labor doing something no one cared about or even doing something destructive.

As a result, it produced the Trabant, a car produced in East Germany before the fall of Communism, which was a value-subtracted product. That is, the metal, plastic, rubber, labor, etc. that went into the product was worth more than the product itself.

From *Transition*, a newsletter of the World Bank, Number 5-6, May-June 1996, page 15:

> With a view to corporate takeover, Volkswagen AG sent a Herr Heuss to Zwickau to find out how the Trabants (relatively cheap East German cars) were made there. He emerged shocked from the huge plant, babbling "My God." The Trabant operation was value-subtracting: valuable material, labor, and capital inputs went in at one end; shabby Trabies came out at the other, their bodies made from compacted trash. The final output was worth less than the sum of the inputs. What was not fully understood at the time was that East Germany's whole economy was value-subtracting and cost-unconscious.

Communism produced somewhat more stable governments than fascism, but worse economic results. And both produced atrocities, from the German Holocaust to the killing fields of Cambodia.

Liberalism, because it is democratic, is more flexible. Leaders who fail can be cast aside without violence. If the system is not producing just outcomes, the system can be changed.

There seems to be confusion on the right as to the difference between social democracy and socialism. Social Democrats are a group of liberals who believe in private property and markets, but want a strong social insurance program to soften the consequences of capitalism. Communism is a kind of socialism that regards it as important that society, usually in the form of the state, should own the means of production. (Marx proposed eliminating private productive property entirely, but since property is the rules, obligations, and rights about how people use objects, this is impossible, as long as people use objects. This basic failure to understand the nature of property is part of the reason for the failure of Marxism.)

Social Democrats, then, are those who wish to preserve capitalism through forms of social insurance that make the system sufficiently just in its outcomes to avoid social unrest. Both fascists and Communists considered them enemies, and suppressed them, in part because they try to achieve their aims by democratic means.

Fabian socialists tried a different approach, trying to institute the social ownership of the means of production by democratic means over a long period of time. When state-owned industries in Britain proved economically unworkable, their project was ended by democratic means.

Some will say that laissez faire capitalism is an alternative, but the idea of laissez faire does not specify a form of government, and in any case I doubt this has ever really been tried. We were still in a mercantilist system when the Grange movement started advocating for anti-trust laws, so we went from the state supporting industry under mercantilism to regulated business without a real laissez faire moment between. In fact, industry still depends upon state aid in matters of credit and infrastructure. The closest we came to laissez faire capitalism was the Gilded Age of the 1880s and 1890s, which featured enough unrest to produce the labor movement and the Grange movement.

Laissez faire capitalism is close to the ideal of libertarianism, but there was substantial government interference in contracts between labor and industry, if favor of industry. Like Marxism, the purist ideal of libertarianism would be the withering away of the state, and this is no more practical than the Marxist ideal of communism without a state. Even most libertarians understand that the state is needed to guarantee property rights. The problem they face is that markets are as much a human invention as governments, and it is difficult to see why, therefore, markets should be privileged over other institutions.

There is a lot of myth-making about the American economy. It might be instructive to take a look at the American Way, sometimes called the American System, as practiced in 19th century America.

Chapter 22: In which we examine the American Way

Back in 2011, David Brooks wrote a column in which he claimed that "The world economy is a complex, unknowable organism, "and that all who think they've found the "magic lever" that will make the economy perform better are wrong.

Paul Krugman replied in a post on his blog, maintaining that "realizing that there's a lot you can do to reverse a short-term slump isn't magical thinking — it's what basic macroeconomics, what we learned through hard thinking and hard experience, tells us. Rejecting all that may sound judicious, but it's actually an act of intellectual amnesia."

He does agree with Brooks that there is little the government can do to improve long-term growth.

I suspect that both men are wrong. Brooks certainly is; economists ranging from Milton Friedman to, well, Paul Krugman, agree that when the country is not in a liquidity trap, monetary policy can stimulate the economy. History demonstrates that they are right.

But what about long-term growth? I maintain that a very old idea, originally called "the American Way," points us to the answer.

Consider the age of our infrastructure. In 1969, the average age of government infrastructure was a little over 16 years. Now it is more than 25 years.

And what are our other competitors doing?

A January 22, 2009 New York Times article tells us:

> The combined national, provincial and local spending for economic stimulus promises to change the face of China, giving the country a world-class infrastructure for moving goods and people quickly, cheaply and reliably across great distances.

In 1919 Dwight Eisenhower had participated in the Transcontinental Motor Convoy, spending 62 days crossing the country, and in the process having to repair 88 bridges. Most of the roads were unpaved, which may help explain why the trucks kept breaking down and crashing.

It has been said that in war, amateurs study tactics, professionals study logistics. Eisenhower knew logistics very well, and knew that for the economy to function efficiently, it needed roads that would permit good logistics. He ramped up infrastructure spending, and signed what he regarded as the highest accomplishment of his presidency, the Federal Aid Highway Act of 1956.

Now, China is doing what Eisenhower did.

Ah, you say, but our roads are already built. Well, yes, but. Remember those bridges the Transcontinental Motor Convoy had to fix before they could cross them? Those were already built, too. Stuff wears out. If you own a factory, you don't figure, okay, I've got my factory, I don't need to spend any more. Or if you do, you are soon uncompetitive. You replace machines that get old, you constantly try to improve your capital stock, and you sometimes tear the whole thing down and start over.

This was actually a problem for the co-op plywood mills that were once fairly common in the Northwest. The workers would often vote to distribute profits to themselves, rather than invest in more machinery. The business managers they hired would have to tell them, no, you can't pay yourself that money, if you don't buy a new peeler you won't be able to keep making plywood.

We're having a similar problem with our country. In essence, it's a big co-op, where we vote on whether to buy a new bridge or keep that money in our take-home pay. We've been putting off paying for the new bridge for so long, some of them are literally falling apart.

Part of the problem is ideology. In 2009, Michael Steele, then Republican National Committee Chairman, said, "You and I know that in the history of mankind and womankind, government — federal, state, local, or otherwise — has never created one job." Republican former New Mexico governor Gary Johnson in 2011 said, "The fact is, I can unequivocally say that I did not create a single job while I was governor." His point was that private industry creates jobs, and his claim is that despite the fact that the state of New Mexico employs a fair number of people, it gets in the way of private industry employing those people.

The problem with this philosophy is that sometimes, government produces goods more efficiently than private industry. Consider lighthouses, which we discussed in depth in Chapter 19, but let's take a more cynical view. First, there were concerned people who realized that on a dark and stormy night, ships tended to run onto the rocks. Some of them built bonfires to warn them that they were nearing the rocks.

Then, the invisible hand of the market intervened, as people found a way to make the signal bonfires pay. They built them in spots that would cause mariners to run onto the rocks, then looted the wreckage after the crews were dead.

Government regulation strangled the private economic enterprise of the wreckers, and competition from tax-supported lighthouses didn't help, either. Thus, a libertarian paradise was strangled in its crib, and the lives of countless mariners were saved.

What this admittedly sardonic account reveals is that sometimes the market fails. Sometimes it's possible to redesign the market so that the incentives align with peoples' needs (the Affordable Care Act is an attempt to do that), sometimes a market failure just means you have to put the matter into public hands.

But the public no longer feels that it has a really direct connection with its government. Part of the reason for this is that since the 1960s, a large number of people have been trying to convince them that the government is an alien thing that only has the capacity to harm them. The mantra that government is not the solution, it's the problem, has a nice ring to it, and we all know instances where government has not functioned as it should.

But a study by Cornell's Suzanne Mettler in 2011 found that 40 percent of Medicare beneficiaries and more than 40 percent of Social Security recipients say that they have not benefited from any government social program. Government is so ubiquitous that people are often not aware of the benefits they receive from it, even when it's something as visible as roads and bridges. So how can you expect people to appreciate the benefits of productive public assets?

Every grade-level crossing delays traffic and trains. If there is enough traffic for this to be a real problem, as is the case in much of the Northeast, the country can be made more productive by building an overpass, but it is not in the interest of any private party to do that for the rest of us.

When the United States was young, men like John Quincy Adams, Alexander Hamilton and Henry Clay believed in something called "the American Way" (the Wikipedia entry refers to it as "the American System.") It was essentially mercantilism, the dominant economic paradigm of the time, and it featured a concerted effort to build first-rate infrastructure.

The American Way featured high tariffs to protect industry, a national bank to foster commerce, and government subsidies for the development of canals, roads, dredged harbors, and other improvements to permit the movement of goods (at the time mainly farm goods) to markets.

Perhaps it's time to revive the term "the American Way." After all, who could oppose "the American Way," especially when it featured the support of the earliest interpreters of what America should be? Perhaps not all aspects of the plan Hamilton and his compatriots pushed worked, (I have my doubts about how useful high tariffs are) but there are some very useful ideas there.

For example, our first national system of roads were the post roads, built to carry mail to post offices. The American Constitution empowers Congress to found a post office, so this was in a way baked into the very fabric of the nation.

And it wasn't just infrastructure the American Way provided for. Government also played a key role in the industrial revolution.

Chapter 23: Myth-making and manufacturing: More on the supply side of public spending

We build the story of our lives on narratives, and do our best to make them like life's supposed to be. But those narratives are not just private stories, they are also the way we build the communities and nations we live in.

The myths that make America are famous and most of the time carry important truths. They also conceal important truths. The self-reliant frontiersman was able to, as Firesign Theater put it in *Temporarily Humboldt County*, "carve a new life out of the American Indian," only because the U.S. Cavalry was prepared to chase the Native Americans off their land. And at a time when land was the most important basis for wealth, this played a major role in the rise of the American economy, essentially transferring wealth from its owners to its invaders in the time-honored manner of pre-industrial empire building.

Clearly, those self-reliant frontiersmen were dependent upon the willingness of the American government to seize and protect the property they settled. The settlement of the West was an agrarian revolution, taking land from hunter-gatherer use to farming and herding use (although there are some interesting things coming to light about the land practices of Native Americans, pretty well explained in Charles Mann's book *1491*.)

The other revolution was industrial. America had, as a British colony, been held back from developing industry. Mercantilist theory held that colonies were to provide the raw materials for the mother country to manufacture, and make that country wealthy and powerful. This was part of the beef between the colonies and Britain: We wanted to develop the resources and manufacturing here.

And when we did, it was private enterprise and Yankee ingenuity that did the trick, right?

Not quite.

The American rise in manufacturing, and the revolution of mass production, had a lot to do with those things, but also depended on bloated defense contracts and publicly owned manufacturing enterprises. In 1852, the British sent a fact-finding mission, touring the government armories at

Harper's Ferry and Springfield to learn about the "American system of manufacture."

Which we got from the French.

Most manufacturing prior to and including the 19th century involved what some scholars call "the craftsmanship of risk." When a craftsman picks up a tool and starts to make something freehand, the product is a functional representation of an idea, and the extent to which it succeeds in making the idea function depends on the skill of the craftsman. The risk is that the product will be flawed because of a lack of skill (or just a bad day) of the craftsman.

In manufacturing, Adam Smith famously chronicled the efficiency of a pin factory based on division of labor, even though the pins were mainly made by hand. This worked quite well, because pins have only one part, which works even if not every pin is quite the same.

Muskets are a different matter. Gunsmiths making each weapon one at a time could produce working muskets, but if a part needed to be replaced, it needed to be shaped by a skilled gunsmith.

French General Jean-Baptiste Vaquette de Gribeauval found that this meant weapons could not be repaired in the field. If you had a stack of muskets, some with one part broken, some with another, you could not assemble a single working musket from the parts, even if they all were built to the same design.

Even with division of labor, the problem remained. Every manufacturing plant had a finishing department, the job of which was to take the parts made by others and shape them so that they could work together in each musket (or clock or sewing machine when those came along).

The *Système Gribeauval* was conceived to solve this problem. Each musket would be made with identical parts so that they could be cannibalized to repair other muskets in the field.

This proved extremely expensive. The reason people were not making identical parts already was that the methods of manufacture available to them involved the craftsmanship of risk. The parts had to be made with far greater precision if they were not to be fitted to the final assembly by modifying them at the end of the process. It took a painstaking gauging process to produce parts that were truly interchangeable, and no individual frontiersman cared to pay for that. Only armies could afford the extra cost, and only in combat was the extra cost worthwhile.

A number of French officers came to help with our revolution against Britain, and some of them stayed. Indeed, some came back after things got hot back home, since many of them were noblemen and feared Dr. Guillotine's machine. This represented an important transfer of skill from one of the most advanced countries in Europe.

It was also a transfer of skills that would not move as easily to England, a nascent industrial powerhouse and sworn enemy to the French. One French engineer, Marc Isambard Brunel, father of the more famous Isambard Kingdom Brunel, introduced the idea of interchangeable parts to the British Navy, in the block-making process he invented. Marc Brunel, by the way, had taken American citizenship and worked as the city engineer of New York, after he fled France because of his Royalist sympathies.

The woman he loved, an English orphan who had been working as a governess, was held as a spy during the Terror. She was released with the fall of Robespierre and traveled to London, where Brunel married her and presented his system of mass production to the Royal Navy, helping win a war against the country he had fled. There's a lesson there for revolutionaries who take the view that you can't make an omelet without breaking some eggs. Sometimes, you end up with egg on your face.

But blocks don't have a lot of parts, and they don't break down much. Speed of production was far more important for block manufacture than precision parts.

The American military became interested in the idea of interchangeable parts for the same reason the French under the royalists were. They went farther with it, and one of the people who promoted it was that old fraud, Eli Whitney.

Whitney, after failing at some other enterprises, managed to get a contract to make a (then) large number of muskets because he had contacts with some of his old Yale classmates, even though he had no facility capable of fulfilling his contract. When he failed to deliver the parts on time, he claimed it was because he was trying to do this very hard thing, produce muskets with interchangeable parts. Although Wikipedia claims he assembled a musket from a bin of parts, this is not the case according to an excellent book by David Hounshell titled *From the American System to Mass Production, 1800-1932: The Development of Manufacturing Technology in the United States.*

What Whitney actually did was show that the flint lock from one of his muskets would fit another of his muskets. Repairing the lock of one with parts from another, however, was the goal.

But his promotion may have helped more able men to get the backing they needed to really implement the idea. Simeon North, a contemporary of Whitney's, seems to have been far more successful in actually manufacturing parts that were interchangeable.

Still more successful was John Hall, a Maine boatbuilder turned inventor who was no doubt familiar with the use of molds and patterns for the building of stock boats. He invented a wide variety of machines for the manufacture of the various parts, and instituted a very complete gauging system for ensuring the quality and interchangeability of the parts. Only a machine could do each action in exactly the same way each time it made a part, and only constant checking with the gauges could ensure that the machine did that. This was the craftsmanship of certainty.

The methods North, Hall and their successors developed automated production to an unprecedented degree, which was necessary to introduce the craftsmanship of certainty. Hall was one of the first to understand that once the system for producing muskets -- or anything else -- was established, the longer the production run, the lower the per-unit production cost. Despite his protestations, the American government kept ordering the kind of small lots (as little as a thousand or two thousand guns at a time) that Whitney had such trouble producing in a timely fashion.

But the revolution that took us from the craftsmanship of risk to the craftsmanship of certainty was the basis for American industrial ascendancy every bit as much as the natural resources bought by our treasury (in the case of the Louisiana Purchase and Seward's folly, Alaska) or conquered by our armies (most of the country,) and the roads, canals and railroads built either with public funds or public assistance. And that revolution would not have happened if the government had not been willing to pay more for weapons than was generally the price because the needs of an army and the needs of a trapper are not the same.

There was plenty of private industry involved. There were contractors working within the armories who learned the methods, invented new machines to automate the process, and carried that knowledge into private industry. But much of the research and industrial experience that supplied our economy with the expertise to succeed was developed on the federal dollar.

And much like the building of roads and schools or the conquest and annexation of nearly half of Mexico, it was a public-sector investment in the supply side of the economy.

Chapter 24: Poor laws: Would the death penalty make poor people get jobs?

One of the fundamental problems with the secular state is, how do you deal with the poor? This has been the case since Henry VIII decided that a church dominated by the state would serve him better than a state dominated by the church.

During the reign of Edward VI of England, the Poor Laws imposed the death penalty for those twice found guilty of vagrancy. First offense was just two years of servitude and being branded with a V, which surely must have helped former vagrants find a new position.

After all, if you want people to stop being poor, you must make being poor more horrible than hunger, cold and want already are, right?

Nowadays, we have political figures who argue that extending unemployment insurance makes people more dependent, causing them to remain unemployed. I believe this reflects our English legal and cultural heritage. They aren't yet heating up the branding iron, though I suppose I should hesitate to bring up that old custom in certain company, lest I give them ideas.

During the recession following the 2008 banking crisis, there were three job seekers for every open job, so it is hard to see how motivating people to look harder for a job would reduce the rate of joblessness. I suspect most people haven't really examined past approaches to the problems of poverty, so perhaps a quick review is in order.

One pipe dream for conservatives is that the poor will be supported voluntarily, preferably through religious organizations. And in fact, in Medieval England, that's how it was done, except that the tithe paid to the church was not voluntary – it was collected by the Crown on behalf of the Church. Monasteries ministered to the poor and the infirm.

This pretty much stopped when Henry VIII broke with the Catholic Church in England, set up the Anglican Church, closed down the monasteries and used the property to reward those who helped him with this high-handed hijacking of things ecclesiastic. I know of no advanced economy where churches have the kind of wealth and power the pre-Reformation Catholic Church had, so that model appears to be irretrievably broken. Let's review the history of England trying to deal with poverty in the absence of such a powerful church.

Henry VIII's move to privatize the monasteries meant that there were no more monasteries to minister to the poor. Instead, their care went to the government, and was paid for by a tax.

Just to be clear, the state was already involved, not in dealing with poverty *per se*, but in dealing with idleness. When the Black Plague wiped out as much as 40% of the population of Europe in the 1340s, there was a labor shortage. The cost of labor went up dramatically, causing the cost of food and clothing to go up, and changing the balance of power between landholder and laborer.

To keep the cost of labor from going up too much, the 1351 Statute of Laborers required that everyone who could work did so and restricted wages to pre-plague levels, so that landowners would not be faced with a choice of raising wages or leaving land fallow.

And it was these laws that the Tudor kings built upon in their approach to the poor. In 1495, under Henry VII, the law was modified so that "vagabonds, idle and suspected persons shall be set in the stocks for three days and three nights and have none other sustenance but bread and water and then shall be put out of Town." This provision led to a system where if you were poor and received any assistance, such as staying in a shelter, you had to walk to the next town to get another meal and another roof over your head. You would, as they say, have to tramp from town to town, giving us a new noun based on the word *tramp*. Now, a person who was poor was known as a tramp.

Some people were still unemployed, so Henry VIII tried substituting whipping for the stocks. You might think, "That will teach the blighters not to be unemployed!" But in fact, people continued to be periodically out of work.

During the short and unhappy reign of Edward VI, the monarch saw that people still persisted in being poor, so in 1547 he instituted the branding and penal servitude for the first offense of vagrancy and the death penalty for the second offense, as mentioned above. You might think that would keep people from being caught unemployed more than twice, because after that they would be dead, but justices proved squeamish about sentencing people to death for not having a job.

English law made no provision for those able-bodied persons unable to find a job until fairly late in the day. Under Queen Elizabeth I, able-bodied poor who refused to work would be sent to a house of correction, where they would be beaten to mend their attitude. But what of those willing to work, but unable to find a job?

The next approach was the workhouse, where people were fed the bare minimum, worked in harsh conditions, and experienced a shortened lifespan, which made them an example to all. It seems throughout the Tudor period and later, poverty was deemed necessary so that people would be motivated to work, so the authorities did not wish to make poverty tolerable. Keep those workhouses in mind the next time someone proposes that the poor should have to work to get welfare.

In fact, the whole root of this approach to poverty was based on those laws passed after the Black Plague, which were aimed not at poverty, but at idleness. A worker able to demand higher pay might choose to spend the money on relaxing for a while, and these little vacations would reduce the size of the work force for their duration, putting further pressure on wages. Soon, the laborer might think himself as good as his master!

This approach was never about the relief of poverty, only about power relationships within society. Under Elizabeth I, the law came to recognize the existence of the "deserving poor," at first called the impotent poor because they did not have the power to improve their situation.

The approach of punishing the poor, the approach of making them work, and the approach of making life as a poor person as difficult as possible have all been tried. We've had debtor's prisons, even indentured servitude for debtors. None of this seems to keep people from becoming unemployed, and many who are unemployed from remaining so.

Laws can change quickly, but culture changes slowly. The attitudes behind those laws are still with us, still bubbling up in our politics. But as Edward VI showed, even the death penalty will not keep people from being unemployed.

Chapter 25: Productivity and the replicator economy

A skilled worker in a hard-pressed part of the economy, the newspaper business. once told me, "I never cared about being rich, but no one told me the alternative was to be poor."

He got a good education, worked hard, and enjoyed considerable success for a while in a profession that used to give people employed in it a living you could buy a house and raise a family on. Then, the magic of a machine that could replicate newspapers and distribute them at virtually no cost came along, and instead of making people in his profession rich, it reduced their ranks to about half as many as had previously been employed, and new hires were getting paid a lot less than the silverbacks in the newsroom. No one was getting raises.

This is odd, because things that increase productivity should make us wealthier.

Robert Solow, a Nobel-prize-winning economist, remarked way back in 1987 that, "What everyone feels to have been a technological revolution...has been accompanied everywhere...by a slowdown in productivity growth."

This has become known as the Solow paradox.

The golden age of productivity growth in the U.S. was between 1939 and 2000, with a slowdown in the 1980s, an increase in the Clinton Administration, and a slowdown again since.

What happened in 1939? Well, we began preparing for war. We didn't just build tanks, guns, ships, and aircraft, we also built roads and airports, and we dredged harbors and improved port facilities. Prior to World War II, flying boats were popular for serving areas that didn't have airports. After the war, there were plenty of airports.

The infrastructure binge continued after the war, and Dwight Eisenhower thought his greatest accomplishment was the Interstate Highway Act, which knit the country together with ribbons of road. Eisenhower understood logistics. He also understood that training was important if you wished to mobilize a large enterprise, and he elevated education to a cabinet-level office.

The federal investment in roads and education set loose the potential of the people and the land. And what have we done with this legacy of supply-side investment in public goods?

We've disinvested. Our public goods are getting old, and we've pushed onto students the cost of financing their education, so that someone can come out of college very easily tens of thousands of dollars in debt. Higher education keeps getting cut while more is spent on other things, like prisons and welfare. Yet providing better education is one way we should be able to spend less on prisons and welfare.

Our bridges are getting old, some of our roads are getting rough.

But why didn't our technology give us the added productivity our disinvestment in public goods was taking away?

Maybe it did, and the drag from the failure to keep up the infrastructure conceals it. Or maybe, sometimes technology is not necessarily useful for increasing measured productivity.

You can measure productivity by seeing how many widgets are produced over a period of time by a given number of people. For example, in the cottage industry of music that existed before recorded music came along, you had to either make your own or hire a musician to make the music for you. Every song required a person making music for the performance to happen.

When recorded music came along, you no longer had to have a musician present to have a song. This meant fewer people would be employed as musicians, but also that people at the top of the profession could provide music for a larger number of people. A musician could sing a song once, and millions of people could buy that song and play it repeatedly. There was more music in our lives, it was made by the best musicians, and the cost was lower. Productivity increased.

But we don't know how much, because we weren't calculating the productivity of musicians prior to this. A few musicians at the top were more productive, but once a record had been sold, it could be played many times. Those repeat performances were taken out of the economic sphere, and not counted as performances in any accounting sense. The metric became the sale of the record, rather than the performance of the song.

But what happened with the digital revolution in music? Well, sales of physical recordings are down to about a third of what they once were, and paid digital downloading has replaced a tiny fraction of the lost sales.

Unless there was a dramatic decrease in the number of musicians, this represents a huge decrease in measured productivity. Far fewer performances of songs are being sold, and if the number of musicians remains constant, their productivity, measured by the usual economic methods, has decreased dramatically.

But we know that this has not been accompanied by an increase in the cost of a song. What has happened instead is that much of the music produced has been taken out of the economic sphere altogether. People are pirating the songs, and getting music for free. There is a cost to this; it's not really as easy to steal a song as to buy it, but those who wish to sell a song are competing with the free copy that can be pirated by acquiring some skill and jettisoning some scruples.

In the realm of classified ads, most of those are free on Craigslist. Until recently, most newspapers have made their digital product free. As a result, whole swaths of the economy have come out of the economic sphere. When you produce something for a lower price, you increase productivity. When you produce it for free, in economic terms you produce nothing.

Thus, we have a different paradox, that of the replicator economy. On Star Trek, replicators can make anything you want for free. But if everything you need is free, how does anyone get paid? Musicians are already facing the replicator economy. Writers may face it soon.

This shows that not all technology produces increases in economic productivity, because some of it takes things out of the economic sphere.

It is also possible to move work into the economic sphere. If someone can stay home and care for a child while collecting welfare, you are not increasing measured productivity. If you provide daycare and require people to work, both the care of the child and the work of the parent are moved into the economic sphere. Mind you, the care of the child may be worse, and having the parent work at a job rather than at caring for children and having the daycare worker work at caring for children rather than at another job may be a wash or even worse in terms of social outcomes: But measured economic activity goes up.

In addition, when new technology moved in, highly-skilled artisans who were more productive than the average person found it impossible to keep making money at their craft. Take the example of weavers and the textile mills that replaced them.

Textile mills increased the number of yards of fabric per worker, and reduced the level of skill required by the worker. Weavers, who had made a good living because they were more productive than average, were put out of work. Some became Luddites, smashing the machinery that was eclipsing their way of life, but in the end, they lost.

They were replaced by low-skilled, low-paid workers, including in many cases children. The price of fabric went down, but the way of life of the people working to make the fabric became worse. And while productivity was increased in the making of fabric, the skilled artisans found their skill was no longer required.

A skilled artisan who ends up working as a laborer or a waiter becomes less productive. And every disruptive technology must have the effect of making some skills obsolete. It takes time for people to adjust, and some never will. Society as a whole may benefit, but in the disrupted industry, there is some immiseration, and among the displaced workers, there will be a decline in productivity. In fact, the immiseration of the obsolete workers removes the incentive for other industries to become more productive, because it drives down the price of labor.

So, what does increase productivity?

Full employment. I know, I know, productivity actually climbs in a recession because you lay off your least productive workers first, but in the long run, only a shortage of workers convinces companies to make capital investments to reduce the number of workers needed. If you have to bid up the price of workers to attract employees, it makes sense to increase productivity.

Right now, we have the spectacle of cash-rich companies buying back their own stock, which is great for managers who have stock options, but not great for productivity. In fact, prior to the 1980s, this would have been viewed as stock manipulation. In 1982, President Ronald Reagan's Securities and Exchange Commission changed the rules. Now, Nobel laureate Joseph Stiglitz tells us in his book, *Rewriting the Rules of the American Economy: An agenda for growth and shared prosperity*, about 70% of pre-tax profits are spent on stock buy-backs. Not only are we disinvesting in infrastructure, we are disinvesting in the capital stock of publicly-traded companies in order to expand the compensation of the top management.

Disinvestment in infrastructure has been bad for productivity. We could kill two birds with one stone by catching up on that, which would increase employment, and build improvements that would unleash some productivity. Investment in public capital goods could increase employment enough to stimulate investment in private capital goods.

But what are the chances of that? We have an entire political party dedicated to the proposition that government spending cannot produce jobs. Until we get better lawmakers, we won't have better policy. Part of the reason we don't have better lawmakers is that markets are a made thing, a human institution that can be structured to transfer wealth from one group to another. We have discussed the fact that money as a system of value tends to corrupt other systems of value, in the chapter on what money is. Once the political system is corrupted by money, you can expect certain people to use their money to rig the game in their favor.

Chapter 26: Porn and market power

In the last chapter, we discussed how changes in the music industry explain a bit of the Solow paradox, the fact that the new technology is being adopted, but productivity hasn't seen much increase. Now we have another example of a way in which technology is suppressing, rather than increasing, productivity growth, also in the entertainment industry.

It also shows how power can transfer wealth from one group to another in ways a free market would not allow, based on monopsony, the dominance of one buyer in the marketplace.

The porn industry, once an economically vibrant part of the economy, has been devastated by changes in the business even as it adopts new technology. Porn stars once had a decent income from their performances, but now many have to work as prostitutes on the side to support themselves. It's a bit like the musicians who used to make most of their money from recordings, and now find they must get their living from live performances.

Like the musicians, part of their problem is piracy. Computer technology allows the rapid and almost perfect copying of music and videos. As a result, many viewings of porn have been taken entirely out of the economic sphere.

But in the case of porn, there is another problem, the market power of the main distributor. The industry is dominated by Mindgeek, formerly Manwin. The company describes itself as being founded in 2013, but that's just when it changed its name back to Mindgeek after a period of being known as Manwin. Each name change came after its owners ran into legal trouble, resulting in the sale of the business.

Mindgeek has something like monopsony power over the porn studios. They own an array of "tubes," the Youtube-like on-line distribution channels for porn. They also own a lot of porn producers, and are essential for the distribution of the works of other porn producers. According to an Oct. 14, 2014 *Slate* article, Mindgeek doesn't always pay the porn producers when they put up a video on one of their sites. From that article:

> Even content producers that MindGeek owns have trouble getting their movies off MindGeek's tube sites. The result has been a vampiric ecosystem: MindGeek's producers make porn films mostly for the sake of being uploaded on to MindGeek's free

tube sites, with lower returns for the producers but higher returns for MindGeek, which makes money off of the tube ads that does not go to anyone involved in the production side.

The result is that performers have to have sex more times to support themselves, performing for the videos and doing their "live" performances as prostitutes. But isn't more work for less money lower productivity as we account for such things? After all, GDP per capita is generally thought of as one measure of productivity.

There was a time when one company in an industry owning most of the production and distribution would have set off alarms in the Justice Department and resulted in anti-trust action. That changed in 1980 with the election of Ronald Reagan.

Word soon went out that the Justice Department would not be worrying about practices such as predatory pricing, (when a larger competitor can use the profits from its other locations to drive a local competitor under by setting prices below costs, then dominate the market and raise prices to monopoly levels.) In fact, the Justice Department was really only worried about monopoly power if it resulted in higher prices to consumers, essentially meaning that the Justice Department was now mainly interested in price fixing in its anti-trust enforcement. This was based on a legal theory advanced by Robert Bork in a book titled *The Antitrust Paradox*.

This radically changed incentives for American businesses. Predatory pricing, a practice that got Safeway in trouble with the Justice Department in the 1960s, became a notorious tactic of Walmart. The key was not to use this power to raise prices, but to dominate its markets and use its market power to squeeze producers and employees.

Mindgeek is using a similar tactic. It is distributing the product for free on ad-supported sites, while squeezing porn production companies and performers to lower its costs. It routinely violates the intellectual property rights to sexual performances, but is so essential to production companies and porn performers for distribution that many say they can't speak out about the problem.

So, why don't the production companies get together and refuse to sell to Mindgeek unless they get paid? Well, if they demand a given price for their goods, that would be price fixing, one of the few aspects of the anti-trust act that the government is still enforcing.

Production of porn films is down 75% from the year before Mindgeek was founded. DVD sales of porn are down 50% over the same time span, because who wants to pay for porn they can watch for free if they tolerate some ads?

Netflix and Amazon are starting to produce their own content (not porn, so far as I know.) We can expect more ethical behavior from them than we see from Mindgeek, but the incentives will be the same. We need to re-examine how our legislation regarding market power affects people selling their wares to distributors or working for them.

The paradox referred to in Bork's book was that antitrust action to increase competition could increase, rather than decrease, prices. What he either failed to realize, or didn't care about, was that monopsony power, the market power of a dominant buyer, interferes with the business arrangements of people who contract to sell their wares or labor to that buyer. This represents a transfer of wealth from one group to another based on power rather than the workings of a free market just as much as price fixing does.

Chapter 27: The nexus of virtue and power

We have examined the seamy side of monopsony and the death penalty for unemployment. Perhaps, now that we've explored the power dynamics of an industry devoted to sin, it is time to discuss the relationship between virtue and power.

For much of human history, we have been ruled by faith and force. It's easy to understand why force – the king with his troops – can rule, but why is faith so important?

Faith is about how we should live. And one of the functions of those who are in charge of faith is to decide who is virtuous, and what actions are virtuous. That is a powerful thing: It means those who interpret virtue can say who is acting rightly, and who is not.

We like to believe we live in a just world, in which virtue is rewarded and vice punished. In a way, the arbiters of what is virtuous are there to reassure us that the world is unfolding as it should. But they are also meant to be a check on those who cheat.

It is therefore in the interest of those who succeed to influence the perception of virtue so that their gains are not regarded as ill-gotten. Kings would rather you believe they ruled by divine right – the will of God – than that they simply control a lot of soldiers. The rich of the Gilded Age liked to believe they were the product of Darwinism, that their wealth was a sign that they were fitter than the poor, just as our modern-day rich like Objectivism, Ayn Rand's reboot of social Darwinism without the bogus biology.

Rand is an interesting case in the study of virtue. She did, after all, write the book on *The Virtue of Selfishness*. Rand as a young woman admired the psychopathic killer Edward Wayne Hickman, because of his selfishness and unwillingness to be bound by social conventions such as not killing people.

Her ideas matured, of course. From the Ayn Rand website (original appearance was in an appendix to *Atlas Shrugged*):

> Man—every man—is an end in himself, not a means to the ends of others; he must live
> for his own sake, neither sacrificing himself to others nor sacrificing others to himself;
> he must work for his rational self-interest, with the achievement of his own happiness as
> the highest moral purpose of his life. Thus Objectivism rejects any form of altruism—

This is a nice philosophy for making a virtue of not helping others, which is fine if you have a nice life and don't wish to be bothered about those less fortunate. This is true not just between rich and poor, but between those advantaged by their race and those disadvantaged by it.

In reality, Rand's notions about morality make no sense in terms of the way people live their lives. Most parents would sacrifice a great deal for the sake of their children, a characteristic that is hardly unique to humans.

Rand's is a philosophy compatible with narcissism and psychopathy, and has no room for idealism, patriotism, or noble self-sacrifice of any sort. It does, however, fit perfectly with the age of the corporation as it now exists.

There was a time when corporations were managed as if they were a person, with shareholders, bondholders, customers and employees all considered as stakeholders. The switch to managing for shareholder value, which started in the 1970s, has remade corporations into a different kind of organization, closer to the Ayn Rand ideal of the selfish individual. And this new version of the right actions for a corporation appear to have seeped into the rest of the culture, with some surprising groups adopting its justifications and notions of what are right actions.

The rise of a libertarian right has given us an entire political movement built around this rather strange notion of virtue. This movement is the strange bedfellow of Christian conservatives who believe Christ dying for their sins is the essence of morality and paleoconservatives who believe in patriotism and the nobility of going to war and becoming a hero.

Our political divisions are as much moral as anything else, but there are deeper and darker emotions at work. To some extent, the morality of libertarians, Christian conservatives, and paleoconservatives are a sham and a justification for things less obviously related to virtue.

When Barry Goldwater, in his 1964 run for the presidency on the Republican ticket, opposed the Civil Rights Act on libertarian grounds, he did something a large part of the country wanted, regardless of how it was justified: He took a stand against civil rights for racial minorities. Strom Thurmond, who ran for president in 1948 on the States Rights Democratic Party ticket, preaching segregation and taking 39 electoral college votes, became a Republican in 1964.

Richard Nixon, sometimes called "the last liberal" for his actual policies, pursued a Southern strategy for election, and continued a transition that made the Republican Party the party of the South.

Now, it's easy to see how paleoconservatives would be attracted to a party that opposed the Civil Rights Act. Many northern Republicans had voted for it, but having Goldwater at the top of the ticket opposing it changed how the party was perceived. But why would Christian Conservatives be attracted to such a party?

Dear reader, you will recall that one thing that happened after the Civil Rights Act passed was integration of public schools. White parents who didn't want their kids in schools with blacks started sending them to a new crop of private schools, colloquially known as "white academies." And many of those were associated with white Evangelical churches. When the nonprofit status of those schools was threatened by a crackdown on those that existed entirely to segregate, those churches became interested in politics, and in limited government.

The libertarian/small government justification for fighting federal efforts to desegregate and put an end to Jim Crow was also attractive to rich people who wanted to pay lower taxes. It was easy enough to demonize government spending if such spending was thought to help Those People, and another group fastened onto the libertarian justification machine like remora on a shark.

Because this is what happens when virtue bestows power. You have to put forward a moral justification for your political movement, and "government is the problem, not the solution" sounded so much better than the 19th century justifications based on race that were no longer acceptable.

Consider an excerpt from the "cornerstone speech" of Alexander Stephens, vice president of the Confederate States of America, in 1861:

> The prevailing ideas entertained by him (Thomas Jefferson) and most of the leading statesmen at the time of the formation of the old constitution, were that the enslavement of the African was in violation of the laws of nature; that it was wrong in principle, socially, morally, and politically. It was an evil they knew not well how to deal with, but the general opinion of the men of that day was that, somehow or other in the order of Providence, the institution would be evanescent and pass away. This idea, though not incorporated in the constitution, was the prevailing idea at that time. The constitution, it is true, secured every essential guarantee to the institution while it should last, and hence no argument can be justly urged against the constitutional guarantees thus secured, because of the common sentiment of the day. Those ideas, however, were fundamentally wrong. They rested upon the assumption of the equality of races. This was an error. It was a sandy foundation, and the government built upon it fell when the "storm came and

the wind blew."

Our new government is founded upon exactly the opposite idea; its foundations are laid, its corner-stone rests upon the great truth, that the negro is not equal to the white man; that slavery – subordination to the superior race – is his natural and normal condition. [Applause.] This, our new government, is the first, in the history of the world, based upon this great physical, philosophical, and moral truth. This truth has been slow in the process of its development, like all other truths in the various departments of science. It has been so even amongst us. Many who hear me, perhaps, can recollect well, that this truth was not generally admitted, even within their day. The errors of the past generation still clung to many as late as twenty years ago. Those at the North, who still cling to these errors, with a zeal above knowledge, we justly denominate fanatics. All fanaticism springs from an aberration of the mind -- from a defect in reasoning. It is a species of insanity. One of the most striking characteristics of insanity, in many instances, is forming correct conclusions from fancied or erroneous premises; so with the anti-slavery fanatics; their conclusions are right if their premises were. They assume that the negro is equal, and hence conclude that he is entitled to equal privileges and rights with the white man. If their premises were correct, their conclusions would be logical and just -- but their premise being wrong, their whole argument fails. I recollect once of having heard a gentleman from one of the northern States, of great power and ability, announce in the House of Representatives, with imposing effect, that we of the South would be compelled, ultimately, to yield upon this subject of slavery, that it was as impossible to war successfully against a principle in politics, as it was in physics or mechanics. That the principle would ultimately prevail.

History can change suddenly, but culture changes slowly. Beliefs such as Stephens voiced did not die with him, they live on, and are part of what many people think of as "right." Those people are now aware that their language and justifications have to change, even as their attitudes remain the same.

Lee Atwater, a Republican political strategist who worked for Ronald Reagan, put it this way in 1981:

You start out in 1954 by saying, "Nigger, nigger, nigger." By 1968 you can't say "nigger"—that hurts you, backfires. So you say stuff like, uh, forced busing, states' rights, and all that stuff, and you're getting so abstract. Now, you're talking about cutting taxes, and all these things you're talking about are totally economic things and a byproduct of them is, blacks get hurt worse than whites.... "We want to cut this," is much more abstract than even the busing thing, uh, and a hell of a lot more abstract than "Nigger, nigger."[*]

The conversation changes, new arguments arise about what is right action, but the old motivation are behind the new justifications. This is the corruption of virtue in the pursuit of power: People who cannot any longer justify the policies they want in honest terms find dishonest ones to make their intentions seem virtuous. One might call it policy laundering; a policy that can no longer be justified by its original moral logic seeks new moral logic to make it seem acceptable.

This is a mask of virtue on the face of an ancient evil, an effort to make a carnival of matters of conscience. But in the end, can they war successfully against a principle of politics? Can the notion that some people aren't worth as much as others because of some feature they cannot control, such as the color of their skin, triumph over the principle that "all men are created equal"?

"The arc of the moral universe is long but it bends toward justice."--
Martin Luther King, Jr.

Chapter 28: The clash within civilizations, between empathy and identity

Talking about virtue brings up the question of why some people kill in the name of religion.

I believe that the answer to this question is bound up in what makes us human, the empathy that gives us our moral sense and the culture that gives us our identity.

Religion gives us a sense of how the world works and of who we are. We define our identity in part by what is included and what is excluded. And while we have an identity as individuals, we are most importantly social creatures. Our identity is bound up in the group we belong to, and is defined, in part, on the groups we exclude.

A psychologist once told me that people need three things to be happy: Someone or something to love, someone or something to hate, and something to belong to. Sometimes this manifests itself in being a fan of a football team and beating up people who are fans of another team. Perhaps we should feel grateful for such petty concerns, because when the thing you belong to is a religion, the battles can get larger.

Religion, for most of the Evangelical Christians I know, is about their relationship with God. But consider the weird world of white supremacists, in which the Christian Identity movement added a whole mythology about race that does not exist in the Bible. They teach that whites are descended from Adam, and that Eve had sex with Satan and conceived Cain. The Bible says nothing about the race of the brothers, and it gives no indication that Eve ever had sex with Satan or conceived a child by him. All the Christians I've known have assumed that they were both fathered by Adam and were obviously of the same race, if such a thing as races existed then.

Yet the mythology of the Christian Identity Church asserts many things that are not in the Bible, but reinforce their belief in themselves as a tribe of the pure, as being better because they are white, even if they are failures as people. Timothy McVeigh, who killed a lot of people when he bombed the Oklahoma City Federal building, was heavily influenced by the Christian Identity movement. It allowed him to think of his victims as somehow less than human, not worthy of his empathy. Their pain and their deaths meant nothing to him.

We could not be social creatures if we did not have a strong instinctive aversion to killing each other.

Human beings have certain safeguards built into them. It's really rather difficult for most people to kill someone, for example. People drive around in powerful wheeled missiles that weigh about as much as a rhinoceros every day, yet most of them manage to get through their day without killing anyone, despite how easy it would be, showing just how kind, considerate and careful people really are. Only recently, terrorists have discovered how much trust we have put into people who drive, and found a way to undermine it.

Our moral sense is based on empathy, our ability to know how others are feeling and identify with their suffering. We can understand the importance of the Golden Rule, to treat others as we wish to be treated, because we have the ability to feel the pain we ourselves inflict. This is why psychopaths are so disturbing – they don't feel the pain they inflict. For most of us, conditioning a person to kill involves a major psychological shift. We have to stop thinking of the person we are killing as human. The means to do this are well established in many cultures. You give the enemy a name -- the Hun, the Commie, the Fuzzy-Wuzzy -- that defines them as different from your group, not quite human. You portray your own side as being on the side of the angels, and pray to God for victory.

Because this is about tribalism, it need not include religion. Portrayals of Germans as "the Hun" in Great War propaganda are as relevant to tribalism as are the Islamic State and Al Qaeda calling American troops "crusaders."

Islamic State's propaganda magazine, *Dabiq*, put it this way: There is "no third camp present: The camp of Islam and faith, and the camp of kufr (disbelief) and hypocrisy — the camp of the Muslims and the mujahideen everywhere, and the camp of the jews, the crusaders, their allies, and with them the rest of the nations and religions of kufr, all being led by America and Russia."

I suppose some in the Arab world are still fighting the Crusades just as some in the American South are still fighting the Civil War. For them, it didn't end with the defeat of the crusaders' Kingdom of Jerusalem in 1291. There was pretty much continuous warfare between Arab and Christian empires for hundreds more years. When the Turks lost the Battle of Lepanto

in 1571, their opponents didn't call themselves crusaders, but they did call
themselves the Holy League. When the expansion of the Ottoman Empire
was stopped at the Battle of Vienna in 1683, it was the culmination of a 300-
year struggle between the Holy Roman Empire and the Ottoman Turks.
While the Reformation resulted in the rise of secular states in the West, the
Ottoman Empire continued to dominate the Arab world until it was dissolved
in 1922, and the impetus for its dissolution came from the West.

This makes it easier to understand why George Washington's
administration negotiated a treaty with the Bey of Algiers that stated that
America is not a Christian nation and has no argument with Muslims. The
language, found in Article 11 of the treaty negotiated under Washington and
approved unanimously by the senate and signed by President John Adams
was as follows:

> As the government of the United States of America is not in any sense founded on the
> Christian Religion, – as it has in itself no character of enmity against the laws, religion
> or tranquility of Musselmen, – and as the said States never have entered into any war or
> act of hostility against any Mehomitan nation, it is declared by the parties that no pretext
> arising from religious opinions shall ever produce an interruption of the harmony
> existing between the two countries.

It may have seemed quaint at the time that the Bey was still worried
about whether America was a Christian nation, and a potential source of
crusaders, but we now have people both in Muslim countries and in America
making exactly the claim that George Washington, John Adams, and the
entire U.S. Senate near the founding of our country rejected -- that America is
a Christian nation.

Osama bin Laden's second fatwa, in 1998, referred to its four signors as
the "World Islamic Front for Jihad Against Jews and Crusaders," and
concerned itself mainly with American activities in the Middle East,
including its support for Israel. Osama bin Laden clearly thought America
was a Christian nation, and opposed its presence in Saudi Arabia for that
reason.

For bin Laden, all Christians were Crusaders, and although secular
states allow people to follow their own religious conscience, only states that
do not do this – states that dictate only Islam is the true religion – were
legitimate. He was worried about the Muslim world being seduced by
Western ways. For him, religion was not just a personal relationship with
God, it defined who were true people, and who were false people. Religion

for him was a tribal marker, not personal salvation.

The problem was how to convince people in his own world of this. He hoped to accomplish this by coordinating a horrendous act – attacks in the United States on the World Trade Center, the Pentagon, and the (failed) attack on the nation's capital – in hopes of provoking a response that would put American troops in Arab nations, and start a war between those nations and America.

This is not too different from Timothy McVeigh's notion that by blowing up the Alfred P. Murrah federal building in Oklahoma City in 1995, killing 168 people and injuring another 880, he could start the sort of race war depicted in *The Turner Diaries*, a novel written by a former leader of the National Alliance, a white nationalist organization. The book, which McVeigh sold at gun shows and sometimes gave away, depicted the overthrow of the U.S. government and ultimately the extermination of Jews, homosexuals, non-whites, and others the author deemed impure.

The objectification of government workers as the enemy enabled McVeigh to suspend any empathy he may have possessed and kill them in large numbers. For bin Laden, the issue was not even that some of the people working in the World Trade Center were Muslim, their association with a global system of commerce dominated by the "crusaders" of the western nations made them less then human, *things* that could be sacrificed to the goal of a conflict between the groups as he defined them.

The lesson I take from this is to make sure we do not suspend our empathy, or make objects of those we must deal with. In World War II, military planners were distressed to find that only about 20% of our troops were actually engaged in shooting at the enemy during battles. By Viet Nam, pretty much all the troops involved were shooting at the enemy, in part because of changes the military made in training.

But consider this. After the battle of Gettysburg, out of 37,000 muskets recovered from the battlefield, about a third contained more than one load.[*] Given the usual cycle of firing a musket, very little of the time would a musket be loaded, and very seldom would someone put more than one load in by mistake. But if you were in a line of infantry with muzzle loaders, everyone could tell if you were loading, but when the guns went off, who could tell if you were firing? Furthermore, who could tell if you were firing high? And when you compare the number of people killed in battles between lines of infantry to the results of lines of infantry firing against non-human targets, it becomes evident that many must have deliberately aimed not to hit their targets.

One would think that such desertions in place would make an army ineffective. But German WW I veterans advised the next generation fighting in WW II to, "Do your duty and surrender to the first American you see," as Kevin Grossman noted in his book, *On Killing*. U.S. Grant's troops may have hesitated to kill their opponents, but he took more prisoners than any other general in the war. Part of this was because he preferred to cut off the enemy rather than annihilate them, but part of this was because the prospective prisoners were more likely to surrender to an army that thought of them as human.

We should also not allow ourselves to be defined by our enemies. Those in my country who wish to define us as a "Christian nation" may not realize it, but they are dupes acting just as the radical Islamists want them to. We do not win by adopting this tribal view of religion as identity, because those are not the values on which this country was founded, and they are not the difference we have from past civilizations. The difference is that we allow freedom, so that people can worship as they wish without the law dictating their faith to them. We win when we recognize other human beings as human beings.

Chapter 29: Ideology, identity politics, and ethnic panic

The unfortunately named Carl T. Bogus wrote a July 18, 2011 article in interview form for the National Review titled *A Liberal Reads the Great Conservative Works.*

The most cogent observation he made was that conservatives talk more about ideology than do liberals:

> One striking difference is that the iconic conservative works are about ideology. By contrast, the most influential liberal books of the era are about policy issues. Those works are *Silent Spring* by Rachel Carson (1962), *The Other America* by Michael Harrington (1962), *The Feminine Mystique* by Betty Friedan (1963), and *Unsafe at Any Speed* by Ralph Nader (1965), which helped launch the environmental, anti-poverty, feminist, and consumer movements, respectively.

Bogus is largely right about the different taxonomies of conservative ideology:

> Conservatives have big appetites for ideology; liberals don't. There are, of course, taxonomies of conservative schools of thought. People on the right classify themselves as libertarians, neoconservatives, social conservatives, traditional conservatives, and the like, and spill oceans of ink defining, debating, and further subdividing these schools of thought. There is no parallel taxonomy on the left. Maybe, in part, it is because a central tenet of liberalism is that ideology should be eschewed in favor of the supposedly enlightened, pragmatic approach of making ad hoc judgments about issues.

Certainly the pragmatism of liberals was on display during the Obama administration, as President Obama adopted the Republican plan for healthcare reform, as developed by the Heritage Foundation and put into Massachusetts law by Mitt Romney, only to have Republicans dub it "socialism."

But if Republicans are all about ideology, why do they object to their own ideas once they are adopted by Democrats? Surely, their ideology has policy consequences, and the policy still passes conservative muster even when the opposing party adopts it.

Ezra Klein, writing in the Washington Post on Nov. 11, 2011, offered two readings of this. One was that partisanship and motivated skepticism are

the reasons. I would agree that partisanship is the reason motivated
skepticism (sometimes called blowback) comes into play.

He added:

> But a more generous interpretation is that because conservatives are more
> concerned with philosophy, they see the motivations of the legislators as much more
> important than liberals do.
>
> So when liberals celebrate a liberal policy proposal coming from a conservative
> president — note the Democrats who joined with President Bush on No Child Left
> Behind and, until the conference committee shenanigans, Medicare Part D — it's
> because their analysis is focused on the proposal. If the proposal lines up with their
> ideas, they support it. When conservatives turn on a onetime conservative proposal
> that's been embraced by a more liberal president, it's because they're looking behind the
> policy to the philosophies of whoever is championing it. For them to feel comfortable
> supporting it, the philosophy of whoever is proposing it has to line up with their
> philosophy, too.

Frankly, this makes no sense to me. An idea is an idea regardless of
who espouses it. If you object to who is supporting it, the problem is identity.

One of the seminal thinkers of conservatism is Edmund Burke, who
provides a better explanation. In Reflections on the French Revolution, Burke
said:

> You see, Sir, that in this enlightened age I am bold enough to confess, that we are
> generally men of untaught feelings; that instead of casting away all our old prejudices,
> we cherish them to a very considerable degree, and, to take more shame to ourselves, we
> cherish them because they are prejudices; and the longer they have lasted, and the more
> generally they have prevailed, the more we cherish them. We are afraid to put men to
> live and trade each on his own private stock of reason; because we suspect that this stock
> in each man is small, and that the individuals would do better to avail themselves of the
> general bank and capital of nations and of ages. Many of our men of speculation, instead
> of exploding general prejudices, employ their sagacity to discover the latent wisdom
> which prevails in them. If they find what they seek, and they seldom fail, they think it
> more wise to continue the prejudice, with the reason involved, than to cast away the coat
> of prejudice, and to leave nothing but the naked reason; because prejudice, with its
> reason, has a motive to give action to that reason, and an affection which will give it
> permanence. Prejudice is of ready application in the emergency; it previously engages
> the mind in a steady course of wisdom and virtue, and does not leave the man hesitating
> in the moment of decision, sceptical, puzzled, and unresolved. Prejudice renders a man's
> virtue his habit; and not a series of unconnected acts. Through just prejudice, his duty
> becomes a part of his nature.

One seldom sees such a defense of prejudice. And I must confess, the
example of the Utopian projects of the 20th century, such as the communist
and fascist regimes that slaughtered millions, give some credence to the

notion that we should not trust "naked reason." But Burke was pragmatic, and some would say a conservative liberal, which in our modern political world seems like an oxymoron, but remember that Frederich Hayek called himself a liberal as well. Burke did not cast out reason, and I'm quite confident that he would not advise, for example, ignoring the conclusions of the scientific establishment on global warming.

The modern conservative movement can abandon its previously held policy positions because it has cast out reason, and indulged itself in prejudice. This is why the conservative movement has become decadent.

A policy that was conservative when Republicans promoted it does not become "socialist" because of ideology, it becomes "socialist" because of what Burke would have termed "prejudice."

The original sin here falls on President Nixon. In his 1968 election campaign, he set out deliberately to divide the country, based on the idea that such divisions would benefit Nixon. In a famous memo to Nixon, one of his aides, Pat Buchanan, wrote that the Republican tactics should include:

> Bumper stickers calling for black Presidential and especially Vice-Presidential candidates should be spread out in the ghettoes of the country," Buchanan wrote. "We should do what is within our power to have a black nominated for Number Two, at least at the Democratic National Convention." Such gambits, he added, could "cut the Democratic Party and country in half; my view is that we would have far the larger half.
> [*]

Nixon was not, by modern standards, a conservative. He used price controls, expanded the welfare state, and took the troops out of Viet Nam. He ran in 1968 as a peace candidate.[*] On a more subtle level, Nixon ran as someone who would stand up for the prejudices of the constituency he was pursuing.

Nixon's chance came because the 1964 Civil Rights Act and the 1965 Voting Rights Act offended the prejudices of Southern Democrats. Although both bills passed with bipartisan support, they did not pass with Dixiecrat support. And in the presidential election of 1964, the conservative flag-bearer, Barry Goldwater, opposed the Civil Rights Act on libertarian grounds. This paved the way for many former Dixiecrats to switch to the Republican Party and bring their constituents with them.

In one way, rank racial prejudice was driving this, but on another level the sort of prejudice Burke was speaking of, the collective wisdom of the culture, was also operating. The anti-war protesters were responsible for ending Lyndon Johnson's hopes of re-election, and Nixon ran as a peace candidate. But Nixon set himself rhetorically against the damned hippies of the peace movement and on the side of the military. One of the more deeply ingrained "prejudices" (in Burke's sense) of the American people is an abiding respect for the military.

Nixon wasn't just appealing to blue-collar whites based on racial prejudice: If he had been, he would not have won the election. He was also running on the more respectable emotions of loyalty to country and respect for law and order, and applying his greatest skill, the ability to exploit hatred, resentment, and fear. His message to whites was not merely that the racial order was being upset, but that their entire way of life was under threat. That message is now usually understood as the culture war.

Very few people regard themselves as racist, but Nixon could appeal to the buried attitudes and fears of the voters. Dog-whistles about race might not even be heard by the voters he appealed to, operating below the level of conscious self-image.

The Nixon model for winning elections has proven durable, and remains the default setting for Republican politics. This is why ideology does not lead to consistent policy positions. The great works of conservatism may be ideological. On an intellectual level conservatives may indulge a rich taxonomy of ideologies. But when it comes to winning elections, all is subsumed by the culture war. That is why Nixon, known in political science circles as "the last liberal" president, is a conservative icon, regardless of his actual policies. He pushed the right culture war buttons, and that is what makes him, by the standards of conservatives, worthy of being called a conservative, despite the ideological gulf between him and modern conservatives. The intellectual underpinnings of modern conservatism may look ideological, but the success of modern conservatism is the result of the ethnic panic of certain whites.

There is a term of art in psychology, "homosexual panic," in which a person fears he may give in to homosexual urges and finds himself acting in an excessively macho manner, attempting to avoid a change to a homosexual identity (this has even been used as a defense for the murder of homosexuals.) Ethnic panic, as I conceive it, works in a similar manner, with people panicking because their country is changing its ethnic identity.

The Democratic coalition is composed of diverse America and those whites comfortable with diverse America. At some point in the not-too-distant future, whites will cease to be a majority in this country. At that point, for those whose conception of what it is to be an American is based on a sort of tribal and racial identity, what it means to be an American will change, as it has already begun to change. For those whose conception of what it is to be an American is not based on ethnic fault lines, what it means to be an American will not change. That is what separates the Republican and Democratic coalitions.

Chapter 30: Rights and wrongs in the incarceration

nation

One of the great disasters of the American experiment was the prohibition of selling alcohol. Making alcohol illegal simply made large numbers of people into criminals, and gave career criminals a steady source of income. Chicago gangster Al Capone would have been a criminal without prohibition, but he would not have been as rich or as powerful.

In the Pacific Northwest, rum running was controlled by a former policeman named Roy Olmstead. Unlike Capone, Olmstead never allowed his men to carry guns. It was much better for business to have his rivals arrested by the police on his orders than to have them attract a lot of attention by killing his rivals.

Olmstead had so many politicians and police in his pocket he thought he was untouchable. He was brought down, in the end, by the then-new technology of wiretapping. Olmstead got a four-year sentence and an $8,000 fine, but he spent a substantial portion of his ill-gotten gains fighting for the principle that it was unconstitutional to wiretap without a warrant. In 1928, the U.S. Supreme Court ruled against him. The decision was overturned the year after his 1966 death, so that now, a warrant is required. But this was the beginning of the intrusive enforcement of the drug wars.

Alcohol prohibition ended in 1933, but it was only part of a larger effort to make all recreational drugs illegal. Many states made marijuana and other drugs illegal between 1900 and the end of Prohibition, and the United States led an international effort to make all opium, coca, and cannabis cultivation, production, transport and sale illegal. By 1937, the effort had largely succeeded.

Alcohol was the favorite drug of most Americans at the time. Germans felt particularly oppressed by prohibition, because beer was such an important part of their culture. Cannabis is commonly referred to by its Spanish name, marijuana. It was a drug favored by American Hispanics. Opium and cocaine were favored, for the most part, by lower-class people who found they could become euphoric at a lower cost with these drugs.

The German immigrants thought Prohibition was in some ways an effort to make their culture illegal. Prohibition of other drugs that appealed to other subgroups was, to some extent, defining those groups as outsiders. And so, when those drugs were made illegal and the same sort of intrusive policing was applied to these groups, it did not worry most Americans, because those practices did not apply to them. Only after marijuana became widely used by middle-class whites did we see a movement to make marijuana legal.

From a practical standpoint, the war on drugs has been a disaster. It has been costly, it has ruined lives, and it has enriched criminals. It has also changed the way the nation is policed.

When there is a great deal of money to be made in doing something illegal, people will take that risk. But illegal activities are not policed the way legal commerce is. I once knew a former smuggler who said he dropped out of the trade when everyone started carrying guns. I also met his former skipper, before and after that individual did time for getting caught with 2,500 lb of marijuana on his boat. (He was caught before I met him.)

When an illegal trade turns violent, this increases the risk of enforcing the law. The result has been a more militarized police force, more likely to break down doors and throw stun grenades, and more likely to fear for their lives and use deadly force as a result.

It has also led to some bad laws. For example, civil forfeiture, a process where police can seize vehicles or cash on the mere assumption that they were involved in the drug trade, which has resulted in some fairly questionable practices that have enriched police budgets. Funds from the seizures can be used for salaries, retirement funds, overtime, and a variety of other police spending priorities. Because it is a civil proceeding, no criminal conviction is required in most states, nor even a criminal charge against the person the property is seized from. In fact, in civil forfeiture, the agency seizing the property takes action against the inanimate object being seized.

Once they have alleged the inanimate object has taken part in a crime, prosecutors file a claim with a title such as *The People vs. $10,000*, and institute a civil action that lacks many of the protections of a criminal case. In the case of criminal forfeiture, the prosecutor would have to prove that the property being seized was the fruit of a criminal act or acts. In civil forfeiture, the burden is on the person whose property was seized, and in some cases if they challenge a forfeiture and lose, they must also pay the state's costs for defending the case.

For most of the history of the United States, civil forfeitures were rare, and used primarily when it was impossible to arrest the owner of the property. Use of civil forfeiture exploded during the 1980s as government at all levels ramped up its war on drugs. Even when the owner is present and could easily be prosecuted if there were proof of a crime, civil forfeiture is used to gain funds for police departments.

Seized property was worth $2.5 billion in 2010.[*]

This has effectively become a back door for circumventing the Bill of Rights, in particular the 4th Amendment, which reads:

> The right of the people to be secure in their persons, houses, papers, and effects, against unreasonable searches and seizures, shall not be violated, and no Warrants shall issue, but upon probable cause, supported by Oath or affirmation, and particularly describing the place to be searched, and the persons or things to be seized.

There are jurisdictions in this country where people cannot be secure in their effects, because a traffic stop can result in the seizure of their car and their cash. No evidence of criminal behavior need be present, only property that is sufficiently tempting, such as plenty of cash. Stops in many jurisdictions tend to disproportionately target African Americans and Hispanics.

It is pretty obvious that civil forfeiture provides incentives for police to seize property regardless of the likelihood it was the fruit of a crime. But this is only one of the corrupting influences on police departments from the war on drugs. Any quick on-line search will find fairly recent instances of police being indicted for stealing from drug dealers, because who are they going to call to report the crime?

I have seen the damage drugs can do. I am not an advocate of their use. But we did not get rid of prohibition because we thought alcohol did no harm, we did so because prohibition did more harm, eroding our liberties, enriching criminals, and corrupting our legal system. Now we deal with much of the harm alcohol does as a public health problem, and some of it in connection with specific harmful behaviors such as drunk driving.

How we are to deal with the problems created by drug use is not the purpose of this essay; I am more concerned here with how the drug war erodes our liberty. And it certainly is not the only threat. The war on terrorism has had a similar effect. And both are tied to cultural outsiders. We made illegal the drugs mainly used by minorities while re-legalizing alcohol, which was the drug of choice for most whites.

Terror again touched the tribal nerve. Conservatives who were in the forefront of advocating a war on terror that would target Muslim militants were outraged in 2009 when the Homeland Security Department issued a report on the threat of domestic terrorism by right-wing militants. The report said the threat was not restricted to hate groups, but said, "It may include groups and individuals that are dedicated to a single-issue, such as opposition to abortion or immigration."

Nothing shocking there. After all, Eric Rudolph, an anti-abortion activist, confessed to four bombings, including the one at the Atlanta Olympics that killed a bystander and wounded 111 people. But the very notion that people on the right who set off bombs and killed people, yet who were white, Christian, and conservative could be classed with Muslim militants because of the similarity of their acts was offensive to those on the right.

This reveals the tribalist element of their emotional reactions. After all, it is often those who worry most about Shariah law that insist that America is a Christian nation, and that its laws are based on Christianity. For such people, it is not merely the behavior, but the identity as well, that matters in defining the enemy.

War is the enemy of freedom, because it causes frightened people to accept extreme measures. And war, all too often, brings out our tribalism and our prejudice against the groups we fight against. It is therefore terrible policy to have a "war" that cannot be won. Drugs will continue to exist and be abused no matter how we make war on it, because who is going to surrender? The drugs? Terrorism is a tactic, not a person, group, or government. It, too, lacks the capacity to surrender.

The U.S. crime rate climbed from the 1960 until the early 1990s, and has declined since. (This also happened in Canada and the United Kingdom, which did not increase their incarceration rate.) One response to that climb was that public officials came to feel pressure to do something about it. One result was that we passed some fairly draconian laws with long prison terms. Another was that prosecutors started charging the maximum they could, and tried to get the maximum sentence. Although crime peaked in about 1991, prison populations continued to climb. At this point, the United States has 5% of the world population, and 25% of the world's incarcerated population. While the probability that a prosecutor would seek the maximum sentence in the 1970s had been one in three, it is now more like two in three, according to John Pfaff, a professor at Fordham Law School, who also observes that,

"Defendants who they would not have filed felony charges against before, they now are charging with felonies."

That would be great if prison terms had the effect of making people who go to them less likely to commit more crimes, but the opposite seems to be the case. To explain why that is, I've written another Likely Story sidebar:

If we trained dogs using the corrections system we have for humans

If we used our corrections system to train dogs, what would be the result?

Consider Jane Doe. She discovers a "gift" from one of her dogs on the bathroom rug. The prime suspects are Spot and Rover.

She dials 911. Since no life is immediately at risk, it takes a couple hours before Officer McGruff arrives. He Mirandizes the dogs, and both put their tails between their legs and dummy up.

McGruff processes the physical evidence and sends a sample off for DNA testing. This takes three weeks, and implicates Spot.

Spot is arrested, booked, and makes bail. Two days later, another "gift" appears on the bathroom rug. Jane, by now fed up with the system, doesn't call this one in, but cleans up the mess and takes Spot and Rover for a walk.

The public defender assigned to Spot has 50 other dogs to represent, so he puts in for a continuance. Three months pass before the trial, and the evidence is damning, which hardly matters, because Spot's lawyer falls asleep during the proceedings.

The judge, who has a great deal of experience in this sort of thing, believes that the best outcome would be if Jane had scolded Spot and, more importantly, got off her butt and took him for a walk before he became desperate. But a public that has lost its patience with Bad Dogs has passed a ballot initiative prescribing a mandatory sentence of six months at the pound. The pound is run by a private dog pound company, which hired signature gatherers to put the Bad Dog initiative on the ballot, and the dog pound employees' union ran advertisements in support of the ballot initiative, helping pass it. Both have an interest in imprisoning as many dogs as possible.

So Spot gets six months, which is 42 months in dog years. His new cell mate, Bowser, has been in and out of the pound all his life. Bowser tends to pee wherever he's standing when he gets excited, hump anything available, and gets in dog fights on a regular basis. He does, however, teach Spot what he needs to know to survive inside – join a pack and learn your place in it, bark without moving your jaw, be ready to fight dogs from other packs at any time.

After two months (14 months in dog years) Spot is eligible for parole. The pound gives him back his collar, sets him outside and tells him he must find a family and must stay in touch with his parole officer.

Not many families want a dog with a history in the pound, nicks in his ears, and a prison tattoo the pack made him get before they would protect him from other packs. He doesn't find a family, and falls into bad company with some dogs Bowser told him to look up if he needs help. They run feral, chase cats, raid chicken coops and poop wherever they please.

Spot's parole officer knows he hasn't checked in, but he's got 128 clients to keep track of and he can't devote much time to tracking down the ones that don't check in. The system doesn't do anything about Spot until he's caught acting as a lookout for a dog who is stealing liver from a butcher shop.

Back to the pound, more education in Bad Dog culture. By this time, Spot has learned that he's a loser, a Bad Dog, that his enemy is The Man, and he knows he'll go feral as soon as he gets out. It's become the life he knows.

Which raises an interesting point. Would our corrections system work better if it was run by dog trainers?

Chapter 31: Language and the social contract

One of the most insightful aspects of George Orwell's *1984* was the attempt to control what people could think by changing the language from "oldspeak" – current English – to "newspeak," in which the number of words is limited in order to limit what people can think.

One of the key concepts of newspeak is doublethink, the ability to believe two contradictory things at the same time, which helps with reality control. One does not want to commit crimethought, that is, thinking things that the Party says are not true. It helps if one has mastered blackwhite, that is, the ability to believe black is white and white is black if that is the policy of the party.

Words give us the categories with which we think. They provide a structure of symbols that we can put together in whatever manner suits our needs. We can embellish the structure by inventing new words or new meanings for existing words. In many ways, we experience our freedom of thought through language.

Orwell perceived that control of language was control of thought.

Now, natural language is not like computer language. It is less logical, its meanings are less clear, and those meanings are constantly being renegotiated. We who speak languages are not dictionaries that, once printed, never change. We have, in fact, a dual nature, part animal and physical, part symbolic, and symbolic thought is one of the distinguishing characteristics of human society. Language is essential for the very existence of this part of human nature.

Natural language is a social construct. The meanings are not the sounds we make to communicate the meanings, those sounds or symbols are arbitrary. It does not matter if I use the English word, water, or the French word, eau, as long as both the speaker and the person the speaker wishes to communicate with know that the word signifies stuff we like so well we have it piped right into the house. For both to know what meaning the sound of a word communicates, there must be social agreement on this meaning.

To my way of thinking, this is the point where the original social contract is made, the point where we negotiate meaning. The fact that the sound of words is arbitrary, and their connection to meanings socially agreed, seems proof to me that this is where human society is constructed. Our symbolic world exists in language, and in ideas. It is in the negotiation of meanings and ideas that the social contract is made. From the basis in language, the contract evolves through culture and beliefs. A shared language and shared religion help define a people. Eventually, a shared religion can become more important than a shared language. But religions evolve over a long period of time, so how do we define a people and still have the flexibility to deal with rapid change?

The genius of liberalism is to see the social contract for what it is, so that we can write the contract to suit our needs. Recall that the ancient Egyptians developed a civilization which allowed them to perpetuate their mythology regardless of whether there was really a dog-headed god or the rest of their pantheon. Language gave us the capacity to build a larger society than a non-linguistic pack, and religion helped build empires. Language, religion, and ethnicity are sufficient to build the mythopoetic state, where custom and authority are integrated with a mythology that doesn't have to make sense, it only has to work. Rapid change exposes the weakness of these slowly constructed, rigid civilizations. What is needed then is a well-thought-out, logical social construct. The modern state cannot be the ethno-religious or mythopoetic state, even if it is an outgrowth of such a civiliazation.

We have then, at least three levels of social contract. The first is the mythopoetic state, in which all authority springs from religion, actions are mainly dictated by custom, often encapsulated in mythology. The second is the ethno-religious state, in which the legitimacy of the state still rests on religion, but there is greater flexibility and a more discernible difference between the authority of the state and that of religion. Although the Greek golden age saw a lot of experimentation in forms of government and a greater reliance on reason, Socrates was killed after being found guilty of a charge of impiety, something we might expect of a theocratic state. The third level is the secular state, either separated by law from religion in an effort to defend freedom of conscience, or, as in Soviet and Maoist Communism, by outlawing religion altogether.

When rapid change came in the late bronze-age collapse, the patterns they had established no longer worked. In the modern, rapidly-changing world, we need a social contract that allows us to redefine ourselves and our society as we adapt to changes.

This means that the modern social contract can only remain valid as long as we retain freedom of speech and of conscience, because only then can we participate in the shaping of the meaning of our lives. Knowing this allows us to travel beyond the tribalism of language and religion, and form political contracts that can unite speakers of different languages and religions based on the needs for freedom of speech and conscience.

Every act of communication is a social act. One person speaks to another, or a group of others, hoping to influence them in some way. They may use language to enlighten, persuade, or deceive. In so doing, they may use words in new and unfamiliar ways, changing the meaning and connotations of the word. The connotations of a word, that is, the feelings or associated ideas it evokes, are as important sometimes as the literal meaning of the word.

Every generation encounters language anew, every new person finds a place in the strange, symbolic world of human society. We have one existence in our animal nature, our mates and offspring, but we are so much more than that. Much of what we are is tied to symbolic thought. Our possessions are ruled by a structure of customs and rules that we call property, our contributions to society are often manipulations of symbols such as our writings, drawings, or made objects. We worry about what we represent. Presidents worry about their legacy, but so do parents and businessmen. Even those who do not physically reproduce live on in their accomplishments, their influence, how they have touched the lives of other people.

This is why the first item in the Bill of Rights concerns the freedom of speech and of conscience. If we are not free to think and speak, and do so in a way that influences other people, we lack the power to shape our lives.

Orwell wrote *1984* after a stint at the British Broadcasting System during World War II. In wartime, propaganda is one of the weapons deployed. Orwell was very aware of this. But even in peacetime, language is used as a political tool.

Consider the issue of political correctness. At its best, it is an attempt to shame those who use language to hurt others. It is now more socially acceptable to say "fuck" than to say "nigger," because our society now is more sensitive to the harm of racism than to any perceived need to conceal the existence of sex.

At its worst, political correctness can seem like annoying nagging about ordinary words. Political correctness is for some reason mainly associated with the left in the United States, but try saying "happy holidays" to a conservative at Christmas and you'll quickly learn that there is political correctness on both sides of the political spectrum.

Lies, concealment, and shading the truth all happen. There is an entire book titled *On Bullshit*, by philosophy professor Harry Frankfurt, which explores the political world in which the truth is treated as irrelevant. For example (this is not from Frankfurt's book) in a 2004 debate, President George W. Bush was asked for a rationale for the Iraq war: He responded, "we had to fight, we were attacked."

He said this as if we had been attacked by Iraq, which was not the case. Every word in that sentence could be true, but the message communicated was false. No true part of that statement justified attacking Iraq.

Truth had been under attack for decades by then, though. Agnotology. the science of creating ignorance, was first perfected by the tobacco companies.

These companies had reason both to affect public policy and to persuade their customers to keep smoking. They deployed polices such as advertising with the healthy, outdoorsy, Marlborough man, hiring scientists to show that substances other than tobacco can cause cancer, and generally sowing doubt about the veracity and the certainty of science.

The word agnotology was coined in 2001 by Robert N. Proctor, a Stanford University professor specializing in the history of science and technology. The idea applies to deliberate efforts to create doubt about science, such as the tobacco company pushback on cancer research, and the unintended consequences of concealing information for other purposes, like the military's classification of research that would have confirmed plate tectonics about a decade sooner than actually occurred.

In 2003, Proctor organized the first conference on the topic, titled *Agnatology: The Cultural Production of Ignorance*, held at Pennsylvania State University.

Proctor and others propose that the flood of knowledge now available may not be creating a more knowledgeable citizenry. When people are overwhelmed by the quantity of information available, they have to look to elites to select which information they need to know. Our increasingly polarized society produces a situation where different groups pick different elites. Those who watch Fox News will be presented with quite different information than those who watch MSNBC, and those who (horrors!) do not watch television may get their information from blogs with names like Red

State (conservative) or Conscience of a Liberal (I think you can figure that one out).

The result is that different groups are judging what is true from different sets of information, often cherry-picked to lead to the conclusion the source wants the viewer/reader to come to. The problem here is not just the flood of information, it is a deeper one involving the splintering of our society and the splintering of which elites different groups choose to regard as legitimate.

In a court of law, a case may be thrown out if the prosecutor is found to have concealed exculpatory information. In the court of public opinion, no such rule applies. As a result, manipulation of information, even outright lies, can be rewarded. If an elite trusted by a large part of the population (I'm looking at you, Fox News) won't report that the politicians it favors have lied, those politicians won't mend their ways. If exculpatory information is concealed (nope, no death panels in this here health care bill) the lie will win the day.

This will only happen if a powerful group takes the Leninist position that the intellectual vanguard must be willing to mislead the masses to guide them to the proper action. I knew people like that in graduate school, where they tended to be Marxists. Now we have recovering Marxists like David Horowitz who are conservatives, and we see some of the methods of the old "new left" adopted by the new right.

Ferdinand de Saussure, the father of modern linguistics, believed that words give us the categories we use in symbolic thought. Steven Pinker even titled a book about language *The Stuff of Thought*. Perhaps now that we have a word for it, we can think more carefully about the practice of agnotology. We should, because that practice has become very sophisticated.

In the political sphere, language gets tested on focus groups. Political consultant Frank Luntz, using this method, discovered that "death tax" got a far more negative response than "inheritance tax," and the word went out that those wishing to end the inheritance tax should call it the death tax instead.

While acting as a pollster for Speaker of the House Newt Gingrich in the mid-1990s, Lutz urged Republicans to refer to their Democratic opponents using words such as "devour," "corrupt," "sick," "greedy," "liberal," and "traitor."

This project succeeded in devaluing the word "liberal" to the point where fewer people identify themselves with it today than did so before the change in language came. Liberals now routinely call themselves "progressive."

Clearly, the part of human nature that belongs to the world of symbolic thought fights its battles on the ground of speech. So why is the basic theory behind the structure of our society so thoroughly tied up with property?

I think it is because the power of language was not fully understood in the 17th century when the foundations of liberalism were laid. Property and speech are quite intimately linked in at least one case, the existence of a free press. Ownership patterns can provide some powerful incentives for bias or impartiality.

Chapter 32: Reality, truth, and facts, versus the will to power

Some on the right seem to regard reality as a mere inconvenience. Donald Trump supporter and CNN commentator Scottie Nell Hughes went so far as to assert that "There's no such thing, unfortunately, anymore, as facts."

It would be interesting to know when there ceased to be facts. Was it during George W. Bush's first term, when an administration official (almost certainly Karl Rove) claimed that, "We create or own reality?" Certainly Republicans had a history long before that of acting as if facts were irrelevant. They have continued to assert that lowering taxes increases tax revenue long after that was shown to be untrue.

Now, there is a philosophical position that "truth" is impossible. In *The Will To Power*, Friedrich Nietzsche asserted as much:

> Against [empiricism], which halts at [observable] phenomena—'There are only facts'—I would say, no, facts is precisely what there is not, only interpretations. We cannot establish any fact 'in itself': perhaps it is folly to want to do such a thing.

> 'Everything is subjective [for example, a figment of your reasoning mind],' you say; but even this is interpretation. The 'subject' is not something given, it is something added and invented ... [Is] it necessary to posit an interpreter behind the interpretation? ...

> In so far as the word 'knowledge' has any meaning, the world is ... interpretable, otherwise it has no meaning behind it, but countless meanings—'Perspectivism'.

> It is our needs that interpret the world; our drives.... Every drive is a kind of list to rule; each one has its perspective that it would like to compel all the other drives to accept as a norm.

Nor is this rather malleable notion of the truth new to the right. German fascism did not consider even science to be capable of objective truth. Each nation had a science natural to them, they maintained, and any science that claimed to be universal was "Jewish" and false. The "science" of racial hygiene was far more acceptable than any science that claimed to be universal.

Nietzsche scholars will object to this link with fascism because the fascists and Nazis relied on a bad reading of Nietzsche. This is incomplete. In the case of *The Will to Power*, it is a bad reading of bad Nietzsche. The book was assembled after Nietzsche's death by his sister, Elisabeth Förster-Nietzsche, an anti-Semite who became a Nazi pretty much as soon as that option became available. Nietzsche had no use for mass movements or nations based on ethnicity, so those who wish to use his work to justify mass movements based on ethnicity are fond of bad readings of his sister's bad readings of his work.

Their error about truth is therefore their own.

I believe the source of the error here is a failure to understand the relationship between reality, facts, and truth.

Truth is a species of belief. It is a word we use in ordinary language to describe that which we believe without question. Reality is what is there whether we believe it or not. Suppose it is winter, and the thermometer in the room I occupy reads 63 degrees Fahrenheit. That is a simple, observable fact. I know that the thermometer in question is not the most precise, but I can report what it says without fear that my interpretation has contaminated the reading, and I can be certain that it accords to a reasonable degree with reality.

Now, lest you think I have taken the statement from Hughes out of context, or that I'm being pedantic about "facts," here is her statement in context. As a call-in guest on the Diane Rheme show, she was asked what she thought about some fact-checking that showed much of what Donald Trump tweets is lies:

> "On one hand, I hear half the media saying that these are lies. But on the other half, there are many people that go 'No it's true,'" Hughes said. "And so one thing that has been interesting this entire campaign season to watch, is that people who say 'facts are facts,'— they're not really facts."
>
> "Everybody has a way—It's kind of like looking at ratings, or looking at a glass of half-full water. Everybody has a way of interpreting them to be the truth or not true. There's no such thing, unfortunately, anymore, as facts," she added.

I think here we see the basic problem between those of us in what Rove termed the "reality-based community" and those in the conservative bubble. We think there are facts – observable, objective representations of reality – while Hughes and her ilk think there is only opinion.

Given the definition of "truth" I've given above, it should be clear that I think it is possible for people to maintain that something is "true" – that they

believe it without question – while not being in accord with the facts –
objective representations of reality. Hughes seems to mean that if people
claiming a thing is true actually believe that, and are not lying, that is as good
as having a belief that aligns with observable reality.

The rather muddled thinking Hughes displayed was based on a
misconception. She seemed to be saying, there is no objective truth because
all is subjective. If people say they believe something without question, that
makes it true.

But what if truth is a social construct? Does that make it less real or
important?

Consider the concept of property. Objects in the world exist whether
they are owned or not. Property is a social construct, a concept about how
people are related to things they wish to possess. It allows society to form
customs and institutions that reduce conflict about who gets to use what, and
to regulate the desire to possess. We would not say, "There's no such thing,
unfortunately, anymore, as property," simply because it is a human construct
or because people disagree about the ownership of something.

Truth can be looked at in the same way. When we used the term in
ordinary language, it means something we believe without question, but we
know that people sometimes believe things for reasons other than their
relationship to reality. The concept of truth is about this correspondence
between reality.

The world exists, and events occur, whether we know of them or not,
just as objects exist whether we own them or not. Truth is a concept that
allows us to build customs and institutions that regulate our desire to know
things, and to share that knowledge. When we speak the truth, we are making
a claim that we have made a good-faith effort to ascertain the facts, and that
we are making a good-faith effort to communicate what we have learned.
Reading a thermometer, for example, is a physical interaction with reality
that can be replicated by anyone who doubts my perception.

We all know how to lie. It is one of those useful social skills that can
save us from conflict or help us get what we want. There are those who think,
because we sometimes have difficulty knowing truth, there is really no such
thing, in which case all language is about power and persuasion, and none is
about truth.

Ms. Hughes was making a claim about facts that is fatuous at best and
bad faith at worst. Her claim is that because many people believe something,

it is true, even though they may believe something said in bad faith by a fabulist with only the most tenuous grasp of truth himself. But strangely enough, people may "believe" something for reasons having nothing to do with truth. Some beliefs become tribal markers. People on the far right tend not to believe in anthropomorphic climate change, regardless of the evidence presented, not because they are sincerely trying to understand what is happening in the physical world, but because in their own social milieu, such a belief is necessary for social acceptance.

Perversely, the more peculiar a belief is, the more effective a tribal marker it can be. To believe President Barack Obama was born outside the United States even after all the evidence of his birth in Hawaii had been presented was to show yourself to be part of a certain group, known as birthers.

But this belief is not based on a good-faith effort to ascertain the facts. It is a belief held in the face of contradictory evidence and in spite of it. People may assert that they believe it without question, but what is lacking is the good-faith effort to align their belief with the known facts. This is a belief that defies facts in the service of a cause: For holders of this belief, Mr. Obama could not be a legitimate president, therefore he had to be in some way disqualified from being a legitimate president. The birther belief system is not about truth, it is about power. It is no surprise that one of its adherents came into the presidency intent on destroying any legacy that may have stemmed from the two terms of our first African-American president.

This is one instance of the astonishing fact that the lies people believe together can be stronger than the truth we know alone, because it can lead to collective action.

Donald Trump first came to political prominence as a birther. It should therefore be no surprise that his strongest adherents are people who would prefer that there should be no such thing as facts, because they get in the way of using language in the service of power.

Truth can subvert power. We can know things about our leaders that disqualify them from leading. We can know things that make their policies seem wrong-headed or even corrupt. Those who would make it seem impossible to know truth are attempting to suppress it.

Truth requires effort to ascertain facts and sincerity in reporting them. A passive and cynical people are easily led, because they will not make the effort or trust the sincerity required for truth. Those who report on Vladimir

Putin's methods in ruling Russia say that he does not so much try to foster a particular set of beliefs as try to create an environment in which no one can discern the truth.

Those of us in the reality-based community tend to think people saying the sort of thing birthers said are in effect claiming their ignorance is as good as actual knowledge. In fact, they think their ignorance is better – if it wins.

That is cruder than Nietzsche's notion of truth. Donald Trump himself, asked if his dishonest and heated rhetoric during the campaign had gone to far, replied in this same mode:

"No. I won," he said.

This is perhaps the clearest statement yet of how conservatives have come to regard claims made in the political sphere. In *Neoconservatism: The Autobiography of an Idea*, Irving Kristol wrote of supply-side economics, "I was not certain of its economic merits but quickly saw its political possibilities."

The political possibilities involved being able to lower taxes on the rich while claiming they were neither cutting programs for those less fortunate nor exploding the deficit. The fact that supply-side economics never worked was a feature, not a bug. It allowed conservatives to argue that the deficit they had created was too large, and we needed to cut programs like Social Security.

Neoconservatives have long believed themselves a sort of intellectual vanguard, who have not merely the option, but the obligation, to mislead people in order to lead them.

Paul Krugman is fond of saying, "Reality has a well-known liberal bias." But why is that? Perhaps it's because conservatives and liberals have a very different relationship with reality and truth.

Conservatives are concerned with conserving traditional values, beliefs, and power structures. Their truth is already established, through long-standing tradition. Liberals are trying to discover the world and human nature, and discover the best way for people to interact with the world. Liberalism is a child of the Enlightenment, conservatism has been with us as long as culture has.

We see this in their relationship with the press, as well. Starting with Nixon, the conservative take on the press has been that the important thing is, are they with us or against us? Prior to the advent of Fox News, when reality conflicted with traditional values, beliefs, and power structures, the press would present facts, which might establish that the truth was not what we had believed before. This is very annoying to people who know the truth without reference to the facts.

This became particularly noisome from the conservative point of view when they were reporting on the civil rights movement or the Vietnam War. Fox News found an opportunity here, providing "news" that did not conflict with traditional values, beliefs, and power structures; if the facts were a problem, they ignored them or changed them.

When Donald Trump claimed he would "Make America Great Again," he was not talking about greatness in the sense of some objectively quantifiable fact. He was promising to restore – wait for that phrase again – traditional values, beliefs, and power structures.

No, he could not bring back the jobs lost in the West Virginia coal mines, and perhaps the West Virginians who voted for him didn't really expect him to. In fact, they may not have expected him to change objective facts in their lives at all. What he represented to them was the will to power for the formation of a different kind of truth, about traditional sex roles, about the power structure that existed in that lost world of the 1950s.

As L.P. Hartley wrote, "The past is a foreign country: They do things differently there." The world has changed too much for us to return to a time when being white and male and willing to work made the world your oyster, or any other mollusk you chose. It is no accident that the 2016 election took place against the backdrop of a controversy over transgender bathroom use and white backlash against the Black Lives Matter movement. Nor is it an accident that the champion of tradition did badly among the young.

The more poisonous our politics become, the harder it is to maintain a place in our public discourse for truth. But politics is the means by which our individual moral judgments become the rules and policies we all must live by. To have that process corrupted would be fatal to our politics.

We must have truth to which we may apply our reason; otherwise, how are we to agree on the rules and policies our moral judgments point toward? Without truth, reason slumbers, and the sleep of reason produces monsters.

Those who can adjust to reality are doing so. For the rest, "truth" is known from tradition, and reality is an inconvenience.

The deep state and the construction of reality

Does a 'deep state' threaten a republic, or actually strengthen it?

One of the complaints of Trump supporters is that the deep state -- a sort of Praetorian Guard that controls who will rule and how -- has frustrated Donald Trump's efforts to remake American government.

This is a fascinating claim. The Praetorian Guard was an elite corps of the Roman army tasked with protecting the emperor. Over the centuries, their power increased, to the point where they were either killing emperors and naming their successors (Caligula, dead, Claudius, emperor) or signalling their support for who would rule after an emperor died (Claudius poisoned, Nero supported for emperor.)

But these were not bureaucrats, nor were they equivalent to the lightly-armed Secret Service. In the reign of Tiberius, there were nine cohorts of 4,500 soldiers each in the Praetorian Guard, three of them stationed in Rome and the others nearby.

The deep state of our time is supposed to be the staff of the U.S. government, whether in the Justice Department, State Department, or intelligence services. The idea is that they may lack loyalty to the president.

How did a large part of the electorate (or at least a noisy part of the internet) become convinced that the existing staff of the American government is a threat to our freedom?

One problem with this belief is that we are a country ruled by laws, carried out by our elected and career government, not a nation ruled by the will of a leader. John Locke, whose writing inspired many of the ideas for the American experiment, said that if the people cannot rid themselves of an oppressive and arbitrary ruler by any other means, they had a right to revolution.

So, our founding fathers decided we needed a republic, which would be governed at the highest levels by people who could be voted out of office.

But if a new regime is to take over, how is it to govern? Won't the personnel of the old regime frustrate the new?

The first answer to this was the spoils system, which allowed each new government to replace large numbers of government workers with people chosen for their loyalty, rather than their skills.

The result was powerful political machines with the ability to reward or punish people according to their loyalty, and a great deal of corruption.

In the late 19th century, the progressive movement started changing this. Their idea was that they could eliminate much of the power and the corruption of political machines by replacing the political hacks with professionals chosen for their skills, and protect those professionals from the corrupting influences of political machines by ensuring they could not be arbitrarily fired.

This was in keeping with the concept of the Constitution. Article VI of the Constitution includes this language:

> The Senators and Representatives before mentioned, and the Members of the several State Legislatures, and all executive and judicial Officers, both of the United States and of the several States, shall be bound by Oath or Affirmation, to support this Constitution; but no religious Test shall ever be required as a Qualification to any Office or public Trust under the United States.

Note that these officials do not swear to support the president. This is the current federal oath of office:

> I, [name], do solemnly swear (or affirm) that I will support and defend the Constitution of the United States against all enemies, foreign and domestic; that I will bear true faith and allegiance to the same; that I take this obligation freely, without any mental reservation or purpose of evasion; and that I will well and faithfully discharge the duties of the office on which I am about to enter.

Donald Trump is reportedly upset that Attorney General Jeff Sessions has recused himself from the investigation of Trump's campaign, and blew his top over the issue, saying that he "needed his Attorney General to protect him."

But Sessions -- and for that matter, Trump -- took an oath to protect the constitution against enemies foreign and domestic. This means that if even the president becomes an enemy of the constitution, his attorney general (and, paradoxically, the president himself) is obligated to defend the constitution from him.

The U.S. Constitution lays out a system of government designed to work, within a set of parameters, for successive governments chosen by the electorate. For that system to work, it has to be a professional government that can work for whichever people get elected.

But this is not how Donald Trump conducts business. He demands absolute loyalty of those around him, and has always relied on his lawyers to clean up any messes he may have with the law. As I write this, his main fixer, Michael Cohen, is in trouble for the way he went about cleaning up those messes.

You can run a business this way, especially a small family firm without the reporting or legal requirements of a publicly held corporation. As a system of government, the Germans had a word for it: Fuhrerprinzip, usually translated as the leader principle. Under that system, at each level of government, the person in charge has total control, and that person's will overrides any written law. The person at the top of the hierarchy is the Fuhrer, whose will overrides any written law and any orders by subordinates.

President Trump, with his admiration for dictators, has shown a preference for the leader principle. Now, the proper control on this behavior is not the democratic norms embedded in the professional standards of the civil service, which has no role described in the constitution for constraining the authoritarian ambitions of a president. The proper control is congress, which passes the laws the executive is charged with putting into action and has the power to remove the president.

There's a problem with that. Not only are most Republican legislators scared of the power Trump holds over the Republican base electorate, many of them agree with his anti-democratic instincts.

From a Sam Tanenhaus article in the July, 2017 issue of The Atlantic[*]:

> (Economist James McGill) Buchanan's theory found another useful ally in the budget-slasher and would-be government-shrinker David Stockman, who idolized Hayek and declared that "politicians were wrecking American capitalism." But Stockman also discovered that restoring capitalism to a purer condition would mean declaring war on "Social Security recipients, veterans, farmers, educators, state and local officials, the housing industry." What president was going to do *that*? Certainly not Reagan. As Stockman reflected, "The democracy had defeated the doctrine."

Tanenhaus was writing about Nancy MacLean's book, *Democracy in Chains*, which explores the influence of Buchanan's public choice theory on American politics. Essentially, the argument is that when it appeared that democracy was a threat to the pure form of capitalism Buchanan favored, his doctrine said that the value system of capitalism should be the one to triumph.

If democracy defeated the doctrine, the solution was to defeat democracy.

We live in a democratic republic. Republics can be undemocratic: The Roman Senate operated more like the English House of Lords than the House of Commons. America's founders thought the best way to have a peaceful and well-governed country was to have its leaders democratically elected, so that if they governed poorly, they could be peacefully replaced.

Over time, we have recognized the humanity of groups like women and former slaves and their descendants by granting them the vote. Rousseau defined freedom as living under a law of your own making. Widening the franchise recognized that previously disenfranchise people were their own masters, and should have a role in determining the laws under which they lived.

Buchanan's theory seems like a throwback to the times when one had to own property to have the right to vote. John Locke theorized that we each are born owning ourselves, and can never sell that property right to anyone else. If you own your own soul, should that not be property right enough to shape the government that rules you? As we've seen in previous chapters, the way we structure our society has a lot to do with the way we construct reality. Ideas become a part of us, and condition our interpretation of reality.

Buchanan said he was applying economic theory to politics. The problem is that he, and those who have financed the political movement that has drawn on his ideas, also applied economic *values* to politics, privileging economic assets and market value above all else.

Buchanan does stipulate that there can be just constitutional arrangements in which people can be rightly taxed. He only stipulates that this arrangement requires unanimity in agreeing to the terms of the constitution. From Chapter 6 of his book, *Limits to Liberty*:

> Under a unanimity rule, decisions if made at all are guaranteed to be efficient, at least in the anticipated sense. Individual agreement signals individual expectation that benefits exceed costs, evaluated in personal utility dimensions, which may or may not incorporate narrowly defined self-interest. With a purely public good, the individually secured benefits, as evaluated, must exceed the individually agreed-on share of costs, measured in foregone opportunities to secure private goods. From an initial imputation of endowments or goods, the multiparty exchange embodied in public-goods provision moves each individual to a final imputation, which includes public goods, that is evaluated more highly in utility terms. Each person in the collectivity moves to a higher position on his own utility surface, or thinks that he will do so, as a result of the public-goods decision reached by unanimous agreement.

<blockquote>
No such results are guaranteed when collective decisions are made under less-than-unanimity rules...
</blockquote>

(A couple of paragraphs later:)

<blockquote>
...We are assuming that the same persons participate in the conceptual constitutional contract and in postconstitutional adjustments. From this it follows that, if a constitutional contract is made that defines separate persons in terms of property rights, and if these rights are widely understood to include membership in a polity that is authorized to make collective decisions by less-than-unanimity rules, each person must have, at this prior stage, accepted the limitations on his own rights that this decision process might produce.
</blockquote>

Now, that's a slightly different position than the "all taxes are theft" position taken by some other theorists, but note that none of the factors that would make the last quoted paragraph apply to the American tax system do in fact apply. While all the states ratified the constitution, they did not do so by unanimous vote. Massachusetts, for example, ratified it by a vote of 187 to 168. While Buchanan theorized that there could be just taxes, no government I know of meets his standards for justice.

Charles Koch became interested in his work, and in 1997 donated about $10 million to finance Buchanan's think tank, The Center for the Study of Public Choice, which is associated with George Mason University.

Public choice theory did much to destroy the idea of "the public good," as understood by political theorists prior to the 1960s. Public choice theory assumes that the people who make up government have their own self-interest. Therefore, any time someone claims to be acting in the public interest, we should assume that whoever is making these claims is acting in their own interest.

Now, consider the first paragraph in section 8 of the U.S. Constitution:

<blockquote>
The Congress shall have Power To lay and collect Taxes, Duties, Imposts and Excises, to pay the Debts and provide for the common Defence and general Welfare of the United States; but all Duties, Imposts and Excises shall be uniform throughout the United States;
</blockquote>

James Monroe claimed the phrase "...and general Welfare..." was meaningless, Alexander Hamilton claimed it was crucial. Hamilton was a mercantilist who believed in government taxing and spending to develop the nation.

The welfare clause became the justification for the Supreme Court's

1937 ruling in *Helvering v. Davis* that held the government had a right to levy Social Security taxes and pay pensions. After all, if Social Security doesn't provide for the general welfare of the country, what does?

Well, who says what the general welfare of the country is? Is it any better defined than "the public good?" Aren't the people promoting the idea just acting in their own interest? A change in the way we conceive of things can change our view of what is just.

One of the problems with the tools of economics is that it is a discipline that makes certain assumptions about human nature, that humans are rational and self-interested. It is a discipline with a decent but mixed record of analyzing behavior in a restricted part of human endeavor, the economic part. It is not really designed for analyzing altruism, heroism, or even the sacrifices a parent will make for a child, seeking to explain all these things in terms of individual self-interest, as defined in a slightly peculiar way.

The self-optimizing individual isn't necessarily selfish. One may have a preference for as much money as possible, or one may prefer to spend a lifetime trying to save the world from whatever you feel threatens it. Economics theoretically treats these preferences as equal, making no judgments as to the moral value of preferences. However, many on the right seem to treat all preferences as selfish, because they are the preferences of individuals. Perhaps this is because they have fallen under the sway of a far more widely known thinker, Ayn Rand, who wrote:

> Man—every man—is an end in himself, not the means to the ends of others. He must exist for his own sake, neither sacrificing himself to others nor sacrificing others to himself. The pursuit of his own rational self-interest and of his own happiness is the highest moral purpose of his life.

This takes the economic assumption in the commercial sphere that people will try to optimize their financial well-being, expands the "virtue of selfishness" to all of life, and changes it from an empirical assumption into a normative judgment.

But we have more than one way of organizing society. There are spheres of human endeavor in which the market is simply not competent to deal with our problems. In fact, markets cannot exist without these other spheres of endeavor. Attempts to run an economy without a properly-functioning legal system have resulted in poor economic performance, and societies only satisfactory to those with enough influence to make sure the courts rule in their favor. Markets were never intended to deal with the problems of those who cannot work.

What sort of parent would fail to sacrifice their sleep to a wailing infant, or their time and money to the education, both academic and moral, of their children? Rand had no children, in keeping with her philosophy that she was an end in herself, but a society of such people would disappear in one generation.

Even in obviously financial decisions, like what one does for a living, people are not financially optimizing creatures. That's not a problem for economics, it just means that the preferences being optimized are not necessarily financial. The problem is with the way this economic explanation is interpreted. The default assumption on the right seems to be that unless one's motives are Evangelical Christian or military, they are selfish, therefore those who seek a profession that gives their lives meaning, like taking a job in the Environmental Protection Agency in the hope of working toward a better world, are really motivated by selfishness.

And if that's the case, the people working for the government cannot be altruistic. Any claims that they are acting for the good of the country can be discounted. People working at agencies because they agree with the purpose of the agencies and the laws that established them are, to this way of thinking, just as selfish as those who want to tear down those agencies so that corporations can make more money.

One of the more troubling ways conservatism has become corrupt is this belief that there are no altruistic people, just hypocrites pretending to have moral standards.

These assumptions would staff your deep state with morally corrupt people whose agenda is not that of the governed, but only of their own corrupt ends. And the solution to this problem would be to elect the Great Man, and make the government subject to his will. The checks and balances built into our government by people who believed there was such a thing as "the general welfare" are useless in this world view, and serve only to frustrate democracy.

But we've seen this movie before, and the ending wasn't funny. In fact, it's a story thousands of years old. About 2,500 years ago, Aristotle wrote the following in *Politics*:

> "When states are democratically governed according to law, there are no demagogues, and the best citizens are securely in the saddle; but where the laws are not sovereign, there you

Plato, his contemporary, thought societies went through a natural progression from oligarchy, to democracy, then tyranny, each stage representing the breakdown of the previous stage. To be ruled by a tyrant is to be subject to the will and the whims of that ruler. Plato said the tyrant arrives as the peoples' champion, telling them only he can fix their troubles, but cannot even govern himself because there is no constraint on his whims and urges. Moreover, because all his relationships are built on domination and submission, the tyrant "never tastes of true freedom or friendship."

If you cannot know friendship, can you know empathy? Trump is Ayn Rand's ideal man, always looking after number one and as a result treating others like number two. He wants to wield the kind of power held by the people he admires, men like Vladimir Putin and Kim Jong-Un. He does not want a government of laws, he wants a government that will do his will.

When his followers refer to organizations such as the Justice Department as the "deep state," they are saying they do not want Trump constrained by the laws of our country. You might think this is just an animal urge on the part of his supporters, most of whom have never heard of James Buchanan, but that would mistake the nature of influential ideas. People who couldn't spell John Locke's name and have never read his work hold his ideas about each of us being born our own master sacred. You don't have to read *The Second Treatise of Government* to feel that way, the idea is embedded in our culture.

The ideas of people like Buchanan and Rand have become embedded in the hive mind of the right, and have become part of their culture.

The concept of the deep state also made some inroads on the left, particularly the far left, where faith in democracy has always been weak. Public choice theory has always had less appeal to this group, because its assumptions are those of capitalist economics. Whereas Buchanan might be said to have made the argument that money doesn't run everything, but it should, the far left tends to think that money does run everything. The deep state of liberal nightmares is the military-industrial complex. The deep state understood by adherents of Buchanan's ideas is government based on laws passed by the people's elected representatives.

Chapter 33: A market-based approach to media bias

Thomas Jefferson famously said, "Were it left to me to decide whether we should have a government without newspapers, or newspapers without a government, I should not hesitate a moment to prefer the latter."

Jefferson considered a vigorous press essential for a nation to have an informed citizenry. So perhaps it should distress us that there are, as of this writing, about 33,000 journalists in America's newsrooms, down from a peak of about 57,000 in 1990. While the number of citizens to be informed has grown, the number of journalists to inform them has fallen by about 42%. So, we are well on our way to government without newspapers.

This is mainly because of disruptions in the news business. There was a time when many cities had multiple newspapers. Then there was a time when most towns had a newspaper, some radio stations, and some television stations. The broadcast media depended heavily on the newspaper to ferret out news stories they could then cover.

Newspapers, during the period when most cities had only one, endeavored to deliver a product that was viewed as impartial by their readers. In practice, this meant that newspapers reflected the politics of the populations they served. You could count on a New York paper being more liberal than one in some small town in Idaho, for example.

National broadcast news for a time consisted of three channels. Again, the incentive was to appear impartial in order to appeal to the largest possible audience. Attacks on the impartiality of the news media were effective in part because of this.

The thing is, it was the limited number of news sources that made an attempt at impartiality necessary. When there were several newspapers in each major city the incentive was to capture a large share of the audience by making the paper interesting to a large group, sometimes in opposition to other groups. You might have a blue-collar paper, and one that appealed more to professionals and business people.

But once the industry settled down to a series of local monopolies, the incentive was to appear impartial so as not to tempt anyone to start a competing paper. In the 1950s through the present, most newspapers attempted impartiality to include as much of their potential audience as possible, and national news networks tried to be as inclusive as possible to avoid alienating parts of their audience.

But one thing about news is that if you tell people what is really happening, you will sometimes end up telling them things they don't want to hear. The mess of the Vietnam War and the big cultural shifts that started happening in the 1960s were replete with stories about things people did not want to have happen, and did not like being told about.

The objective of impartiality became problematic in part because of the forces tearing society apart. Impartiality consists of telling stories that are full, fair, and accurate. Two of the three standards there are subjective, and I doubt Noam Chomsky and Dick Cheney could even agree on whether a given news story was accurate.

Fox News recognized this as an opportunity, rather late in the day, I'd say, when they launched in 1995. CNN had shown that a cable-based news network could be viable, and it occurred to Rupert Murdoch that there was an under-served audience of conservatives who did not like being told that the country was changing in ways they did not like. He got Roger Ailes, a former Republican Party media consultant who had also been an NBC executive, to run his new network, which was designed to appeal to conservative viewers. The formula has been very successful, but now faces a demographic crisis because the average age of its viewers is 68.

At about the same time, the internet, which had been non-commercial in the late 1980s and early 1990s, became fully commercialized. Soon, the cost of starting a news organization fell, and the cost of distribution fell to almost nothing. However, actually getting paid for news on the internet was practically impossible. Many news organizations started putting their stories online for free, and news aggregators soon began to skim off what little money there was in internet news. One major source of income for newspapers, the classified ads, moved onto the internet, most of it for free.

Most internet "news" sites didn't hire a lot of reporters to get their stories, because they couldn't afford them. They became free riders on the reporting done by the declining news industry, and put their own spin on it. In fact, while the newspapers' stock in trade had been accurate reporting and attempted impartiality, the internet news sources' stock in trade is their bias. Appealing to a small part of the potential audience might limit their reach, but it guarantees them at least part of the audience.

This is what happens when you have a lot of voices: More shouting. The economics of the news industry is the key to whether it attempts to be impartial or to give its readers red meat for their existing bias.

What I hear from people still working in the newspaper industry is that staffs are still shrinking. Positions go dark and stay dark, or a command comes down from on high that the budget must be cut by approximately the salary of a staffer. Newspapers, once cash cows, are being starved for resources. Fewer reporters means less actual news, and more competing outlets means more bias. We are less well informed, by more biased sources.

What would Jefferson think? Probably that it was a lot like the newspapers of his time, that labeled him the "negro president." The press in his day could be vicious, and often carried their political bias right on the masthead.

While a diminished press will not end democracy, it can lead to us being less aware of what is happening, and of what can actually put an end to democracy.

Chapter 34: How democracy ends

The Polish-Lithuanian Commonwealth was once a force to be reckoned with, a country more powerful than Russia and far bigger than most of the countries of Europe. What happened to that empire?

Well, the commonwealth was one of the few countries in Europe that had a really influential parliament. It was called the Sjem, and it operated as a legislative body starting in 1493 and became the legislative body of the Polish-Lithuanian Commonwealth when that was founded in 1569. It was, like many republics prior to the modern era, not particularly democratic. Its members were indirectly (by regional bodies) elected by the nobility, which amounted to about 10% of the population.

For much of its existence, any member could nullify legislation that had just passed and end the session by shouting "*Nie pozwalam!*" (I do not allow.) This is known as a liberum veto.

Harvard political scientist Grzegorz Ekiert argued that:

> The principle of the liberum veto preserved the feudal features of Poland's political system, weakened the role of the monarchy, led to anarchy in political life, and contributed to the economic and political decline of the Polish state. Such a situation made the country vulnerable to foreign invasions and ultimately led to its collapse.[*]

For one thing, foreign regimes discovered they could bribe legislators to use their veto, thereby paralyzing the government. This led to the partition of the empire and foreign occupation.

In Germany the Wiemar Republic had a rough start, but after the hyperinflation got tamped down in 1923, there were some very good years – until the crash of 1929. The American banks that were helping Germany pay its reparations for WW I had to call in their loans, unemployment went up just as it did in other countries, and the people responded by throwing the bums out. Unfortunately, the bums they threw in tended to be people who did not believe in democracy, like the German National Peoples' Party, the Communists, and the Nazis.

Unable to form a majority coalition, Heinrich Brüning formed a minority coalition. But he was forced to often rule by emergency decree, because the Reichstag could not pass legislation. Unfortunately, his policies for dealing with the Depression were exactly wrong – he tightened credit and rolled back wage increases, making him unpopular with the electorate and the Reichstag and making the economy worse.

Since his decrees were actually ruining the country, Brüning opened the door for the election of populists like the Nationalist Party and the Nazis. Even business interests turned against him, though it must be admitted that some started financing Hitler long before Brüning became chancellor.

In each case, democracy failed because it could not govern. Francis Fukuyama, in *Political Order and Political Decay*, argues that American political order is decaying because it has become too easy for special interests to veto decisions. He claims this leads to a government unable to function well enough to address the nation's challenges, which undermines the peoples' faith in the ability to address their problems, which leads them to deny it the resources to address their problems, which leads to...well, you get the idea.

The destruction of the Polish Commonwealth and the descent of Germany into the totalitarian hell of Nazi dictatorship had this in common – democratic, representative government ceased to function. When democracy can't address the peoples' problems, people will turn to a strongman or watch things get worse and worse.

So it is with real dread that I read this (from a Matthew Yglesias post on Vox):

> To prevent Obama from becoming the hero who fixed Washington, McConnell decided to break it. And it worked. Six years into the affair, we now take it for granted that nothing will pass on a bipartisan basis, no appointment will go through smoothly, and everything the administration tries to get done will take the form of a controversial use of executive power.[*]

Sound familiar? This is one way democracy is destroyed. As long as politicians find they can increase their clout by making sure government does not address peoples' problems, and not take the blame for how things turn out as a result, our democratic system is in danger. The next step is to gather enough power – say, both houses of congress, the presidency, and a substantial part of the judiciary – that you can change the rules so that the rulers choose the voters, rather than the other way around. This is the beginning of a shift from liberal democracy to illiberal democracy, in which the rule of law and the ability to choose your leaders or even criticize them disappears.

This strategy works best if voters view the wreckage and say, "A curse on both your houses, I will vote no more forever!" Disillusioned, passive voters, disenfranchised by their own inability to see who did the wrecking, are the ally of those who seek to undermine democracy.

When we have all branches of government in the hands of one party, the question becomes, will majority rule trump democratic norms? Faith in democratic institutions is already on the ropes. If the party in power will not act as a check on an executive who is the leader of their party, who will? Remember, the courts are reliant on the executive branch to enforce their orders.

Our constitution and our democracy exists only so long as we believe in them.

But this is not the only aspect of the tragedy of the Polish-Lithuanian Sjem that resonates today. Remember, the liberum veto was not just used to prevent policies some legislators objected to for their own commonwealth, but some also took bribes to utilize the liberum veto on behalf of foreign powers.

As a country whose politics are being influenced by foreign powers, we need to pay attention to this aspect of things.

One of the more surreal moments in the presidential campaign was when Donald Trump, at a rally in Tampa, Florida, June 11, 2016, walked across the stage and literally hugged an American flag -- even though his campaign is now being investigated for colluding with the Russian government and its minions to win the campaign.

In retrospect it might be more accurate to say he molested the American flag while working with the Russians to subvert what it stands for. He campaigned on a promise to make America great again, but he's been hollowing out the State Department in a way that reduces American power abroad.

Sen. Chris Murphy (D-Conn.), a member of the Foreign Relations Committee, recently tweeted, "The purposeful gutting of American power abroad is mystifying. If you didn't know better, you'd think some rival government was running our foreign policy."

And Rod Dreher, a staff writer for The American Conservative, recounts this quote from an interview with Northwestern University Prof. William Reno about an exchange with the former foreign minister of an East

African country:

> We spoke several months ago while I was in his country to meet with army officers for my research on civil-military relations. Well read and well informed, he expressed distress over what he saw as the Trump Administration's attack on the foundations of American power in the world. He compared Trump to Gorbachev...

> He explained that Russians know Gorbachev as the man who destroyed a superpower. He said that "Trump is your Gorbachev" because he is also destroying his country's global power. He noted that Trump was systematically undermining the architecture of American power, such as NATO and all sorts of other arenas of cooperation that make America essential in the calculations of other countries. He pointed to people like Sebastian Gorka and took the time to find out who he and some of the other advisors actually are. His country, he explained, prefers to get advice from "reality-based professionals" and wondered how others in the American political establishment could tolerate people who are so harmful to American power.[*]

When a publication like The American Conservative is worried about a Republican president destroying American power, you know things are getting bad.

> *The Hill* reports that:

> "These people either do not believe the U.S. should be a world leader, or they're utterly incompetent," Dana Shell Smith told The New York Times. Smith was the ambassador to Qatar until she resigned in June.

> Aides for Tillerson have also reportedly depleted much of the department's diversity by firing most of the department's leading African-American and Latino diplomats.

Having a diplomatic corps that looks like the world could only help deal with the world, but the Trump administration doesn't want that.

Very few Republicans (Sen. John McCain (R-Ariz.) is an exception) have raised an alarm about this, and that may be related to the fact that some on the right see as their greatest enemies not foreign powers, but their fellow citizens of the opposition party.

I mentioned above that foreign governments were bribing members of the Sjem to use their liberum veto to serve the interests of the commonwealth's enemies.

This has become more relevant to our present-day politics as the story of Russian interference in the most recent presidential election unfolds.

Certainly much of what happened in the Polish-Lithuanian Sjem had to do with divisions within the polity, but part of the problem was the willingness of legislators to advance the interests of other countries with the exercise of their veto.

It showed a lack of patriotism. And part of what we are now experiencing is a lack of patriotism.

This is hardly our first rodeo. Prescott Bush, father of George H.W. Bush and grandfather of George W. Bush, was a director and shareholder of Brown Brothers Harriman, an investment bank set up for German industrialist and Hitler ally Fritz Thyssen, who helped finance Hitler's rise to power. (Thyssen was big in coal and steel, and benefited financially from Hitler's rearmament of Germany. Brown Brothers Harriman helped him set up front companies to move money around the globe.) BBH was seized under the Trading with the Enemy Act, but strangely was not dissolved to benefit the taxpayers but returned to its stockholders after the war. Far from being prosecuted, Prescott Bush was able to sell his stock for a fortune after the war and use this wealth as a base for his election to the U.S. Senate.

We all remember Charles Lindbergh, who was widely praised in Nazi Germany for his efforts to keep America from aiding Britain in its war with Germany and advising America to negotiate a neutrality treaty with Germany. When President Roosevelt criticized his position, he resigned his commission as a colonel in the the U.S. Army Air Corps. Lindbergh even considered moving to Germany as late as 1939, but German friends advised against the home he wished to lease because it had been owned by Jews.

Lucky Lindy also had some pretty racist views, but seems to have been motivated more by anticommunism than antisemitism. He was active in a group called America First, a term which has cropped up again in the Trump administration.

The thing is, we had a House Un-American Activities Committee to investigate people suspected of being fellow travelers with Communists, but we never had such an agency to help deal with Quislings.

Those on the right have never felt they had to answer questions about their patriotism, even when they have aided hostile foreign powers. Those on the right seem to get a pass on the issue of patriotism from pretty much everybody. The right was happy to accuse President Barack Obama of deliberately reducing American power, but it now appears those accusations were aspirational, and they were really voicing what they intended to do.

One definition of a political gaffe is "accidentally telling the truth." When Rep. Chris Collins (R-NY) said about tax cuts, "My donors are basically saying, 'Get it done or don't ever call me again,'" he was doing just that. His donors are very rich people who care more about money than about their country. They don't care if the deficit explodes, they don't care if the foreign service is so decimated that foreign ministers don't even know who to talk to at the local embassy.

Because the wealthy Republican donor class don't care about their country, they care more about whether a president will sign a tax cut than whether he is destroying American power.

It's not just the Republican donor class. Many of the votes that put Trump in office were supplied by Americans who hate their fellow Americans so much that they elected Trump to battle against "liberals" with the aid of Russia.

Anyone who talks to conservatives on line has run into people who don't care that Russians hacked the Democratic National Committee's emails, as long as it nobbled Hillary Clinton. I've run across some who didn't care that many of the things said during the campaign were lies, because, "It worked, didn't it?"

These are people who have more common feeling with the ethnic and religious aspects of Vladimir Putin's Russia than to Americans in San Francisco. They are more conservative and more tribal than they are American. The American flag represents something that was new in the world when this country was founded, a nation based on ideals rather than on ethnicity and religion. From the first we imperfectly embodied our ideals, proclaiming that all men are created equal, yet enshrined slavery in the Constitution. But we've made progress over the years, and during the Cold War America came to be seen as a beacon of freedom.

We've come to represent an international order that seeks consensus rather than conquest. Our military adventures have often been either futile or have boomeranged against us, but our soft power has been consistently important and beneficial to the nation and to the world.

Trump's treatment of the diplomatic corps shows that he does not understand American power, does not understand why we are seen as the essential nation – or worse, that he sees this and rejects it, seeking to reduce us to the sort of gangster state Russia has become, a state that prefers conquest to consensus and kleptocrats to democrats.

Chapter 35: The State of nature, the allure of the authoritarian, and life among the delighted

Thomas Hobbes, in *Leviathan*, argued that the basis for the social contract is that in a state of nature, we see a war of each against all, so we must form a social contract to have a leader in charge of enforcing order, or we will die a violent death. I believe that was a description of the breakdown of order during the 30 Years War, just ending when *Leviathan* was published. John Locke, for reasons we explored in the chapter on him and his radical activities, argued that we form a society to protect property, which includes our own lives.

Both wrote in the 1600s. I believe it may be time to update the notion of the state of nature. First of all, the Hobbesian notion that we formed society to avoid violent death would apply to any animal capable of fear, and I think human society is fundamentally different from most or all other animal societies.

Second, property is a term Locke never really defined. It cannot be objects, which exist whether they are owned or not. Property is the concept behind the rules and customs regulating the human use of objects. It is, if you like, what objects mean to people. It is a province in the realm of meaning, and meaning is what makes human societies different from those of other social animals.

The Hobbesian notion that we form a society to free ourselves from the threat of violent death explains why we have been ruled so long by force. It does not explain why we have been ruled so long by faith and custom, as well. The answer to that lies in the symbolic side of human society. What makes human society a civilization or a culture is this symbolic world, a sort of virtual realm consisting of meanings, which is invisible to animals other than humans. Human culture is one of the strangest things on the planet, and religion is one of the strangest and most powerful things in that ethereal, symbolic world. Moving beyond the symbolic world of religion to and ideology based on reason and experience, as liberalism is, requires an enormous change in the way we think about who we are.

Reason is not the basis of religion. In fact, it is not the basis for civilization. People learn to live together by living together, and codify what they have learned into institutions, culture, and stories. The most important of those stories, such as the origin story that binds the community together and the story of what happens to the wicked in the afterlife, are in the keeping of one of the most powerful institutions, religion.

But where did religion come from, and why do virtually all human societies have one?

Humans, relative to other animals, have giant brains. The brain is an expensive organ, consuming about 25% of your body's energy when it is in a resting state, but it pays dividends. One result is our ability to solve problems, such as how to get a piece of fruit down from a tree without breaking our necks. Another is our use of language, and symbolic thought.

We see signs of tool use as much as three million years ago. That is a sign of instrumental thought, problem solving. Symbolic thought is much more recent, appearing and disappearing a few times before it finally "took" permanently (we hope) about 35,000-40,000 years ago.

Language must first have been used instrumentally, to warn of danger, coordinate defense, communicate what plants are edible and how to prepare them, and talk one's lover's mate out of killing you.

But we see the revolution of symbolic thought in the creation of jewelry, and tools that are beautiful as well as functional. We see these as signs that our ancestors thought these things were not just useful, they had meaning.

We are creatures who make meaning; it is the essence of being human, and allows us to have larger civilizations that would otherwise be possible.

Most animals only coordinate with others of their species who are relatively closely related to them. Humans are different, in part because of their dual nature. As Richard Dawkins wrote in *The Selfish Gene*, living creatures can be seen as things that exist to perpetuate their genes. These are chemical strings of information that define what the creature is.

But we have other strings of information, symbolic ones that define who we are as much as our genes do. Dawkins used the word *memes* to describe them. They are a major part of what our minds are made of, the brain's software that has evolved to allow us to function in society. They give us, for example, ideas about honor and decency that prevent us from acting badly and selfishly.

Our minds are made up of the memes we have been in contact with.

You might say, what we accept into ourselves defines who we are, and what we reject defines the boundaries of the soul. But in the end, a large part of what we are made up of is each other, everyone we've known, spoken to, read, or watched as they went about their lives around us. In fact, so much of what we are is in our memes, we can transmit much of what we are to those with whom we share few genes. We certainly feel closer to our friends than to our second cousins, and feel they share more of who we are.

But there are divisions within the symbolic self as well. We have ideals, which we can share with those who do not share our language, and we have the spiritual part of ourselves, which can also transcend language.

But how does the symbolic link up with the spiritual?

Consider what a wonder language is. You have a tree, you know its smell, recognize its shape, perhaps eat its fruit or nuts. The tree is a solid thing, growing in one place and firm in its reality.

But then, you have a word for the tree. In fact, you have a word for trees. It is as if the tree, and all trees, have grown a new dimension. The tree now has an existence in the physical world and another existence in the new, symbolic world. This must have provoked a sense of wonder that we have long forgotten.

How are we to interpret this?

One way would be to regard that second existence as spirit. The tree now has a spirit, perhaps we could speak of it as a wood nymph, the brook has not just the sound of moving water but the babbling of the water sprites.

This is a mythopoetic understanding of the world. We understood this new dimension in the world by calling it spirit, and inhabiting the world with a new sort of creature that existed only in the realm of magic.

In our materialistic age, we tend to think of the world and society in materialistic and instrumental terms. But this would not necessarily be the dominant mode of understanding for all of history. In a slowly changing world, we could construct a society of customs and myths that caused people to act in ways that made the crops grow and the social order remain stable without them corresponding to literal truth in the physical world. This would be a world Edmund Burke could admire, in which the customs and myths society imbued its members with were the cumulative wisdom of the society.

There is a branch of philosophy called pragmatism, which says ideas have an evolutionary life, in which the fittest ideas survive. For millennia, this could work slowly, and the ideas only had to work, they did not need to be literally true. Humanity could live by its myths.

When the world changed quickly, as in the late bronze age collapse of about 1200 BCE, this system did not work well enough. The new technology of iron meant the old powers fell. In the following dark age, many cities were leveled, never to be built again on those sites. Populations fell, civilizations failed.

It took around 800 years for civilization to recover. And from that dark age came a flowering of reason we now think of as the Greek golden age. Instrumental logic, combined with language, became philosophy. It was a precursor to the age of reason.

We entered a new dark age when Rome fell, and society relied more on religion and custom for centuries. Then came the Enlightenment, and we began to try to reason our way to the good society again.

So here we are, with reason and faith often at odds. The world is changing too rapidly for mythopoetic systems that have evolved over the ages to adapt quickly enough, but there is great resistance to leaving them behind, and for good reasons. The Enlightenment, after all, produced philosophies that led to the Terror, the Stalinist purges, the killing fields. There is enough wisdom in myth to make it still useful. Its claims to truthfulness are usually not testable, and beside the point in any case.

But reason and faith are not the only things at odds. Both can be used to justify either authoritarian or democratic regimes. The violent regimes justified in the name of "science," such as the fascist and communist governments, have been pretty thoroughly discredited at this point. But we are now seeing violent reactions against liberalism from people motivated by religion and tradition. We are used to thinking of democracy as a better form of government to live under, but there are plenty of people fighting for or living under authoritarian regimes. The rights to life, liberty, and the pursuit of happiness are not valued in these societies, and a surprising number of people seem to be just fine with that. But what is the appeal of this?

The allure of the authoritarian

Those who define their people in terms of tribal markers such as religion, race, and culture tend to want a government that pursues the interest of the society so defined against outsiders. Part of the allure of the authoritarian leader is that they won't be namby-pamby about pursuing their nation's interest, right?

But that perception is puzzling in light of the evidence that democracies win a lot more of their wars than autocracies do. If you're interested in results rather than bravado, the strongman who leads his country into battle isn't the best choice.

Benjamin A. T. Graham, Erik Gartzk, and Christopher J. Faris, have written a paper that explains this in terms of a bar fight.

In *The Bar Fight Theory of International Conflict: Regime Type, Coalition Size, and Victory,*[*] they raise the question, "Who wins a bar fight?" The answer is, usually the person with the most friends in the bar. Think of how many more allies Britain had than Germany during World War II. When Saddam Hussein invaded Kuwait, the U.S. led coalition had 32 members aligned against him.

One reason that was possible was that other countries knew that, unlike Hussein, the United States did not intend to keep Kuwait. Standing up for the little guy, it turns out, is more popular than taking his lunch money and his oil fields.

And consider the web of alliances in which America is a prominent member. NATO, SEATO, and other alliances are certainly better than the paltry alliances our old opponent, Russia, has managed to muster. Those who admire Putin for taking decisive action in seizing Crimea should remember, Russia's whole conflict with the Ukraine goes back to the fact that when it came time to choose between getting closer to Russia or the democratic West, the people of Ukraine made it clear they wanted it to be the West. Putin took action because he was losing to the soft power of the democratic nations of western Europe, and his "decisive" action was made necessary by his weakness, not his strength.

Graham and his fellow researchers write:

> The biggest martial asset of democracies may well be that they are better at making friends, not that they are better at vanquishing their enemies.

Not that vanquishing your enemies is anything to be sniffed at. In general, wealthier countries beat poorer countries. But why are they wealthier?

Daron Acemoglu, Suresh Naidu, James A Robinson, and Pascual Restrepo, in the 2014 study *Democracy Does Cause Growth,*[*] argue that – spoiler alert – democracy does cause growth.

In an introduction to the study, they state the following:

When we disentangle what components of democracy matter the most for growth, we find that civil liberties are what seem to be the most important. We also find positive effects of democracy on economic reforms, private investment, the size and capacity of government, and a reduction in social conflict. Clearly all of these are channels by which democracy can increase economic growth, and a great deal of further research is needed.

So, it isn't voting that matters, it is freedom that matters. Not that you are likely to keep civil liberties if the rest of the institutions of democracy, such as rule of law and rule by the consent of the governed, disappear. You need those institutions to ensure that you can keep civil liberties, but the freedom to think and say what you want is, according to Acemoglu and his co-authors, the real spur to economic growth.

We shouldn't be surprised. After all, the strength of democracy is not in executing policy, it is in deciding what policy is worth pursuing. If the example of the Soviet Union showed us anything, it is that the ability to produce the most steel is not as important as being able to decide what to produce. Consider American capitalism without the input of *The Wall Street Journal* and other commentators on the economic scene. Without them, who would embarrass inept executives, or question company policy? And if you say, well, dissident shareholders, they need freedom of speech as well. Consider that the youth of the Soviet Union wanted Levi jeans, not Soviet work pants. Free speech gives you fashion magazines and other means of deciding what to wear, therefore free speech helps us know what is worth making.

But freedom of speech is not the only civil liberty. Being secure in your property is not a feature of many authoritarian regimes, who seize the property of anyone they deem an opponent. If you cannot be secure in your property, why invest in it?

And as for the reduction in social conflict that the study cites, that has a lot to do with John Locke's insight in *A Letter Concerning Toleration*: That it is not people believing different things that causes social upheaval, it is trying to get them to believe the same thing. Given freedom of conscience and freedom of speech, a great deal that used to cause violence ends up just causing arguments.

Arguments may not seem productive, but they are at least not as destructive as kristallnacht or other ethnic conflicts that result in the destruction of the businesses, homes or temples of the targeted groups. The destructive tendency of authoritarian regimes has everything to do with their definition of who is inside and who is outside the controlling group, and what can be done to control others. That is actually how societies have been run for much of human history.

Traditional societies' reactions to Enlightenment ideas can be violent. To many people, tribalism and religion are their identity, and they feel the secular state is a threat to that. Both al Qaeda and Islamic State are examples of this. Both are anti-democratic because they see democracy as fundamentally wrong, and freedom of conscience as fundamentally wrong. If you don't believe what you are supposed to believe, you are wrong, and deserve to die, in their view. Certain things could, in the view of Islamic State, make a Muslim an apostate, and one of them was voting in elections. Another was simply being a Shiite Muslim.

Islamic State was not atavistic merely because of the doctrines it espoused. It espoused those doctrines as a return to an earlier state of civilization, in which we are ruled by force, faith, and custom. They disapproved of voting because they disapproved of the very notion that government should serve the governed. They believed, instead, that it should serve God, just as most human civilizations have through the ages. And, rather conveniently, the leaders of Islamic State considered themselves the experts on what God wants.

When you see a pattern repeated with different justifications, such as the authoritarianism of disparate regimes such as Stalinist, Fascist, and Islamist, you may assume that the pattern, not the justification, is the point.

All of this fits with what Theodore Adorno, who fled Germany in the 1930s and returned after World War II, referred to in his 1950 book, *The Authoritarian Personality*. From that authoritative book:

> The most crucial result of the present study, as it seems to the authors, is the demonstration of close correspondence in the type of approach and outlook a subject is likely to have in a great variety of areas, ranging from the most intimate features of family and sex adjustment through relationships to other people in general, to religion and to social and political philosophy. Thus a basically hierarchical, authoritarian, exploitive parent-child relationship is apt to carry over into a power-oriented, exploitively dependent attitude toward one's sex partner and one's God and may well culminate in a political philosophy and social outlook which has no room for anything but a desperate clinging to what appears to be strong and a disdainful rejection of whatever is relegated to the bottom. The inherent dramatization likewise extends from the parent-child dichotomy to the dichotomous conception of sex roles and of moral values, as well as to a dichotomous handling of social relations as manifested especially in the formation of stereotypes and of ingroup-outgroup cleavages. Conventionality,

rigidity, repressive denial, and the ensuing break-through of one's weakness, fear and dependency are but other aspects of the same fundamental personality pattern, and they can be observed in personal life as well as in attitudes toward religion and social issues.

On the other hand, there is a pattern characterized chiefly by affectionate, basically equalitarian, and permissive interpersonal relationships. This pattern encompasses attitudes within the family and toward the opposite sex, as well as an internalization of religious and social values. Greater flexibility and the potentiality for more genuine satisfactions appear as results of this basic attitude.

Looking at a few lists of the characteristics of authoritarian personalities, I'd boil it down to this:

Rigid conventionalism and a tendency to think in rigid categories.

Uncritical submission to the moral authority of the group to which a person belongs.

Authoritarian aggression, that is, looking for those who violate conventional norms in order to condemn them, reject them, and punish them.

Opposing the subjective, imaginative, and empathetic or sympathetic.

Superstition, that is, a tendency to believe in mystical things that affect peoples' fate. An example would he Benito Mussolini's insistence on changing airplanes if he thought one of his fellow passengers had the evil eye.

A preoccupation with toughness, identification with those who seem powerful, and with the powerful/weak, winner/loser, dominant/submissive dimensions of character.

Hostility and vilification of human nature, projecting unconscious urges, therefore a belief that horrible and dangerous things are going on, and a cynicism about the world.

A focus on sex, sexuality, and what sexual things others are doing.

There is some question in my mind whether any of this is innate. There is no question in my mind that society can choose to be ruled by the authoritarian among them or by the more flexible alternative that Adorno described. It strikes me that as civilization has developed, we have gone from the small band, to the tribe, to the village, to the nation, and at each stage our definition of who is "one of us" has become broader. The greater our inclusiveness, the greater the size of our cohort. Acceptance of the "other" into the cohort increases the power of the cohort, so in the end, those who are suspicious of outsiders are less likely to increase the power of their society than those willing to include them. The bluster of the nativist is a defensive posture based on fear. Every new group of immigrants to the U.S. has been opposed by nativists, before being accepted and considered an asset. Those who demonize outsiders are exposing their weakness, not displaying their strength.

One caveat I wish to offer is that like many psychological terms, "authoritarian personality" seems pejorative. This is in part because of the history of the term and its invention after World War II and the Holocaust, which reflected the excesses to which this particular personality type is vulnerable, and in part by the tendency of psychology to pathologize whatever it studies (the exception is positive psychology, which studies what makes people thrive.) Efforts to rebrand this analytic category with another term have failed, so we seem to be stuck with it. Something like 40% of the population would be called authoritarian by some standards, and yet they do not advocate dictators, for the most part. As long as those with this personality type were evenly distributed between the political parties, we were unlikely to get an authoritarian party. Unfortunately, since the Republican Party re-branded itself as the party of law and order in conjunction with Nixon's Southern strategy, the type has gradually sorted into the Republican Party. At this point, about 65% of people who test highest as "authoritarian" are in the Republican Party.[*] Faced with a sufficient threat, non-authoritarians tend to act like authoritarians, which means that if enough voters can be scared, we could see the election of an anti-democratic, authoritarian regime. Once you get them in office, they tend to break democratic norms and eventually, institutions.

Stanley Feldman, a political science professor at State University of New York at Stonybrook, came up with some questions not obviously political to detect this personality type in surveys.

1 . Is it better to have a child who is independent, or respectful of

elders?

2 . Is it more important for a child to be self-reliant, or obedient?

3 . Is it more important that a child be considerate, or well-behaved?

4 . Which is more important for a child, curiosity or good manners?

Quite reasonable people might answer that children should be respectful, obedient, well-behaved, and well-mannered, and all of these answers would lead them to being labeled authoritarian. (Full disclosure, my answers were all non-authoritarian.) Perhaps the only way to avoid a prejudice based on the pejorative term is to give people like me an equally pejorative label, such as libertine. The problem, in any case, is that just as "libertines" like myself are prone to tolerating excessive disorder, authoritarians are prone to excesses of order. Some sort of balance is needed. Since people who want power usually want it to impose the sort of order they prefer, the balance has usually tipped in the direction of excessive order throughout history. Freedom, for most of humanity's existence, has been in short supply.

Now, it strikes me that any ideology or in-group can contain people with these traits, from self-righteous hipster assholes to fire and brimstone preachers and "citizens for decency." Many will be attracted to conservative causes, because of the conventionalism of the type, but that also depends on the conventions they are raised with. It is also quite common for people who have generally conservative views to be kind, empathetic, and accepting. How conservative or liberal you are depends more on your upbringing than your temperament, but how authoritarian you are depends more on your temperament.

Consider the following passage, from Sayyid Qutb's *The America I have Seen*:

> ...the American girl is well acquainted with her body's seductive capacity. She knows it lies in the face, and the expressive eyes, and thirsty lips. She knows seductiveness lies in the round breasts, the full buttocks, and in the shapely thighs, sleek legs – and she shows all this and does not hide it.

In this brief passage we have on display lust, disgust, condemnation, envy, and a concern with the sexuality of others. It seems safe to say that Qutb, an early firebrand of the Muslim Brotherhood, was an authoritarian. He reacted to the open society with revulsion. Qutb was one of the founding figures in the jihad movement, an advocate of religious law over secular law, and wanted women to know their place (and everyone else, as well.)

What Qutb wanted was a return to the old system of governance by force, faith, and custom. He would be more comfortable if everyone knew their place, instead of trying to shape their own lives. If Allah is the ultimate source of truth and good, why would you rely upon the judgment of people, who after all might be seduced by the licentious freedom of the libertine West?

Culturally, this was happening around him. Egypt's last king was an obese playboy given to pleasures of the flesh. Farouk I died at the ages of 45 and the weight of 300 pounds, collapsing after a heavy meal. In his defense, he may have been poisoned, though it is not necessary to suppose this is the case, and no one bothered with an autopsy.

Egypt's dictators at the time were secular. The Muslim Brotherhood was having none of this. They believed God's law was above man's law, and wanted a society where God's law overruled man's law. This is only a problem if you don't happen to belong to the same church as Qutb and his brethren. If, for example, you happen to be a Coptic Christian, under the rule of religious fanatics of a different faith, it sucks to be you.

Every civilization needs some degree of conservatism, some value placed on tradition and order. But for a civilization to learn and grow, it must also be open to new ideas and new experiences, and in a time when the world faces rapid change, these needs are in conflict. The psychologically conservative will be disturbed by the disorder of rapid change, while those with minds more open to change, the need to adapt society and leave behind old prejudices will lead them in a different direction.

When people look at Islamist extremists, and tell me that this is a clash of civilizations between Muslim and Christian civilizations, I think of the Christians in our own civilization who want religion to overrule secular law. The clash is not between religions, it is between tolerance and intolerance, between liberty and authority.

What we are seeing is not a clash between regions or cultures or religions. We are seeing a clash between people who want to conserve traditional values and people who want to open society up to new freedoms. Tip the balance one way, you have the Islamic State, tip it the other and you have San Francisco, or at least the San Francisco of a conservative's nightmares.

Those who want America to be a Christian nation have more in common than they might wish to believe with those who want an Islamic state.

When the world changed slowly, those who wanted order and traditional values and those who wanted to be open to new experiences were not much in conflict. New experiences were rare in Egypt's Old Kingdom, and the need to adapt to a changing world was rare. We no longer live in that world, and many people are made profoundly uncomfortable by this, while others delight in it.

Count me among the delighted. I am happy to see that surveys of young people show them sharing more and more of my views as I get older, because they are adapted to the changes that have occurred. I find that more and more, I live among the delighted. But I still recognize the need for a counterbalance, even if I sometimes become impatient with the way people cling to what I feel are outmoded views. I only ask that they use persuasion rather than force when they attempt to get people to follow their older ways.

As society changes, we must reinvent ourselves. That is difficult for those who have already invented themselves, much easier for those who are still young enough to be inventing themselves.

Humanity's dual nature, animal and symbolic, is the essence of what makes human society specifically human. The state of nature for mankind is the state in which we invent our symbolic selves. Ontogeny recapitulates phylogeny mentally as well as physically, as each of us encounters symbolic thought and we become, not just mature creatures of a genetic inheritance, but creatures as much defined by what we know as by what we physically are. We often have more in common with those who know what we know and think about the things that trouble our minds than with people who are more genetically similar. That is what it is to be human, to be defined more by your symbolic self than any other creature we have yet encountered can be. Hobbes said that we form the social contract to preserve ourselves from violent death, but looking at all those who have been killed to silence them, perhaps we preserve ourselves from violent death so that we may define our symbolic selves, and help define our society.

We now are aware of the social contract, and can make explicit political contracts such as the U.S. Constitution. We can now have a rational society that does not rely on the natural tribalism of a shared language, a society that relies instead on shared ideals. The most basic of those ideals are freedom of conscience and freedom of speech, which cannot really exist without each other, and the notion that government serves the governed, which cannot effectively exist without those two freedoms.

Freedom of conscience allows us to define ourselves. The symbolic self, the most distinctly human part of a person, will flourish most when freed to speak and listen to others the most. There will always be restrictions. No two people communicate perfectly, and barriers of language and culture exist even between generations within the same community, or even between siblings. There are secrets we feel we must keep, and lies we will tell. But the way to grow our communities and grow ourselves within communities is to have as much freedom to communicate as possible.

The logic of democracy, of equality before the law, and the rest of the American experiment all flow from the essentials of freedom of speech and of conscience. We must not lose sight of these at a time when tribalism is attempting to reassert itself.

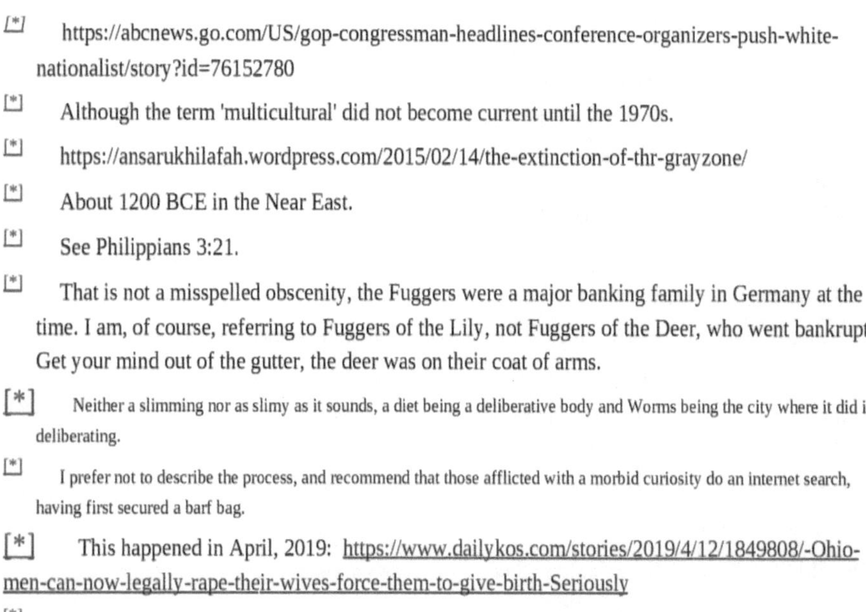

[*] https://abcnews.go.com/US/gop-congressman-headlines-conference-organizers-push-white-nationalist/story?id=76152780

[*] Although the term 'multicultural' did not become current until the 1970s.

[*] https://ansarukhilafah.wordpress.com/2015/02/14/the-extinction-of-thr-grayzone/

[*] About 1200 BCE in the Near East.

[*] See Philippians 3:21.

[*] That is not a misspelled obscenity, the Fuggers were a major banking family in Germany at the time. I am, of course, referring to Fuggers of the Lily, not Fuggers of the Deer, who went bankrupt. Get your mind out of the gutter, the deer was on their coat of arms.

[*] Neither a slimming nor as slimy as it sounds, a diet being a deliberative body and Worms being the city where it did its deliberating.

[*] I prefer not to describe the process, and recommend that those afflicted with a morbid curiosity do an internet search, having first secured a barf bag.

[*] This happened in April, 2019: https://www.dailykos.com/stories/2019/4/12/1849808/-Ohio-men-can-now-legally-rape-their-wives-force-them-to-give-birth-Seriously

[*] In his book *Anarchy, State, and Utopia*, published in 1974. Nozick had some views that clashed with Locke, including the idea that people could sell themselves into slavery. Locke wrote at a time when people still sold themselves into indentured servitude, including at least one of my ancestors (another was abducted from the streets of Glasgow and sold as an indentured servant in America, a

practice that was surprisingly common at one time.) Locke certainly understood that people *did* sell themselves into servitude, he just didn't think they could become objects. In America, indentured servitude was outlawed by the 13th Amendment to the constitution after the Civil War. Personally, I think the concept Nozick advanced of 'non-coercive slavery contracts' is incoherent, given the coercive nature of slavery. Granted, this is a tiny part of Nozick's philosophy, but I think it illustrates how different his libertarian conception of the nature of man is from Locke's.

[*] Walter Johnson, King Cotton's Long Shadow, New York Times, March 30, 2013. In part, this was an artifact of the financial system. Slaves could be mortgaged, the mortgages could be the basis for bonds, and the bonds could be sold all over Europe, competing with bonds for railroads. Much as with the securitization of housing in the early 21st century, this made for the possibility of a financial bubble.

[*] Our unreliable narrator (me, the author) is making two mistakes here. First, he is thinking of pelicans, not penguins. Second, he is confusing pelicans with storks, and while a pelican may superficially look like a short-legged version of a stork, the two are not closely related. For purposes of properly informing our youth through sex education, it is important to remember that it is storks that bring babies (see Disney, Walt, and Goose, Mother.)

[*] Sometimes, and more accurately, called the Funding Act of 1790. The actual title was "An Act making provision for the payment of the Debt of the United States."

[*] https://www.vox.com/2015/7/2/8883307/merkel-nsa-wikileaks-greek-crisis

[*] Page 336,Plato: General issues of interpretation, edited by Nicholas D. Smith, 1998, Routlage, London.

[*] http://www.firstprinciplesjournal.com/articles.aspx?article=871&theme=home&page=2&loc=b&type=ctbf

[*] http://www.nytimes.com/2012/02/19/us/politics/santorum-criticizes-education-system-and-obama.html?_r=1&hpw

[*] Kennedy gave this speech to the Greater Houston Ministerial Association on Sept. 12, 1960.

[*] "Remember, Remember, the fifth of November, Gunpowder treason and plot. I see no reason why gunpowder treason ever should be forgot." Guy Fawkes, among other Catholics, plotted to blow up King James I, with barrels of gunpowder concealed underneath the House of Lords. Fawkes was found guarding the barrels and the plot was stopped before the fuse could be lit.

[*] In an 80-year war. Guy Fawkes fought on the Spanish side under the name Guido Fawkes.

[*] Jim Bramlett, *The U.S. Supreme Court Radically Reverses Itself!* Part 5 of a series of posts, Choicesforliving.com.

[*] Whereas Social Democrats, who advocate a market economy with social insurance to alleviate the worst effects of unfettered capitalism, are as much within the realm of liberalism as business conservatives, and seem able to govern capitalist countries without difficulty.

[*]   This ignores the issue of effective demand, which becomes a problem when, for example, there is a famine. The farmer loses not only the food raised for consumption, but also the food raised for cash, and without cash the farmer cannot buy food for consumption. As a consequence, most famine areas export food, because the locals can't afford to buy it.

[*]   In 1878, with the passage of the Posse Comitatus Act, which prevented federal troops from enforcing the voting rights of people the state and local governments wished to disenfranchise.

[*]   Journalist Jane Mayer wrote about the Powell memo in an August 30, 2010 issue of *The New Yorker* titled *Covert Operations*.

[*]   *The Real Origins of the Religious Right*, Randall Balmer, Politico, May 27, 2014.

[*]   The source of the above chart is the Fedreral Reserve Bank of Atlanta (public domain.)

[*]   Fed Chairman Jerome Powell, in a speech given Aug.27, 2020, indicated that the Fed may be shifting it's views on the NAIRU. He noted that in the long recovery that started under the Obama administration and continued under the Trump administration until the Covid-19 shutdown, with unemployment "well below most estimates of its sustainable level" for about two years, did not spark inflation. https://www.federalreserve.gov/newsevents/speech/powell20200827a.htm

[*]   The Case for a Progressive Tax: From Basic Research to Policy Recommendations, Peter Diamond, Professor Emeritus of Economics, Massachusetts Institute of Technology, Emmanuel Saez is Professor of Economics, University of California, Berkeley, California, Journal of Economic Perspectives—Volume 25, Number 4—Fall 2011—Pages 165–190.

[*]   http://www.nytimes.com/2012/03/04/business/capital-gains-vs-ordinary-income-economic-view.html?_r=1&

[*]   Like anything involving taxes, it gets more complicated as you look into it. The rate is higher, but still below the top marginal rate for ordinary income, on commercial buildings, collectibles, and certain kinds of small-business stock.

[*]   In the case of preferred stock, 90 days.

[*]   http://taxvox.taxpolicycenter.org/2012/03/19/no-obvious-relationship-between-capital-gains-tax-rates-and-economic-growth/

[*]   https://hbr.org/2014/01/we-cant-afford-to-leave-inequality-to-the-economists/

[*]   An economic axiom used to describe the relationship between inflation and unemployment.

[*]   http://insideclimatenews.org/news/15092015/Exxons-own-research-confirmed-fossil-fuels-role-in-global-warming

[*]   An 1857 uprising that put an end to East India Company rule of the subcontinent, replaced with British government rule.

[*]   This was at one time accepted as a defense in murder cases, as a form of temporarily insanity, but in a society that does not consider homosexuality an unacceptable perversion, this argument no longer makes sense. Modern juries tend to hear this argument as, "of course I killed him, I'm a bigot."

[*]   He was interviewed by Alexander Lamis, a political scientist then teaching at Case Western. See The Nation, Nov. 13, 2012. Interestingly, The Nation was founded the day before the conspirators in the Lincoln assassination were hanged, and still finds itself publishing stories about racial conflict.

[*]   *The Army of the Potomac: Glory Road*, Bruce Catton, Doubleday & Company, New York, 1952, page 325

[*] *The Fall of Conservatism*, George Packer, The New Yorker, May 26,2008

[*]   while, according to Lyndon Johnson's presidential tapes, sabotaging the peace process so that it would not conclude before the election (The Lyndon Johnson tapes: Richard Nixon's 'treason', BBC, http://www.bbc.com/news/magazine-21768668

[*]   JOHN R. EMSHWILLER And GARY FIELDS (August 22, 2011). "Federal Asset Seizures Rise, Netting Innocent With Guilty". Wall Street Journal. Retrieved October 11, 2014. ...New York businessman James Lieto ... Federal agents seized $392,000 of his cash anyway....

[*]   https://www.theatlantic.com/magazine/archive/2017/07/the-architect-of-the-radical-right/528672/

[*] Grzegorz Ekiert, "Veto, Liberum," in Seymour Martin Lipset, ed. ''The Encyclopedia of Democracy'' (1998) 4:1341

[*] http://www.vox.com/2014/11/4/7158293/mitch-mcconnell-strategist

[*]   http://www.theamericanconservative.com/dreher/trump-america-gorbachev/

[*]   The European Political Science Association, 2015

[*]   NBER Working Paper No. 20004 Issued in March 2014

[*]   http://www.vox.com/2016/3/1/11127424/trump-authoritarianism